A WORLD
OF TEACHING

A WORLD OF TEACHING

Personal Journeys Through the
World's English-Speaking Classrooms

*Edited by John A. Hansen
and Evan M. Smith*

BERGIN & GARVEY
Westport, Connecticut • London

Library of Congress Cataloging-in-Publication Data

A world of teaching : personal journeys through the world's English-speaking classrooms
/ edited by John A. Hansen and Evan M. Smith.
    p. cm.
  Includes bibliographical references and index.
  ISBN 0–89789–874–5 (alk. paper)
    1. Teachers, Foreign.   2. Teacher exchange programs.   I. Hansen, John A., 1972– II.
Smith, Evan M.
  LB2283.W65   2002
  370.116'3—dc21   2002018211

British Library Cataloguing in Publication Data is available.

Library of Congress Catalog Card Number: 2002018211
ISBN: 0–89789–874–5

First published in 2002

Bergin & Garvey, 88 Post Road West, Westport, CT 06881
An imprint of Greenwood Publishing Group, Inc.
www.greenwood.com

Printed in the United States of America

∞

The paper used in this book complies with the
Permanent Paper Standard issued by the National
Information Standards Organization (Z39.48–1984).

10 9 8 7 6 5 4 3 2 1

Contents

Acknowledgments

The success of this project required much hard work and cooperation in addition to invaluable assistance from many people. I would like to extend my gratitude to Dr. Curtis J. Bonk, for planting the seeds of this project; Dr. Hans O. Andersen for his support and encouragement to travel to Venezuela; Mr. Jack Marino, who inspired me to teach; my partner, Evan Smith, from whom I have learned a world of lessons about interpersonal relationships; the contributors and international teachers around the world to whom this book is dedicated; my mom, who nurtured my budding interest in writing; and to my dad, who unfortunately passed away during my two-year assignment in South America, whose lessons of hard work and discipline have helped me shoulder such a challenging project.

—John A. Hansen

I would like to thank Geoff Irvin for his professional advice and assistance in the early stages of this project; my colleague and friend John Hansen whose professional skills, creative spark, and enthusiasm have been a constant source of support to me during this partnership; all of our contributors who have devoted time to this endeavor; my parents for their support, challenging questions, and advice; and my wife Cristina, who supported my move to Venezuela and continues to support my writing projects with interest, patience, and love.

—Evan M. Smith

Introduction

Evan M. Smith

I have strange power of speech;
That moment that his face I see,
I know the man that must hear me:
To him my tale I teach.
  "The Rime of the Ancient Mariner," Samuel Taylor Coleridge

For every teacher who makes the leap to leave his or her home culture to
venture somewhere new, there is an instant camaraderie with those who
have done the same. Regardless of how different their newly adopted environments may have been, these former expatriates share something that
seems to defy description. With time, stories surface and when there is no
one with whom to exchange cultural anecdotes and life-changing insights,
there must still be a listener; and in that way, the returned expatriate is
similar to the ancient Mariner. This Mariner develops a glittering eye, a
symbol of his life-changing voyage and the important story he must tell.
As with the ancient Mariner, an overseas teacher wants to arrest your attention and use any part of a conversation as an opportunity to tell another
captivating detail about his or her life working abroad. Every detail of life,
from the bill at a restaurant to the way people say hello, reminds these
teachers of their journeys.

A journey is more than a trip or vacation. The experiences of being
overseas teachers differ from those of the seasoned travelers who even stay
in one locale for two or three months, learn some of the language, and
acquaint themselves with locals. Working and living in a country for a year

or more means enduring a marriage to a new environment following the honeymoon of your first few months, when cultural idiosyncrasies that you initially found endearing and funny, become frustrating and tiring. Living in a country means relying on a local postal carrier to bring news and love from home; it means going through a process of coping with frustrating local perspectives. And most of all, living as a teacher in a different country means forging bonds with students who, whether local or foreign like you, are ultimately the biggest, brightest, and most unforgettable welcoming and good-bye committees a teacher will ever have. Being an expatriate means forging beyond the tourist veneer of a country, not in a physical sense, as many tourists are capable of and actually prefer to do, but in a psychological, emotional, and intercultural sense. Teaching overseas, then, becomes a personal journey.

Describing such a journey for the purposes of educating others can seem a daunting task, but it comes naturally to the returned expatriate because, like the ancient Mariner, one is compelled to tell people his or her story. It is through narrative, from character and plot to atmosphere and tone, that one's listeners can understand and learn. Indeed, stories fulfill the aims of this anthology more than formal essays or a textbook could perhaps ever do. Each of these essays engages the reader in a dialogue, a conversation in which the reader follows the successes and failures of individual teachers in their daily routines. While, fortunately, there are no albatrosses hung around the necks of our teacher-storytellers, as is the case with the ancient Mariner, there is an honesty and candour to each story. Jeri Hurd's description of visiting a Turkish bath has both these things and more. Her humor is infectious, and it is echoed throughout the anthology. The ability to laugh at oneself in new situations is a hallmark of the international journey. Without it, a teacher would rush home, disarmed by change and frustrated by people. This tone makes these essays all the more real—all the more successful in realizing the goal of this book: to inform and entertain, motivate and provoke, educate and inspire.

Like the Mariner's glittering eye, then, this book is a beacon attracting listeners who are also learners, which highlights another dimension of the word journey. A person who teaches as a profession, perhaps even a vocation, a poignant distinction made by Ross Laing in his essay, "A Canuck Down Under," understands what it is like to be a learner. Since a knowledge of learning styles is commensurate with a knowledge of teaching styles, moving to a new country becomes professional development in its fullest sense, as the teacher now becomes a student of culture putting the message, professional development, first. Debbie Boucher highlights this issue as she explains a pattern of international teaching in Latin America spanning a long career that few could have thought possible. She explains the process of taking the first adventurous steps to such visceral learning, while other contributors take that step for you—in front of you—with an invigorating outcome. Balanced with each teacher's pedagogical stories are fascinating cultural observations and insights that reveal the extent to which these educators are themselves avid learners.

Unlike the texts from faculties of education or school libraries, a book about teaching in another country must address many divergent issues; there are as many variables in the life of an expatriate teacher as there are lesson plans and tricks up the sleeve of an experienced teacher. Because prospective overseas teachers have either an overabundance of questions or too few due to lack of knowledge, each essay, by virtue of its authorship and our editorial selection, offers a different point of view; we have chosen essays from people with different levels of experience, different concerns, and different types of employers. (An interesting illustration of this strength is the variation in spelling between the Canadian and American contributors.) The scope of this anthology ranges from the concerns of a fresh graduate to an experienced teacher with a stable job and family. While private American and international schools are the most common destination for these teachers, many people decide to teach, as some of our contributors have, with ESL institutes or nongovernment organizations such as the British-founded Volunteer Services Overseas (VSO), which raises an important issue.

The majority of the essays in this anthology are not about the Western, English-speaking world. They are in worlds that are developing—less technologically advanced than our own. The rationale for having chosen the following selections is threefold. First, attention is given in this anthology to those areas of the world offering the most overseas posts. Second, positions demanding the most adjustments from the teacher, professional and personal, require the most description. The perils of reading only one perspective about a given part of the world are as serious as relying on only network news to formulate an opinion about a conflict, let alone an entire country or culture. Mike Kielkopf raises this issue in his discussion of media stereotypes in the United Arab Emirates as does Daniel Davis in "Risky Business," his provocative paper about teaching in politically sensitive areas. Davis's essay, along with Shirley Hooper's, is particularly relevant given the political and social climate since September eleventh, when teachers may give much more careful consideration as to where they will feel safe. They may also consider whether they seek new experiences that are primarily cultural or professional in nature. For an exploration of nuances in pedagogy, school administration and curriculum, teachers may opt for schools in more "Western" countries. Karen Newman, for example, focuses on curious school procedures in Vienna, which were certainly more disarming for her than the cultural differences she experienced. Her beloved ritual of drinking gourmet coffee at a popular café is a common experience for both North Americans and Europeans alike. In non-Western countries where exotic differences shock the expatriate's senses, professional aspects of the assignments are either completely eclipsed by culture, or the schools operate on an American system that is very familiar to North American teachers. In those cases, the school offers stability and familiarity that an expatriate needs when even a simple walk to school becomes a slog through a dense brush of cultural curios.

Mentioning the West, which is a sociopolitical designation rather than a hemispheric one, raises the colonial issue implicit, and at times explicit, in teaching overseas; this political third reason for selecting the essays in the anthology is inadvertent but significant. While children of wealthy petroleum engineers or diplomats in developing countries still carry lunch bags, Barbie backpacks, still grudgingly copy their homework assignments, just as they do in North American schools, they do not go home to a house that is typical of the area. On their way home in a bus or their parents' sport utility vehicles, they pass the students of local, national schools, students who eventually turn down the dusty lanes where banana plants hide their small square houses made of rough brown construction blocks and corrugated metal roofs. The bilingual, international school students, however, continue on until they reach a gate where an armed guard monitors the traffic around large air-conditioned houses. In Latin America there is an evident disparity between these two standards of living. The small metal-covered houses may not have glass in the windows, washing machines, or anything more than bare cement for a floor. These students can't afford to attend an international or American school. In the parts of the world they may not be able to attend reliable local schools, as in areas of Namibia, which Liz Wigful discusses in her essay about teaching through the non-government not-for-profit organization VSO, a British cousin to the Peace Corps. There, students not only learn how to speak English, but also study their other subjects in English.

So where does this difference leave overseas teachers? Is their choice between altruistic social development on a subsistence-level salary or of a well-paid professional post in a privileged, well-equipped facility? It is neither that simple nor our aim to discuss such morally and politically charged questions. Teaching is a noble profession wherever it is practised, and, as Debbie Boucher notes, democratic principles and provocative questions should enter every classroom. Shirley Hooper, who teaches in Bolivia, takes this idea a step further when she explains that she is just waiting for her students to "do something for their country by giving it honest leadership," the kind of leadership that may eventually lead to sound education for every citizen. In the meantime, teachers can only do what they do best, and that is something Vici Egan has been able to do in both the volunteer and private positions. She plainly explains her reasons for changing as she dazzles us with the possibilities of limitless global exploration through teaching.

Returning home to their familiar realities, following the acquisition of deepened vision, is not easy for our world travelers. As the Mariner is fated to have a glittering eye, and travel ceaselessly in search of the appropriate listener, the returned expatriate teacher must deal with reverse culture shock and the seemingly provincial attitudes around them. The problem, however, is gradually erased by memories, recited, reinterpreted, and recorded. Trevor Dodman recapitulates a moment in his journey in Japan through memory: bowing to the pressure to perform Western songs by his students at a karaoke bar, he writes: "through the light-hearted mix of languages . . . singing, I knew what it was to be in harmony." Vernon Olson felt in harmony with something incredible in Egypt when he watched the swallows in their "flashes of aeronautical poetry with the Nile as a backdrop." These memories are beautifully rendered by our contributors and give us confidence that culture shock is simply one step in a fulfilling journey that does not end with the return to North America.

These experiences and insights—both prior to and after the return—are all made possible by the one facet of the overseas journey to which this introduction gives only scant attention: the students. They can only be adequately described, with the detail and insight they deserve, by those who have formed personal bonds with them. Time and again these contributors return to discussing the students, regardless of how marvelous the trips they took were, how fascinating the cultural events they experienced were, or how much money they saved. Students, and the growth they achieve and represent, form the rudder of a teacher's fulfilling overseas journey. Let each of our contributors, then, with their glittering eyes, take you by the hand and tell you a wonderful story.

WORK CITED

Coleridge, S. T. (1964). "The rime of the ancient mariner." In J. Hayward (Ed.), *The Oxford book of nineteenth-century English verse* (pp. 139–161). London: Oxford University Press.

PART I

Asia

1

Education in Japan: Developing Citizenry, Celebrating Harmony

Trevor Dodman

"Please try this one," Kimura-san invites. "It is delicious and very healthy for you. In Japan, we say *inago*." He smiles broadly as he passes the container across the table to me. "It is a locust."

"A locust. How interesting. Now, how do you prepare a locust?" I ask, once again marveling at the curious way that Japanese delicacies consistently manage to join my conversation classes. One month into my teaching experience, it seems as if I'm given something new and exotic to try every day.

"The process is quite simple," says Kimura-san. "Catch the locusts, break off their legs, boil them, and then soak them in soya sauce. Although they are expensive, I prefer to buy them at the store. I am too old to run after locusts!"

Having established that the locusts have been cooked, I reach into the container and make my selection. The locust is sticky and quite brittle; I notice that one of the legs is still attached. "Kimura-san, this locust still has one of its legs."

Laughing, Kimura-san replies with a knowing glance that this must be my lucky day. I gaze down at the brown creature and consider his unfortunate repose in my palm. Hoping that recourse to an idiomatic expression will put off the sampling a bit longer, I offer, "Well, as we say in English, there's a first time for everything."

Kimura-san, however, accustomed to my tricks, remains unyielding, and matter-of-factly states, "Yes, this is your first experience with a locust." He folds his arms across his belly and stares at me expectantly.

He smiles broadly again as I devour his one-legged ambassador.

Before I went to Japan, I never even considered the possibility that I would one day find myself snacking on locusts in the classroom. Instead, I pictured myself enjoying the gentle grace of a traditional tea ceremony. I saw myself admiring the carefully sculpted form of a bonsai tree set within a tranquil garden. I imagined myself amid a throng of conservative business suits pressing their way through crowded Tokyo streets. I pictured myself teaching uniformed workers within the sterile, hallowed confines of a massive automotive company.

While I did manage to experience many similar scenes during my year and a half in Japan, I quickly realized that such compelling media images—which have come to represent Japanese society and culture in the West—do not reflect the whole of the story. Japan is, of course, much more complex than any generic juxtapositioning of bustling streets and quiet rock gardens would suggest. Much to my delight, every day during my time abroad I explored the Japan that exists in between such stereotypical extremes. Both in the classroom and on the street, I encountered a Japanese people intent on blending memories of a rich past with dreams of a bright future in a harmonious, if sometimes perplexing, present.

Harmony. At the mere mention of the word I am reminded of my employer Uchida-san's insistence that I abide by the traditional Japanese custom of acquiring a *hanko*. He explained to me that each Japanese carries an official wooden stamp that has identifying characters carved into one end; after blotting the *hanko* on an ink pad, a bright red, oval seal is left to dry on a document in the place of a signature. Without a *hanko*, Uchida-san noted, I would encounter unusual delays at the bank and post office—I would disrupt the harmony of the workplace. He felt, however, that if I carried my own *hanko*, everyone would be impressed that I had chosen to respect a long-standing Japanese custom. Since many of my younger students had already discovered the challenges posed by the unusual combination of consonants and vowels in my first name ("r" and "v" are notoriously difficult sounds in Japanese), Uchida-san set about designing a *hanko* for me with their hilarious pronunciations in mind. After discarding the likes of "Torebu" and "Turabo," Uchida-san decided on "Toriba," a handle that roughly translates into "Bird Plantain." Needless to say, after opening my account at the bank and sealing the deal with my unusual *hanko*, the tellers never looked at me in the same way again! For Westerners raised on a Japanese diet of sumo wrestlers, kimono-clad geisha, and Sony televisions, the sudden introduction of *hankos* at thoroughly modernized banks—not to mention locusts in the classroom—can be disconcerting. However, for new teachers preparing to come to Japan, I believe that a better understanding of "harmony" and its place in Japanese life will serve to make the difficult transition to this very different culture a smoother and less perplexing one.

My own immersion into Japanese culture began with the early discovery that the Japanese, to the great surprise of my naive Western sensibilities, share many of our proverbs (or, as I began to wonder, do we simply share many of theirs?). In any event, while the direct translations of such proverbs are, in many cases, roughly equivalent, the Japanese deploy these expressions according to vastly different rationales.

Selecting one from the many proverbs and expressions which repeatedly came up in my classes, "Silence is golden" (*Chimoku wa kinari*), I might suggest, encourages one to embrace and welcome a moment or two of silence, to bask in the proverbial chirping of birds in the trees. Alternatively, in this expression I can hear the admonitory words of my grandfather reminding me that an economy of speech is an admirable quality in today's hectic talk-show world. In Japan, however, neither of these definitions neatly applies. While the Japanese do embrace moments of silence in conversation—and would seem to possess astonishingly high thresholds for enduring such gaps—the proverb does not reflect a cultural premium on the sounds of silence. In Japan, the words *Chimoku wa kinari* function instead as a reminder that opinions are strictly private matters and that to express them candidly and without reservation is to disturb a delicately existing harmony.

A student's reluctance to offer personal feelings and thoughts takes on a particularly strong resonance for teachers coming from more open teaching practices in the West that emphasize and encourage class discussion. To ask a question of a group of students and stare out into a sea of attentive but entirely unwilling participants is indeed an unsettling experience. In Japan, the educational pathways are decidedly one-way: teacher to student. From an early age, students are encouraged to listen to and learn from the teacher—teachers ask questions and students provide answers. However, as Uchida-san would often tell me, in Japan the student is told that the best answer is the correct one, the next best is to remain silent, and the worst response is the wrong answer.

This approach to educating students can lead to frustration and despair for the newly arrived teacher. Any attempt to develop an issue-driven dialogue or debate in class will likely be met with resistance. For many children and adults alike, the thought of openly offering an opinion on something as seemingly innocuous as a favourite pop star, can be both troubling and distasteful. My Thursday evening class of thirteen-year-old girls proved, at times, to be a weekly hour of frustration. Here is a typical exchange:

"So who likes pop music?" I ask plaintively. Maho puts up her hand and responds, "I do, Toriba-san. I like pop music."

"That's great, Maho. Who do you like?"

"I don't know."

"You don't know who you like?"

"Yes, I don't know."

Setting aside the general confusion about how to respond correctly to a question asked in the negative (another area of particularly painful confusion for Japanese students of English), students' acute awareness of their own limitations in a second language, combined with fears that their particular opinion may differ widely from those of their teacher and classmates, can result in an atmosphere of complete trepidation in the language classroom.

Initially, I found myself spending much of my class time encouraging, cajoling, or even begging my students to utilize their English skills: "Please, Maho, please tell me which pop singer you like!" However, as my own inexperience as an educator abroad eventually gave way to a better understanding of my teaching environment and the needs of my students, I realized that greater efforts on my part to create a more relaxed atmosphere in the classroom would translate into dramatic increases in student participation. Moreover, along with my students, I, too, began to relax more; as I felt my frustrations ebbing away, I encountered a heightened awareness of the culture about me. A few of my experiences stand out, captured like still shots in my mind: the sense of accomplishment that I read in the face of a six-year-old boy as he finally made the connection between the symbols and sounds of our alphabet; the confidence that I felt in the handshake of a businessman I had spent months preparing for his new life in the Philippines; the sincerity that I heard in the voice of a middle-aged housewife with advanced language skills who used to delight in telling me that as soon as she stepped into the classroom for our private lesson, she felt free to speak frankly and directly in ways that Japanese social mores and language patterns would not ordinarily permit—"In English, I feel as if I can be me!" Although she proved to be the exception rather than the rule as far as my students and their willingness to openly communicate went, I look back on the connection we made together in English and see that through our lessons together I was able to realize my greatest hopes as an ESL teacher. Moreover, not once did she suggest we try locusts with our green tea and conversation.

A week before the end of October, and well into my stay in Japan, I announced to my adult conversation classes that I would be hosting a Halloween party. Unaware that the Japanese do not celebrate Halloween with the same kind of dedicated seriousness as we do in the West, I learned that most of my students had never heard the words "trick or treat" before. Many of them had never even dressed up for Halloween when they were children; moreover, none of them, certainly, had ever been to an official costume party thrown by a Westerner.

Tensions ran high as my students considered the details of the upcoming event. Always attentive to the formalities of any festival or occasion, they first wanted to learn about traditional party costumes. Although I mentioned a few of the classics—witch, devil, monster, superhero—I emphasized that any costume would do, so long as some effort was put into its creation. "Use your imagination!" I suggested to groans and anguished looks of reluctance.

"But what should I wear?" they each asked in a state of total panic. More questions flooded my way. What if no one at the party recognized them? If a person were to arrive at the party dressed as an alien, would the person be obligated to act as an alien in some way? What disguises had I donned in years past? Why is the holiday called Halloween? Shifting to finances, many wondered about the costs of an appropriate costume. I replied that because buying or renting a costume can be expensive—particularly in Japan, I laughed to myself—many people decide to make their own. "In fact," I added, hoping to lead by example and get them in the spirit of the event, "I will be making my own."

Incredulous at such a show of brazen initiative, my students probed for more information: "But what will you be? What will you make? How will you make it?" Ill-prepared to answer such questions, I responded with a hint of the mysterious: "It is a secret. Come to the party on the 31st and you will have your answers!"

Preparations for the big night proved to be somewhat trying for me. Failing in a desperate, community-wide quest to acquire a pumpkin, I purchased the largest melon that I could find, concluding that a meagre green jack o' lantern would be better than nothing at all. Disheartened by the complete scarcity of ready-made Halloween decorations, I took scissors in hand, unpacked my rather rusty cut-and-paste skills, and feverishly set to work. Before long, handkerchief ghosts were suspended from the ceiling with fishing line, two-dimensional spiders were scaling the walls, and a trio of goblins—made all the more macabre by their crude rendering—were stationed at the front door.

Having already decided that I would transform myself into a fearsome, mustachioed pirate for the party, I next waded into the complexities of buying the face paint to complete my ensemble. Unable to speak or read Japanese, I found myself brandishing an imaginary sabre and play-acting a high-seas adventure for a bemused cosmetician in the town's biggest grocery store. My utterly ineffective theatrics, however, soon gave way to waning enthusiasm and the discouraging act of settling for a black magic marker instead. Naturally, it proved to be indelible.

Decorations and eye patch in place, I greeted, in turn, a black cat, a Japanese yakuza gangster, a karate practitioner, two mice, a bumblebee, a high-school student, and three samurai warriors. All were duly impressed with their buccaneering host and his cramped apartment of horror; I was thrilled that everyone showed up in costume and that the samurai didn't take it upon themselves to disarm the uzi-toting yakuza.

After several drinks, the bumblebee pointed at one of my hanging ghosts and asked, "Why did you make such a thing for this Halloween party?" Surveying the vigorous nods of approval from the rest of my guests, I surmised that they had all been wondering the same thing. Cautiously, I offered a brief explanation. "Well, a ghost is scary."

One of the mice squeaked, "That is a ghost?"

"Of course it's a ghost," I replied. "What else could it be?" I looked from face to face, taking in the laughter and bracing myself for yet another wonderful colliding of worlds.

"In Japan," the spirited bumblebee buzzed, "children will hang up a small white sheet if they do not want it to rain the next day." She paused and looked up at my host of ghosts hovering in the cigarette smoke. With a straight face she added, "Perhaps it will not rain here again for many months."

I laughed the hearty laugh of a pirate far from home, collecting untold treasures.

Long before I showed up to class for days straight with remnants of a pirate's mustache on my face, I encountered a proverb that I believe sums up the Japanese educational ethos: "*Deru kui wa utareru.*" An ESL classroom full of students tempered by the notion that "The post that sticks up will be hit down," can make for less than entertaining discussions. Emphasizing, once more, the need for harmony in society, this proverb manifests itself in an educational system that primarily caters to the needs of the average student. For students who fall behind the rigid demands of their school schedules, teachers and school administrators put in extra time to ensure that those same students will continue to pass through all of their exams. In Japanese elementary and junior high schools (the mandatory schooling required of every citizen), students very rarely fail a year of school and miss the chance to move on with their classmates to the next level. For those students, however, who are ahead of the class or are unchallenged by the work they are given, little is done to keep them occupied or to help them further develop their skills in new directions. This is where the significance of "The post that sticks up will be hit down" can best be seen. For not only are students encouraged to remain silent unless they know the correct answer to a question, but even if they do know the right answer, there is an overriding pressure to remain silent exacted by the group as a whole upon the individual who continually raises a hand to provide all the answers.

How do the Japanese cope with a system that seems to suppress individual pursuits and encourage a flattening out of differences? How can the Japanese have managed to survive and flourish in such a constrained environment? Harmony. And just how is this harmony achieved? In large part, the Japanese word *gaman* (patience, endurance, forbearance) is responsible for a vital society that is relatively free of crime, a world economic leader, and a living storehouse of traditional practices and modern advances coexisting peacefully and naturally.

In the West, before starting an unpleasant chore or service, we might offer a timeworn adage about perseverance and then steel ourselves to the task at hand, hopefully with the knowledge that with the completion of the job there will be some kind of tangible personal reward: a minor celebration of the self. In Japan, however, enduring the societal pressures and constraints that have evolved over time is deemed to be a constant and necessary personal responsibility, shouldered in order to preserve a harmonious community. Japanese society depends upon frictionless relationships in the home and workplace, and the ability to bend the will, to sacrifice degrees of personal freedom. The implicit trust that everyone else is continually exercising forbearance and suffering together is a precept that helps to tightly bind Japanese communities of people together.

In education, this idea translates into long hours spent in the classroom followed by mandatory after-school commitments to sports or other club activities. Additionally, many parents, in order to prepare their children for the difficult entrance examinations that are given before high school and university (and even some kindergarten, elementary, and junior high schools!) rely on afternoon and evening "cram" schools for extra guidance and tutelage. Such institutions provide instruction in all subjects ranging from geography and calligraphy, to mastering the intricacies of the abacus.

In my case, as an ESL teacher in a small, private language school, I witnessed firsthand the demands upon my young students' time and energy as they dragged themselves into my classroom at 7:45 P.M. after a long day at school. Afforded precious little free time, Japanese students must do their best to come to grips with the realities of their busy schedules and the pressures associated with preparing for their all-important examinations (not to mention learning how to be teenagers!). Their constant state of fatigue, combined with the fact that Japanese culture has none of the Western social stigmas associated with sleeping in public places (particularly in small English classes!) will provide the new teacher with a rather chronic source of motivation to prepare interesting and stimulating lessons as much as possible. My students, especially the occasional adult student who would manage to surreptitiously nod off in the middle of an exercise, were always apologetic about their naps and I did my best not to let their mild cultural narcolepsy erode away too much of my budding, yet still fragile, confidence and comfort levels as a newcomer in the field of ESL instruction.

Although teachers in Japan may be forgiving about sleeping in the classroom, the Japanese need for *gaman* or perseverance is tightly woven into the previously mentioned one-way teacher/student relationship. Japanese society through the ages has always been very stratified and the echoes of that long history can still be felt today. In big companies, executives and managers from top to bottom in the hierarchy adhere rigidly to traditional methods of delegating responsibility and handling problems all the way down the chain of command. In schools, the principal lords over all major school decisions and educational issues. In the classroom, the teacher has total control and is expected to provide direction and leadership at all times, with little, if any, feedback from the students themselves. To maintain harmony, teachers must lead and the students must follow, and all parties must have *gaman*.

It is in this area that I believe teachers new to Japan will find themselves making adjustments in how they approach their classroom hours. In my particular case, I quickly discovered that my students, both young and old, became noticeably uncomfortable when I asked them questions about their goals for the class and how they thought it best to achieve them. While all of them were quick to identify dreams of fluency or better pronunciation, an increased vocabulary or grasp of survival travel English, they grew utterly uncooperative when I pressed them for more information. For instance, when it came to something as simple as commenting on the seating plan, or specifically identifying the kinds of exercises they enjoyed doing, or discussing the structure of the class—"Would you prefer to have twenty minutes of textbook work and forty minutes of free-talking, or vice versa?"—they would invariably refuse to offer suggestions for fear of overstepping their bounds.

Countless times, in an effort to circumvent this familiar impasse, I enthusiastically welcomed any and all of their comments and advice. I explained to them that, in fact, they could help me to become a better and more effective teacher for them if they would only let me know how they were feeling about the class. All of this, however, was to no avail. They continued to leave everything up to me and remained consistent in this regard for my entire stay in Japan. Their own finely-tuned hierarchical sense, along with their highly developed capacity for subjugating their own personal desires, left me completely in charge and always wondering whether or not they were happy with my classes and truly satisfied with me as their teacher.

At times, I found the one-sided nature of my relationships with my students to be wonderful: they completely trusted me and all of my classroom decisions, never questioned any of my lesson plans, and always left me knowing just who was responsible for keeping the class moving forward. Other times, I found myself longing for a student's subjective critique of my class, or, at the very least, a suggestion for a juicy discussion topic! New teachers, therefore, should be mentally prepared to step in and take charge of the classroom. Despite what usually amounts to minimal ESL training prior to commencing with classes (or total lack thereof, as in my case), expect little, if any, feedback from either students or employers. Outwardly exude confidence and be enthusiastic; inwardly embark upon a journey that will hopefully reveal, given time, the educational approaches and teaching styles that suit you best.

It is my final class with the employees of the Akebono Brake Company and we are enjoying our first and only group outing. The décor of the Japanese-style pub is typical: thin square pillows rest underneath low tables set upon tatami mats; walls covered in small white cards display neatly inscribed menu items; wooden chopstick pairs, joined at the thick ends and sheathed in paper scabbards, wait patiently for their mealtime divorce. Looming in the corner is the karaoke machine. I know only too well what the night will hold: toasts will be made, beer and sake will flow, pub food will be eaten, and I will perform solo act after solo act. A request for Whitney Houston will come up on the monitor—I will not refuse. Enthusiastic demands for "Bridge Over Troubled Water" will be voiced—how could I say no? Someone will want an encore performance of "My Way"—I will not let them down. Jon Bon Jovi will need to be heard—I will not hesitate in stepping to the mike. And then, several locusts later, through the smoke and the music, through the lighthearted mix of languages, through the clinking of beer mugs; through it all I will suddenly hear my own voice rise in song. Listening, I will know what it is to be happy; singing, I will know what it is to be in harmony.

2

China: Education, Culture, and Western Misconceptions

Michele E. Gordon

As a teacher of English as a second language, I envisioned myself standing in front of a large classroom, speaking English and doing various activities that involved the entire class. I thought that the students would be somewhat shy and reserved. After my first term in China, I was able to realistically sum up my teaching experiences: I was a foreign teacher whom students loved but I was also a dentist, pulling teeth trying to get even the best students to speak. Eventually, the students in my class were shouting outlandish ideas, singing, role-playing, and even, for two brave souls, getting married the Western way. They attest to the true warmth and vigour of the Chinese people that made my experience so enjoyable.

Zhaotong has approximately 100,000 people, a small town by Chinese standards and until shortly before I arrived, it had been a "closed" area, meaning no foreigners were allowed to visit without special permission. The town is located in the foothills of the Himalayas, at an elevation of 1,800 meters (just over a mile high). Many of the houses are poorly insulated, without centralized heating, offering only modest shelter from the cool and windy climate. Located in Yunnan Province, Zhaotong is in the southwest of China. There are over fifty official "ethnic minorities" in China; about two dozen of these reside in the Yunnan Province.

I had heard that classes in China would be big, reports of over one hundred students were not uncommon. Fortunately, my classes ranged from thirty-five to thirty-eight students. I had eight different classes in three grades, teaching them oral English, listening comprehension, British and American culture, and writing. My students were studying to become English teachers in rural junior high and high schools. They were young adults, aged 18 to 25. I was the first foreign teacher any of them had ever had; in fact, I was the first foreigner most of them had ever met. As the year began, the students were afraid of me. They did not dare to speak to me in or out of the classroom. And although I imagined there were questions about our cultural differences, they were never asked. I quickly realized that I had a lot to learn about the Chinese educational system, teaching in China, and the Chinese culture.

The travel bug bit me when I was eighteen. I had taken a year off between high school and college to work and study Hebrew on a kibbutz in Israel. Still with a strong desire to travel, I spent my junior year abroad in England. Then, after receiving my BA in psychology, I went back to Europe to teach. Two years later, with a master's degree in International Education in 1996, I wanted to experience a new culture and lifestyle different than my own. Ultimately, the opportunity to teach English at Zhaotong Teachers' College in Yunnan Province, China presented itself.

I prepared for this trip the same way I had prepared for the former ones, searching through two books: *Alternatives to the Peace Corps* (Becky Buell, Victoria Clarke, and Susan Leone, eds., First Food Books, Institute for Food and Development Policy, San Francisco, 1992) and *Travel! The Comprehensive Guide to Voluntary Service in the U.S. and Abroad* (Council on International Education and Exchange, 1995). After several months of writing letters, filling in applications, and waiting, I agreed to a two-year contract to teach English in China through an organization called Voluntary Service Overseas (VSO). VSO provided several training courses both predeparture as well as in China. Additional preparation came from speaking with numerous individuals who had been to China, reading, and research on the Internet.

The school's campus had two teaching buildings with large classrooms equipped with a teacher's stage, movable blackboards, and plenty of seating. The dining facilities included a bakery and a "dining room" consisting of long counters with three-foot diameter serving dishes and an open floor where students squatted down to eat out of their individual bowls. Outside the college gate, many street vendors catered to the students. The town had ample restaurants, shops and department stores, and large markets, karaoke bars, discos, and even some English movie theaters. My main entertainment, however, was spending time with my students, in my home, in their dormitories, or taking trips with them to town or the countryside.

The provincial capital, Kunming, is about three hundred miles away. A forty-minute flight was available, but prohibitively expensive, costing over one-third of my monthly salary. So like most Chinese, I took the bus, which was a fifteen-hour ride, trundling through winding, narrow, unpaved roads and over several mountain passes to the capital where I would stock up on

Western supplies that were unavailable in Zhaotong, such as yogurt, oatmeal, and pasta.

The contract with VSO and Zhaotong Teachers' College was clear and complete. My apartment had entirely new furniture including a television, refrigerator, hot water tank and washing machine, and a telephone that was installed after one term. It was clean, big, and in many ways more comfortable than my U.S. apartment. My volunteer stipend was low by Western standards; however, it was double or triple what the Chinese teachers earned, and I lived very comfortably. The cost of living in Zhaotong was very low, and although I spent money on clothes, shoes, and gifts, I still had enough money to travel during the six-week breaks twice each year.

The students also lived on campus, in one of three large dormitories with eight students to a room. They had no hot water, and electricity at only certain hours. Nonetheless, all were grateful to be there. They were receiving a good low-cost education, meals, housing, and a job as a teacher guaranteed after graduation. Many of them were from peasant families, and their acceptance into the college ultimately helped bring the family out of poverty.

Teachers in China are highly respected. They are considered experts in their field, and the students rarely question their knowledge or authority. When I arrived in China, I was given a Foreign Expert's Card, which certified me as the most expert of all the experts teaching English in China. I was not a certified teacher, but because I had a college degree and was a native English speaker, the Chinese qualified me as such. In addition to this status, I unwittingly became a dentist pulling teeth in a system with which I was unfamiliar and unhappy.

The Chinese teach English (and many other subjects) by rote, repetition, and memorization. Generally, when a new lesson begins, the teachers play a tape with the passage being studied. The students repeat the entire passage individually and in small groups with everyone in the classroom repeating the new text. Another common practice is to ask questions which can be answered quite easily by looking at the passage being studied. A sample text might include: "Tom goes to the market every day to buy vegetables." Questions would include: "Where does Tom go?" or "What does Tom buy?" They would not include questions like: "What vegetables does Tom buy?" or "How much does Tom spend at the market?", which require more lateral, independent thinking and a deeper understanding of the text to answer them correctly.

I looked through books that were used before I arrived, and found each unit was nearly identical to the last, following the same pattern and using the same types of exercises. I had to introduce variety into the lessons, hoping that the more interesting the lessons were, the more interested the students would be, and the more enthusiastically they would approach the classroom environment. My lessons were based on communication as the primary tool for language. Speaking, in any way, shape, or form, was most important, regardless of speed, pronunciation, or grammar. I felt my lessons were successful if the majority of the students spoke. I rarely corrected mistakes, and emphasized that you learn from your mistakes. My motto was "Mistakes are not important," which I wrote in huge letters on the board at the beginning of each term. The students understood my meaning, and laughed at my intentional mistakes, but it was extremely difficult to get them to follow this.

"Face" is an extremely important issue in China. Face is a form of honor for oneself, one's ancestors, and one's family. Losing face means bringing dishonor to oneself and those around you. Proper face implies not bringing attention to oneself in any way. Hence, Chinese students are unwilling to make mistakes, because this would mean bringing attention to themselves by having the wrong answer. Both the teacher and the student lose face if a student gives a wrong answer; it demonstrates that the teachers are not teaching well and the students are not working hard enough. Therefore, students will readily answer if they are certain they are correct. However, they will remain silent, rather than guess and risk being wrong, thus losing face for themselves and the teacher. Silence and reticence, especially when faced with adversity, is honorable, and thus, face-saving; making mistakes and guessing is not.

I attempted to counter this cultural bias by providing examples to follow and encouraging creativity and openness as much as possible. My main methodology followed the pattern of demonstration, practice, and presentation. First I demonstrated the exercise on the blackboard with the entire class, then the students practiced on their own, and finally the students presented their results to the class. For example, if we were making up stories from pictures, the students worked with the teacher to write a story together. In looking at a picture of a woman sitting on a bed reading a book, I encouraged outlandish ideas such as "She is reading about her husband's trip to Mars" or "They bought the bed with a million dollars they just won." If the exercise was to make up a dialogue with a certain topic, an example dialogue was written together on the blackboard, with students shouting out as many ideas as possible, and never discouraging or laughing at any of them. At the end of the lesson, they read their stories or dialogues to the class.

We sang songs. We did role-playing. We told stories. We played games. Most importantly, we laughed and had fun. In a culture lesson, we discussed and compared weddings in the U.S., UK, and China. At the end of the lesson, I performed a marriage ceremony for two students, following the U.S. traditions. The class referred to them as husband and wife for the rest of the year. One speaking lesson was spent taking a walk to a local reservoir. I gave them several potential topics but allowed them to discuss anything, as long as it was in English. I warned the students that anyone speaking Chinese would get a zero. Although I repeatedly sneaked up on groups to try to catch them, I only heard English spoken for the entire two hours. After that lesson, the students asked to have a lesson outside whenever the weather was nice. All these activities encouraged communication while making learning fun. The activities usually allowed a wide range of answers so that weaker students could participate as well as more advanced ones, all working at their own level but all also learning.

During my summer break, a group of foreign teachers came to the college to retrain English teachers from the area. Among those studying were several of my former students. The teachers later told me they were able to identify those who had studied with me. Their English command was better, they were more active, and they communicated more freely and creatively. Seeing this impact played out so clearly in those classrooms made all my efforts, frustrations, and difficulties in China worthwhile.

While I tried to encourage the students to have fun in the classroom, I also tried to demonstrate that teaching can be fun. They were students, but they would soon be teachers upon graduating, and if they enjoyed using the language, they would enjoy speaking it, and later, teaching it.

Teaching and learning English also occurred outside the classroom. There was a weekly "English Corner," an hour-long gathering of all the English department students where they could speak freely on a given topic. I also spoke to the students as much as possible outside of the classroom. During the breaks between lessons, there were always students around me practicing their English. I also visited the dormitories and participated in class trips, dances, and sports games.

Students were also welcome in my home, and I often invited them to my house for dinner. We went to the market together, prepared a delicious Chinese meal, and ate and chatted all evening. This arrangement was beneficial for everyone, as they practiced their English in an informal setting, and I learned how to cook authentic Chinese food. On these occasions, I was a friend rather than a teacher. In this relaxed, small-group atmosphere, each student was able to participate more fully and to learn as much or more than in the classroom.

During the college breaks, I was fortunate to be able to visit some of my students' homes. Transportation in the area was by bus, and the ride was always long and bumpy; yet, the enthusiasm of the student far outweighed any discomfort of the bus ride. They were bringing home their foreign teacher, bringing great face to themselves and their family. They served as my interpreter. They would be the talk of their town, and it was all they could do to not jump up and down with sheer excitement.

Sometimes they did actually jump up and down. Although my students were young adults, they often acted with a childlike maturity level. Their lives were simple and uncomplicated, and they took great pleasure in basics that Westerners take for granted. On a class trip, a student burst into my room flushed with excitement, proudly showing off the jar full of fireflies that she had just caught. They played musical chairs and patty-cake and seemed to enjoy them more than we did when we played them as young-sters. Theirs was a beautiful innocence that was extraordinary to watch.

My days spent in their homes are some of my fondest memories of my two years in China. If I thought that the Chinese were reserved in any way, it was simply because I had never visited their homes. They are generous in a way I have never seen before, killing a chicken for our dinner, going to the market to buy what they know I liked, setting no limits on what they should do to make me feel comfortable, happy, and respected. They gave up their beds, borrowed a car to take me to local scenic spots, offered me gifts all along the way, and of course, took countless photographs to be able to remember this noteworthy event. They introduced me to every-one they knew, and in each of their friends' homes, I was always warmly welcomed. Although the families were poor and the homes were not as clean or modern as Western homes, I never felt uncomfortable or unhappy. I always ended my visits with a much deeper appreciation of the wonderful (albeit hidden) nature of the Chinese people.

I traveled to many places in China besides my students' villages. Trav-eling in China is challenging at best. Train tickets are sold out before the ticket window opens, bus rides are long and cramped, timetables unreliable. Finding hotels and restaurants is often made easier with the help of locals, but occasionally requires great effort due to language barriers.

Communication is undoubtedly the biggest barrier for foreigners travel-ing in China. Although Chinese students are required to study English, many of them do not speak well or are afraid to speak. Learning Chinese is a must for foreigners, and all attempts at trying to speak this most dif-ficult language are greatly rewarded. Nonetheless, even a working knowl-edge of the language does not necessarily mean an easy trip; yet, the effort required to travel is well worth it. China has a fascinating culture with a long, rich history and people from a variety of backgrounds.

The lifestyle in China is also one that can be frustrating for a Westerner, but once understood and accepted, fully enjoyed. Most of the country shuts down from noon until 2:30 P.M. so that people can return home, cook and eat lunch, and sleep for an hour or so. As a result, the afternoon is cut in half, and the remaining time is slow, since people are just waking up. Added to this is a "no-need-to-hurry" attitude. Chinese society guarantees workers a job for life, extra effort is not often rewarded, and there is little personal motivation to excel. Yet people are unencumbered by watches, deadlines, and annual reviews, so they are much more relaxed and free. Once I re-alized that I had a long lunch break every day, I began to take full advan-tage of it by taking walks in the nearby fields, writing long letters home, and taking naps. It was acceptable to drop in on people any time, and they were usually free and willing to go to the local vegetable market, sit and talk all evening or play mahjong, a Chinese game played with tiles and dice, similar to the card game rummy.

Living and teaching in China was an unforgettable experience, although not an easy one. If given the opportunity to do it again, I would do so without hesitation. During my two years at Zhaotong Teachers' College, I met extraordinary people who taught me about China. I visited parts of its vast country. I gained deep insights into a different teaching methodology and helped three hundred students improve their English. I also learned about my country and culture through their questions and comments. Most importantly, I came to understand that China is not the "Big Brother Watching You" communist state full of reserved, shy people that I had expected it to be.

PART II

Africa

3

Letters from Home and a Man on the Moon: Lessons in Culture a Step at a Time

Elizabeth Wigful

I bent down to look through the cracks between the post office boxes. "Hello? Mr. Immanuel?" I called. I knew he was there. I could hear him shuffling and sorting letters behind the metal wall. Without interrupting his rhythm, the postmaster replied, "Yes, Miss Liz. How are you?" And so began our weekly ritual of me standing on the outside of Ombalantu post office waiting for Mr. Immanuel to finish sorting the mail and Mr. Immanuel on the inside giving me updates on the sorting process. "I think you'll have a letter this time," he would say every week.

The first few times he said this to me, I got excited, thinking that someone from home had remembered me. And, indeed, sometimes he was right, and a friend or family member in Canada had taken time out of their hectic lives to whiz off a letter to me in Namibia, far away on the other side of the world. But, usually, I waited on the steps of the post office next to my little box in vain. Mr. Immanuel didn't want me to lose hope so he always told me what I wanted to hear, that there must be at least one, if not several, epistles from home. When I would ask him how many letters he had left to sort he would always say, "Oh, about twelve or ten." Twelve or ten. I quickly learned that these words could mean twelve, ten, fifty, or even a hundred. Mr. Immanuel, kindhearted soul that he was, didn't want me to lose faith and trudge home through the dust just because he had a thousand letters to sort. Not one of which was addressed to me, mind you, but that wasn't really the point. It was being hopeful that counted.

Hope was something I learned a lot about in Namibia. The place was full of it, and I was especially aware of it when I first moved there in late

1994. I lived in the North of the country where guerrilla warfare had been waged for nearly thirty years against the then-ruling South African government. Ombalantu had been one of the areas hardest hit by the war, as could be witnessed by the abandoned South African army camp, the land mine field now surrounded by barbed wire and the bullet holes puckering the walls of my house. After years of oppression by the apartheid regime, Namibians had won their freedom from South Africa and joined together to form their first democratic government. Ordinary Namibians were very optimistic about their future and the people of Ombalantu were no exception.

The children of Namibia, especially those living in the former homelands, had been deprived of a basic education and were far behind their counterparts in Canada. I had come to Ombalantu as a Voluntary Service Overseas volunteer, part of an effort to raise the standard of English in schools where all subjects were taught in this alien tongue. It was a daunting task. The students had only a few years of English under their belts and had been taught mostly by untrained teachers who were far from fluent themselves. Some of their teachers had only a grade twelve education. Namibia had decided to take on Cambridge University's International General Certificate of Secondary Education (IGCSE) as its standard of education. The students had to pass formal exams at the end of their two years of senior secondary school; all subjects were studied in English, but they were not very good at it. Needless to say, it was an uphill battle.

Some of the teachers, faced with this arduous task, felt overwhelmed by it all, but several of them, the ones who had attended university or college, as well as the principal, seemed keen to take on the challenge. They saw the IGCSE as a way to a better life. And the students were very hopeful. "Education is the key to development," they would say to me, repeating the slogans of the new democracy. "Now is our chance! And you have come to help us!" I felt welcome and important.

Their enthusiasm was catching. When the first term of 1995 started, I launched myself into my job. During my first year at the school, I taught English to four classes of grade eleven and twelve. The IGCSE syllabus called for an intermediate level of proficiency in reading, writing, listening, and speaking. Some of the students weren't too far off the mark, but it quickly became obvious that the great majority of them had below standard language skills. How were we going to get them to improve their skills enough by the end of grade twelve to enable them to pass not only the English exam but all their subjects? There was no easy answer.

Not only were their skill levels impediments, but their lack of knowledge about the outside world prevented my students from understanding much of the cultural context of the British exams. Ombalantu was flat with nothing in the way of construction but one-story buildings and the groups of traditional wood huts as far as the eye could see. The concept of elevators and escalators was far beyond the students' imaginations. "How strange!," one of them said to me as I tried to explain a passage from their textbooks. "Why would people want to build rooms on top of other rooms when they can just build them side by side? Isn't that easier?" Images of packed New York skyscrapers and the crammed-together tenements of Rio flooded my head. "Well, you see . . ." I began and stopped. She was right, of course. It didn't make a lot of sense to build tall buildings in Ombalantu with so much wide, open space to utilize. I made a mental note to ask someone at home to send pictures of such wondrous things, just so we could gaze at them together.

The apartheid regime had been so thorough in its oppression of ordinary Namibians that my students hadn't even heard of the great historical events we in the West take for granted. One day I was walking past another classroom when Severin, one of our science teachers, caught sight of me and waved at me with great urgency to come in. His class was gathered around him, pointing and staring at a large picture book Severin was holding. They were murmuring excitedly in their mother tongue, Oshiwambo, many of them laughing as well. "They just don't believe me!" Severin declared in exasperation. "Tell them!"

"Tell them what?" I replied, puzzled.

"Tell them," Severin gave me a direct look, "that it's true that man has been to the moon." At this request, several of Severin's grade eleven students tsked and grumbled in English that this ridiculous piece of information must be a lie. People standing on the moon? Honestly, who had ever heard of such a thing? But, nevertheless, all eyes turned on me. They were waiting for the white foreigner to give her answer. Never mind that Severin had a Bachelor of Science from the University of Wisconsin and was certainly far more knowledgeable than I in such matters. I considered the grade elevens carefully.

"Yes," I said gravely after a few seconds of silence, "it's true." A collective gasp of delight and wonder filled the room. The students, amazed, pestered us for more information. Severin and I followed with an impromptu lesson about Neil Armstrong, NASA, space shuttles, and moon landings. I still didn't think they really believed us but it was fun trying to convince them. Obviously, more pictures needed to be sent from home.

The lack of resources in the school and surrounding village proved to be a problem that first year. We were lucky enough to have textbooks and several English language resource books in the English office. We had tape recorders and some listening practice cassettes as well, but at times these could be very temperamental. Many schools didn't even have that much. At first perusal, the textbooks for grades eleven and twelve seemed to be quite good, following a learner-centered philosophy, emphasizing equally the four skills of reading, writing, listening, and speaking. But it became obvious after a short time that these textbooks were too difficult for all but the most advanced students. After a few weeks of frustration, we English teachers decided to buckle down and help fill in the gaps. We had to do a great deal of adaptation and supplementation with our own materials. The Namibian English teachers were the best speakers of English in the school and for the most part, were also trained teachers in something, although not always English! Together we came up with ideas. Over the three years I was at the school, we built up an arsenal of weapons against the inequalities of our students' junior school educations. We organized ourselves as an efficient, interdependent unit. We planned our lessons together. We created schemes of work for the year that included frequent grade-wide tests to help the students get used to sitting for formal exams. We marked tests together to maintain the same standard. We gave additional lessons in listening practice, the skill in which they seemed to need the most help. We gave prizes to the most improved students to motivate our classes. We started a drama club, a Scrabble club, and a debating club. The school bought a televideo (a television and videocassette recorder in one) and we asked my family to send over videocassettes of ordinary things—newscasts, music videos, children's science programs, travel shows, episodes of The Simpsons. Another volunteer had her friends and colleagues send over almost a thousand children's books over the two years she was there and she started an informal library in our house. And then, in 1996, NAMAS arrived.

NAMAS (Norway Association of Namibia) was a Norwegian NGO (non-government organization) that had targeted our school, Outapi Senior Secondary School, and another school in Northern Namibia for a pilot project. NAMAS poured vast amounts of money into our school. They stocked the library, which hitherto had contained only a few ancient, unread classics and old magazines. They paid for the school buildings to be renovated. They provided a small number of computers for the secretaries and teachers to use. After my departure, they even brought in satellite TV and are now on e-mail. The miracles of the modern world brought to the isolated African village. The principal was extremely pleased, the students were thrilled, and we felt that this was going to make our job a bit easier. But new equipment brought new problems. In a school not used to having such expensive items, people were extremely protective of them. When I wanted to show my students one of the new computers and how the CD-ROM worked, the principal was reluctant to let me take it out of the staff room. What if one of the students dropped it on the way to the classroom? What if one of them touched a key they shouldn't and the whole system crashed? What if . . . ? It took me a long time to convince him and even then, he was still uneasy. The students, on the other hand, were awestruck by this incredible piece of machinery on which they could watch a short video of Nelson Mandela giving a speech after his release from prison—

not to mention the fact that you could use it to learn other languages, even Greek! The students' worlds were suddenly bigger.

The renovation of the school, as well as the gift of NAMAS, sounded wonderful at the beginning; but problems with the supply of materials, shipped in from South Africa, 2,000 km away and the worldwide tendency of builders, plumbers, and electricians to disappear in the middle of a job, made this a very slow operation indeed. I was lucky. My classroom was one of the first to be completed—before the plaster, nails, and what-have-you ran out and the builder whisked himself off to bigger places to find more. For months, my colleagues were forced to teach outside, vying for impromptu classrooms under the shadiest trees. This was fun for the first few days. Between classes, endless streams of students carried their chairs from one spot to another where their teachers sat waiting, chattering happily about fresh air and cool shade. After several weeks of this, however, they seemed far less cheery, having to trudge in the heat and write on their laps, particularly difficult when they were working on their geometry. It's not easy to use a compass without a desk to lean on. The teachers had to make do with few resources, not even being able to rely on that old standard, the chalkboard. Eventually, though, the school was restored to the original, beautiful state it possessed before the bombs and bullets. Everyone returned to their classrooms, much relieved and very pleased with the new boards and freshly painted walls.

Not all of our new-fangled ways were well received by the local teachers, however. The English department, usually a mix of volunteers and Namibians, was a highly motivated team that worked hard. This determination was not always viewed as a positive thing by our other local colleagues. Many of them had received little or no teacher training and were not well paid. They had ended up at our little backwater school because they had either been sent there by the government or had been unable to obtain a post in the city. They were not the most motivated teachers in the world and it's hardly surprising, considering the difficulties they faced teaching undereducated children a syllabus as difficult as the IGCSE. Volunteers tend to be very keen people, determined to "make a difference" despite the difficulties. Often, we had dreamed for years of coming to such a school in such a different place to "help." (I must point out that many of the new teachers, those first graduates of the new University of Namibia, were also keen to jump in with enthusiasm.) This combination of people often led to misunderstanding and frustration.

One day, early on in my time there, the principal asked me and my two volunteer colleagues to give a mini-workshop on the intricacies of learner-centered teaching. The new government had declared that all schools were to teach in this way, replacing the old "chalk and talk" routine. Mr. Kanyangela asked us the question at a staff meeting in front of all the teachers. We, of course, felt we couldn't refuse, and indeed, were secretly pleased that we'd been asked to dispense our good, Western wisdom in teaching methodology. "Yes! We'd love to help you!," we said. Then looking around the room, we added, "that is, if everyone is interested." Our Namibian colleagues beamed at us and nodded vigorously. "What a good opportunity!" someone said. "We can learn from our qualified teacher colleagues from Canada, Australia, and America!" "Yes!" others chimed in. "Let's set a date." A date was chosen for the following month. I and my volunteer colleagues, Jan and Kimberly, sprang into action. Wouldn't it be great, we thought, if some of the teachers who had been to teachers' college could deliver part of the workshop? We approached one or two people who seemed very excited at the prospect of instructing their fellow Namibians. We booked a room. We sat down together and made our plans. We were doing something truly worthwhile! Sharing skills! Helping our colleagues understand new methodology! This was important.

The appointed day rolled around and after school, we went to the classroom we'd booked and organized all the desks in nice little groups of six, group work being an essential facet of learner-centered teaching, we told each other. We put up pieces of flip-chart paper and arranged our colored markers. We waited. No one came. Oh well, no matter. People were often late to these things. We made a joke about "African time." We adjusted the desks and rearranged a few chairs. We waited some more. Still no one. Finally, I walked to the staff room to see if I could find our colleagues. It was practically empty. Where was everyone? The few people I did see there all had grandiose excuses for not being able to come to our workshop, even the two teachers who were supposed to be giving sessions! Someone's grandmother had to be taken to the hospital. Another teacher had just heard that there were important visitors at his house. Someone else had rushed off to the regional capital to go to the bank. In the end, absolutely no one showed up to our little workshop, except the vice-principal who dropped in to see how it was going. His eyes widened in surprise. "These people," he tutted, "how can they learn if they don't come?" He walked away shaking his head.

We tried not to feel too hurt by the lack of enthusiasm for our tutelage. In hindsight, it's not surprising that no one showed up. Besides the usual reasons—it was after working hours and people had family responsibilities to see to—we were still new at the school and hadn't built up enough credibility to be considered authorities on any subject, Bachelor of Education degrees notwithstanding. Anyway, why would anyone want to take on a new way of teaching when the old way seemed to work just fine? (Later on, two years later, I ran workshops for English teachers in the area but in partnership with my Namibian counterpart, Mr. Kashindi. His presence and reputation added value to our methods and ideas for tackling the new system and the workshops were much more successful.) And as to why everyone said they'd love to attend a workshop put on by their esteemed foreign colleagues when they had no intention of showing up? Well, that's called saving face and it is a very important aspect of everyday communication in Namibia. People are anxious not to offend and will always tell you what they think you'd like to hear. I don't think the Namibians we knew ever understood our need for direct answers. Because we never got them, we had no choice but to adapt! It took me a long time to get used to this new way of communicating.

At the beginning of my time at Outapi Senior Secondary School, the students' behaviours in the classroom were a bit puzzling to me as well. Outside the class, some of them were very friendly, coming to visit me at my house or in the staff room, but in class, they were so very, very quiet, especially the girls. I would greet them at the beginning of the period and they would just stare at me in silence. Later on, they said that they really couldn't understand a word of what I was saying when I first arrived, and besides, they weren't usually expected to say anything in class. In Namibia, as in many African countries, students only speak when called on by the teacher. They then stand up and very formally give an answer. And I was expecting them to talk? To discuss things with their neighbour? In English?! It took several weeks to get them started. By the end of grade twelve, though, I couldn't get them to stop talking which led to a few complaints from other teachers who were giving tests and practice in algebra or history readings. But this I viewed as a good thing—a solution to one of my challenges.

Then there were class sizes, another problem to solve. My smallest class was twenty-seven in grade twelve (after almost a third of them had dropped out after grade eleven) and the largest was forty. Most classes had about thirty-five students, not at all ideal for the teaching of a second language. It made keeping track of their progress an exercise in efficiency as I had to be very organized, giving assignments to each class on alternate weeks in order to have time to mark. My approach was to use peer evaluation, in which the class members would correct each other's work. There just wasn't time, otherwise. When evaluating speaking activities, I'd choose one or two people a day—without their knowing—and give them an individual mark at the end of the month. To encourage them to speak English as much as possible each week I'd give prizes to the group in each class which spoke the most English without lapsing into Oshiwambo. This ploy worked well—as all the students loved fruit candies!—but again, recording their individual progress was very time-consuming.

The grade twelve students' results of my first year at Outapi weren't promising. Only 62 percent of the students had passed their English exams. It was heartbreaking to see them in tears when they came to pick up their results. Independence had given them such high hopes. Now they would have equal access to education. Gone were the days when only white people were able to go on to "further studies" in Namibia. Black people too could go to university and teachers' college, but the reality was that they just couldn't get the marks to gain entrance to tertiary institutions and there weren't enough places for them. Results improved quite a lot over the three years I was there—due partly to our regimented methods of teaching and partly to the higher quality of students coming in as time went on. Most of my students, however, were members of what could be called a lost generation. A handful of them achieved their dreams and went on to higher education. These were the particularly bright students who could do well, not only in English, but in their other subjects as well. But most of them were to return to their homesteads to work the land as their parents had done before them.

A few months before I left Ombalantu, one of my former students, Junias, returned for a visit. Junias had been an exemplary student in all subjects. We had high hopes of him going on to university, but he was unable to get into the program of his choice. Instead, he opted to work for a year before reapplying. Junias, having been a star pupil, got a job easily at a junior secondary school where he became an English teacher. He popped into one of my grade twelve classes unexpectedly one day. Not knowing that he had become a teacher, I was thrilled to hear his news. After we had chatted for a while, Junias smiled and said, "I want to tell you something. The way you taught us last year was the good way. Now I am using the same methods to teach my students. I don't let them sit quiet in the class. Oh no! They are forced to speak, just like you made us. I'm practicing learner-centered teaching! That way, when they come to Outapi school next year, they will already be ahead." I recall that day being a particularly tough one—extremely hot and dry, with students starting to panic about the upcoming exams—and these words were like a tonic. Junias, despite the devastating results that many of his classmates received the previous year, despite his own failure to win a place in the program of his choice at the country's one and only university, was still hopeful. People would get ahead, bit by bit. These things could not be achieved overnight. Junias' peers would not be part of the high-flying, super-educated generation of Namibia, but perhaps their children would live in better times—better educated and with more opportunities to obtain a higher standard of living.

Such optimism in the face of adversity had a profound effect on me. We teachers, both volunteer and Namibian, often felt defeated by the enormous task we had of raising the standards of English at Outapi. But, the standards did improve over my three years there, and whether it had anything to do with our restructured English department and all the new equipment or not, the improvment occurred very, very slowly. Whenever we teachers felt like giving up, something would happen to make us push ahead: our grade-wide tests would yield good results; we would make a connection with another local school; people like Junias would return to encourage us.

These positive signs, I suppose, lead me back to Mr. Immanuel, the Ombalantu postmaster. As he sorted out his letters inside the post office and I sat outside waiting for some good news, we would chat through the metal barrier of five hundred post office boxes. He would tell me the news of the town, I would tell him what was going on at school, and we'd chat about the weather. As I sat there, the sun would usually go down at the normal hour of 6 o'clock, providing me with a beautiful sky to look at, alive with colour. And, sometimes, Mr. Immanuel would suddenly say, "Miss Liz, there is one for you!" I'd rush back up to my box, open it, and retrieve the crumpled envelope that had traveled so far to find me. Thanking Mr. Immanuel profusely—"*Tangi unene!*"—I would then race home through the evening dust, clutching my letter tightly, anxious to savour the news from home.

PART III

The Middle East

4

"Come with Me to the Casbah": Romance and Reality in Turkey

Jeri Hurd

I stood before the oak door wondering what in the hell I'd gotten myself into this time. Wrapped in a flimsy muslin towel that just barely cleared my derriere, I tottered precariously across the floor, my size eleven feet hanging at least an inch over the end of the size nine flip-flops the attendant had dropped in front of me. Exposing myself in the middle of the street wouldn't have left me feeling more defenseless than standing in the entrance hall of this Turkish bath, all but naked, fuzzily eyeing my two friends since my glasses were locked safely away with my clothes. I stood uncertainly before the door, not knowing whether to push through into the baths, not knowing whether that wooden shield was all that stood me between me and utter humiliation. Filled with people I didn't know, in a culture I didn't understand, this moment seemed the culmination of my first two months in Turkey, and my only thought was a loud, emphatic, "I want to go home."

Four months previously, safe in my coastal home of Aberdeen, Washington, where I'd been teaching in a small, rural school for eight years, Turkey had seemed like a marvelous idea. I was tired of looking at the same students, tired of talking to the same people, tired, frankly, of my boring old self. The surrounding forests of this logging community closed in relentlessly as I surveyed the stagnant pool my life had become. Dreams of camera safaris on the Serengeti, moonlit strolls along the palm-lined Casablanca boulevards as romantic strangers murmured "come with me to the Casbah," lay under the thick sawdust of a secure job in a town that may have been only two hours from Seattle, geographically, but millions

more in every other sense. Listening to the stories told by ex-pat pros at
the overseas job fair I attended—reaching out your kitchen door in Cyprus
to pick an orange off the tree, midnight evacuations from strife-torn Mo-
rocco, waking to watch elephants bathe in Namibian dust—the sameness
of my own life, clotted over with predictability and routine seemed all but
unendurable. When I finally received an offer from an international school
in Turkey, I hesitated for a moment, then plunged. What the heck? Who
cared if I only had a vague idea of where Turkey was? I mean, I knew it
was next to Greece somewhere, that it was 99 percent Islamic and that
Istanbul/Constantinople/Byzantium had played a large part in writing various chapters in history, but that was about it. I shoved my doubts aside,
reminded myself that "When you're green you grow; when you're ripe you
rot," signed on the dotted line and faxed off the contract.

Then panic struck. Change is always hard for me, and once the move
became real, all the romantic dreams gave way to worrying about leaving
family and friends behind: my pregnant sister, the romantic fling that had
started a few months earlier. "Hurd," I admonished myself, "You are
thirty-nine years old. Is this really the time to change your nice American
way of life, to trade in your Camry for a camel?" Determined to stretch
my horizons, I knew I had to plan ahead for facing the emotional difficulties
once I arrived in Ankara.

When preparing for an overseas move, you must be completely honest
with yourself about your normal response to stress. Whatever you normally
feel at home in safe, known surroundings will be amplified three times once
you're overseas, whether you're in London or Laos. Planning for that
greatly increases your chances of a successful sojourn overseas. I don't want
to sound like a doomsayer, but any guide to living overseas will tell you
of the surprisingly high ex-pat failure rate—people who break contract and
run for home, unprepared for the day-to-day struggle of coping with an
alien culture. Obviously, nothing can completely prepare you, but reading
several of the available books on culture shock can at least make you aware
of what you're feeling and why, which gives you a good chance of dealing
with it successfully.

My troubles started early. Intermixed with the occasional bouts of an-
ticipation came bouts of crying over deciding what to get rid of, crying as
I said good-bye to friends, crying as the plane took off. Once I arrived, the
drive from the airport thrilled me, with its views of towering minarets, *simit*
sellers with their wares perched atop their heads, and even the occasional
donkey cart trotting complacently down the highway, unperturbed by the
Renaults and Audis speeding by (no camels).

Then we arrived at the apartment and I learned the first rule of ex-pat
life, teacher style: accommodations will probably fall below the standards
you're used to at home. The apartment earlier described to me as spacious
and modern made my college dorm room look like a suite at the Ritz. It

didn't help that I tripped over three carpet-covered holes in the floor when I walked into the living room. And the decor! White walls, beige carpets, beige furniture that looked like a reject from the Jetsons and beige curtains—completely barren. Thus, I discovered rule number two for overseas living: Resist the urge to panic at the last minute, removing everything nonessential from your luggage. Be sure to pack items that will help make your apartment comfortable and homey, whether it's a favorite afghan or comforter, pillows, or whatever. Sure, you don't want to take "home" with you; you want to go out and experience the new culture. However, it's nice to have a retreat, especially in those first few months when everything is a challenge, whether it's learning how to squat over a floor toilet or spending an hour trying to figure out how the washing machine works.

With all the changes, once alone in my apartment, surrounded by its emptiness, I succumbed to a long crying jag, which lasted for three months on an almost nightly basis. However, because I knew about culture shock, I could devise ways to deal with it.

First and foremost, I told myself it was fine to be depressed and that it would pass eventually. It really is just a phase, and a result of moving from a place where you understand how to function as an independent adult, to a place where you don't recognize a box of milk when you see it, are terrified to cross the street since no one seems to be obeying any recognized traffic rules, and a place where people stare at you as if something were hanging out your nose as you walk down the street. Individually, you'll find these occurrences amusing, great fodder for delightful e-mails home (if you have e-mail!) to wow those without your adventuresome spirit. As they lose their newness, however, and you realize that, after spending three hours to get to and from shopping, and the company that promised you six weeks ago to have your phone in within five days still hasn't shown up, these incidents not only lose their charm, they grow increasingly frustrating. So, rather than thinking, "I HAVE to stick this out for the full two years" (most international schools offer two-year contracts), I said, "Okay, you can go home at the end of the year, if you want." Within a week, this changed to "You can leave at Christmas!" Naturally, the entire time I gave myself permission to leave, I knew that by the time Christmas came around, I wouldn't need to leave. But you do what it takes to help yourself through the rough times.

You'll also find that once the students arrive, your general outlook will improve immensely, if only because school will keep you as busy as ever, if not more so, though it does come with its own set of frustrations. In Turkey, there are basically two types of schools, the "International" schools, usually based on either British or American curriculum, and the national schools with their own curricula, but with some subjects taught in English. My school, as far as I know, is the only one in Turkey that accepts both, offering both a national and international track. Moreover, it's a very selective school; thus, for me, while I had to adjust to some philosophical differences between British and American education (our school uses just enough of both to frustrate both the Brits and the Americans!), the students themselves were reassuringly familiar. Friends who teach at Turkish schools, however, don't have it so easy.

Turkey reveres its children, certainly an admirable trait. For many Westerners, however, there is an apparent lack of discipline for fear of "psychologically damaging" the child. In public you'll see children of all ages out until eleven or twelve at night, bundled up even in warm weather against disease-causing drafts! (Westerners stifle on buses in Turkey, because Turks hardly ever open windows or turn on the air conditioning, for fear of drafts.) Mothers may still be feeding seven-year-olds by hand, and I once saw a woman wheeling a child of at least eight in a stroller! In movie theatres during intermission, children may charge up and down the aisles, climb over seats, and bang on the screen with only an encouraging smile from Mom and Dad. (By the way, most movies are subtitled, not dubbed, so you can see most of the new releases, and often only a few months after they're out in the states.)

You can see what problems this may cause when students enter a classroom that expects more restrained behavior, especially if you're one of only a few foreign teachers. Many Turkish teachers, quite honestly, resort to yelling and screaming as their predominant disciplinary tool. But what about the school system itself? Interestingly enough, it's all but forbidden to flunk a student, regardless of how little work the student completed. In fact, students and their families can actually sue a teacher over a poor grade. I've never seen this happen, but, at national schools, there is considerable pressure to give students good, or at least passing, grades. As an example of Turkish fear of harming a child through failure, a friend just told me yesterday that her school gives an end-of-the-year achievement award to *every* student. They are afraid of the "psychological damage" to students who wouldn't receive awards if they were only given to high achievers!

As a result of these fears, many schools have few consequences for poor behavior: students, the darlings of their parents at home, ignore teacher requests, wander around the room talking on the ubiquitous cell phones, and seldom complete assignments. Moreover, Turkish educational style encourages rote memorization rather than independent learning, and students often resist teaching styles requiring more thought on their part, a problem exacerbated by the lack of a reading culture here. Newspapers abound, but few people read books on a regular basis.

On the other hand, teachers at most international schools, which train students to a different work ethic, couldn't be happier. At my school, for instance, my worst discipline problem is an eighth-grade class that sometimes talks too much. Unlike some students at home, few Turkish students are deliberately malicious. I can't imagine being called here some of the names my students in Aberdeen called me, or any of my kids here throwing a desk across the room in a temper tantrum. Moreover, most students at international schools go through a rigorous set of entrance exams for admission, guaranteeing bright and motivated students (mostly). Two of the most prestigious schools in Turkey accept only the top 2 and top 5 percent of students who apply. As an added bonus, thanks to Atatürk, the much revered founder of the Turkish republic, most people here feel a deep respect for teachers, and you'll find the average person on the street perking up when s/he discovers you teach. In fact, teachers receive discounts at movie and theatre events (I just went to the opera for seventy-five cents) and, for those in national schools, most major cities offer special discounted hotels just for teachers.

As for Turkey itself, you couldn't ask for a better experience as your first overseas country. It's exotic enough to feel you're in a foreign country, but modern enough you don't have to suffer for it! Turkish people exude warmth and hospitality; almost every shop owner will urge you to join him in a glass of delicious apple tea as you bargain over his wares. The food, though sometimes monotonous, is almost always wonderful. Turks stuff almost every vegetable imaginable, and produce the best fruits and vegetables you'll ever eat. Think Greek cuisine, only better!

Geographically, the gods blessed Turkey profoundly, with everything from snow-capped mountains to warm Mediterranean coasts. The country boasts a long and meaningful history, from the early Hittites, through the Greeks and Romans, and on to the Byzantine and Ottoman empires. In one day it's possible to see Troglodyte caves, Greek temples, Byzantine mosaics, and Ottoman mosques!

Like any developing country, Turkey has its social problems. Inflation is rife. A million lira was worth $13 when I arrived in 1996; three years later, it's worth just over $2. You'll also find the poverty unnerving at times. I'll never forget the three-year-old girl I saw trying to sell pencils outside a McDonald's one cold January night, her thin body shivering as she begged me to buy from her. I bought her a happy meal and some hot chocolate instead.

Also, while Turkey receives some pretty heavy media bashing for human rights abuses, some fairly, many others are grossly exaggerated. Women's rights, in particular, have made broad strides forward. Turks even voted in a female head of state, which is more than the United States can claim!

Having begun my two-year adventure with intense fears, I'm now entering into my fourth year here, completely hooked on the ex-pat experience. I still feel anxious in new places, but I'm confident in my ability to cope with any problems that arise. As an Irish friend here says, "As long as you have money and your passport, no problem is overwhelming!" Teaching overseas offers unlimited opportunities for both personal and professional growth, as long as you're not afraid to risk looking foolish on occasion. Or, to put it in more exotic terms, looking foolish can be enchanting:

As I stood before the *hamam* door, the dilapidated state of the place had me worried. Did I really want to put myself in one more situation where I didn't understand the rules and couldn't ask what they were? However, all doubts fled as I opened the oak door and stood, stunned. A cavernous marble room confronted us, its large domed ceiling covering recessed arches spaced evenly around the walls and a marble platform spacious enough for several bathers to lie on. Grey marble basins filled with water stood in each of the recessed arches, while steam hung pleasantly in the warm air. Moving rather timidly toward one side of the platform, my friends and I almost yelled in surprise as we sat down: the marble was heated to just bearably hot. Wrapped tightly in our towels as our sole defense against the foreignness of the place, we felt more than a little awkward as we wondered what we were supposed to do. We surreptitiously observed the other women, some being scrubbed down by attendants clad only in black lace panties, others lying on their towels, backsides bared for all to see. What the heck! Muttering a determined "When in Rome . . ." (or Istanbul), we cast our inhibitions aside. As we lay on our stomachs, sweat from the steamy heat trickling down our faces and between our breasts, the bath attendants began to sing, the melody's haunting Middle-Eastern cadence echoing and mingling with the splashing water.

Another attendant entered and, grinning, jumped onto the platform, breasts and pelvis swinging, feet stamping, and hands beating time to the tune her coworkers sang. We clapped and cheered; one attendant dumped out the water in her bucket, turned it over, and drummed a counterpoint to the music and the dance. What a marvelous moment! This woman didn't worry about her pendulous breasts or flabby stomach—she danced with an infectious humor that we all caught as we whistled and cheered her on.

Soon, however, all settled down and a well-muscled woman beckoned me over. I walked cautiously over the wet marble to where she dipped nearly scalding water out of one of the marble basins. She poured bowls of it repeatedly over my reclining body until, loofa mitt in hand, she scrubbed me up and down, the accumulated grime of Turkey's pollution rolling off my skin. Oddly enough, as I watched the dead skin sloughing off my body, my past anxieties seemed to wash off with it. I didn't know this woman, couldn't speak to her at all, yet my muscles relaxed and tensions eased under her ministrations. Maybe I could handle all this foreignness after all. As she lathered me down by filling what looked like a cheesecloth pillowcase with air, grabbing the top ends and twirling the "bag" to form a balloon, then squeezing out the air and resulting suds, I felt a growing confidence. Who needed home when I had this?

That bath and massage were the most luxurious and decadent experiences I've ever had. I'd bet anything baths were the high point of the day for those harem girls. A sense of well-being and camaraderie settled among us as we laughed and chatted, relaxing against the warm marble, buck-naked with women we'd never seen before and would probably never see again. Afterwards, sipping freshly squeezed orange juice—and feeling rather freshly squeezed myself!—my earlier anxieties seemed silly and the remaining time in Turkey seemed full of promise.

5

Surviving the Soviet Legacy

Ken Lockette

The building is dark and virtually empty when I arrive at 7:45 A.M. The morning is gray outside and seemingly grayer inside the drab rectangular structure, a cheerless building typical of Almaty, Kazakhstan. The Soviets, until recently the urban planners for Almaty, loved rigid, uniform concrete buildings, and this former preschool building is no different. It is oppressive really. Despite efforts to gentrify the grounds with new elementary playground equipment and fresh paint, the bars on the windows and the massive blocks of crumbling concrete make the school look and feel like a prison. My first impression, and nearly everyone's, was a horrified gasp, a first impression that has entirely faded for me because of what is happening inside.

I pass through the cloakroom, flip on the lights, and look around my classroom. I have been engaged in a glorious and hard fought battle to beautify the room, a battle where major strides have been made, but the room with all its years still can't help but show its age. Multiple layers of paint continue to chip, and posters hang down from the wall as they do every morning. The windows too are old and wear dust that has long left its mark and can't be removed.

The bathroom door inside my room is wide open, left that way as it always is by the night cleaning lady. I shut the door and release the CD player from its imprisonment in the padlocked storage closet. I put in a CD by Cecilia Bartoli. A lidded trash can sits in front of the chalkboard next to the bathroom, another item never put back by the cleaning lady. Each bathroom is provided with a lidded bucket or large trash can because no one is allowed to throw toilet paper in the toilet. The pipes in this building are too old and narrow to accommodate the extra waste. I return the trash can to its proper place in the bathroom and sit at my desk. Cecilia greets me with a soaring aria as I go through the school mail and plot out my course for the day.

The students slowly start arriving in shifts. Sasha, a seventeen-year-old Russian youth, ambles in, his presence preceded by the stale stench of cigarette smoke. Sasha has been with the Almaty International School from its inception five years ago when foreign companies poured in and embassies opened at a furious rate. He struts in with his backpack slung over his left shoulder, his long-sleeve, button-down shirt meticulously pulled out and draped over his belt. He is somewhat quiet this morning, trying to wake up as he fetches a chair from the adjoining room.

With a total of only twenty-five students in the entire high school, it didn't take long for everyone to get to know each other. Lines were drawn and friendships formed within the first week. Throughout the year, students trickle in and may upset the mood that has been established, but usually the new kids find their place in the high school social order. And with the diversity of eleven nationalities in all (Korean, Japanese, Taiwanese, Kazakh, Russian, American, Israeli, Turkish, Filipino, Pakistani, and Indian), there are virtually no discipline problems. Everyone gets along. An Indian girl is friends with a Pakistani girl. The American students mingle with the Asian students. The local students, both Kazakh and Russian, mix with the rest of the group. This cohesiveness makes sense once you think about it. Everyone is in the same boat; that is, living in a post-Soviet culture, a culture that is struggling with its own identity as are these adolescents.

Sasha, however, remains somewhat on the periphery, proudly so; he is proud of his independence and heavy metal attitude. He is popular though in the way he wants to be, which is as the class clown and hooligan. Nevertheless, he never bothers anyone and certainly is not a bully in any sense. The image is more of an attitude he likes to project. It brings him attention and notoriety that he suspects he would not get in any other way.

When Sasha first started, he knew very little English, and the words he did know were not exactly appropriate for a school setting. He struggled through the first couple of years taking intensive English classes, mainly one-on-one tutoring, and struggled to find his niche in what was a foreign environment in his own country. He despised being away from the rest of the student body and would occasionally act out in defiance by smarting off or by being uncooperative. It was not until Sasha was "mainstreamed" into the regular high school classroom that he truly started to develop.

The transition did not occur easily. Sasha's spoken language skills had improved through his intensive English classes, but at sixteen, his written skills were still weak. Understanding the bulk of the reading in his classes was difficult, and many thought that he would flounder and fail. Frustration poured from his face and voice as the words would swim around him instead of sinking in, absorbing into his vocabulary and understanding. This was the Sasha that I met last year, a struggling young man trying to embrace a "foreign" culture while, at the same time, trying to figure his own place where everything had changed.

Since Kazakhstan's inception as an independent country in 1991, ethnic Russians have lost power and opportunities. Russian was replaced by Kazakh as the official language. (It has since been restored because less than half of the country knew Kazakh. Now there are two official languages.) All the street names have been changed from Russian names to Kazakh, yet most people still don't know the new names and will refer to the old ones. All Russian statues have vanished and in their place are Kazakh artists and leaders. An ethnic Russian would even have a difficult time running for president since a new law was passed requiring candidates to pass a Kazakh language exam. Many Russians with the means and money to leave have done so. But where is Sasha to go? What is his place in this society?

I met Sasha the first day of school last fall. There was a huge turnover in the teaching staff and a fairly large turnover with the high school student body. Everyone was trying to establish their own identity. Sasha thought he would instigate a challenge and wore a black Nirvana T-shirt with a mopey-eyed portrait of Kurt Cobain on the front. His black jeans had a long chain-wallet that noisily dangled at his side. It wasn't Nirvana that I objected to. I too was attracted to loud, angry music as a kid. It was the quotation emblazoned with large white lettering on a black surface, a quotation that read "Don't tell me the FUCK what to do," that I had a problem with. I had to hand it to Sasha for having the guts to test the waters so thoroughly the first day. We quickly got acquainted and since then have established a rapport with each other. The relationship is a funny one. This shirt serves as a resounding anthem for Sasha but not one without a little irony. He does not want to be told what to do; but, at the same time, he does not know what to do.

Sasha hands me an essay entitled "Pop Music Sucks," a makeup draft of a persuasive essay. His point certainly comes through, but the paper is riddled with grammar and syntax errors and is not well organized. We talk about the differences between formal and informal writing, and Sasha works on his diction until he leaves satisfied that he will at least make a decent showing during the writing workshop later that afternoon.

First period begins. I have all of the graduating seniors in British Literature except for Sasha. British Literature is a required course for the "academic" diploma; that is, a degree geared to those going on to further study. All of the seniors in the class have mapped out their immediate futures. One student has been accepted to Stanford. Another has chosen a bible college. A local Kazakh girl is heading to the new Kazakh/American University in Almaty. One student is going to complete his Mormon mis-

sion before attending Brigham Young University, and yet another is going
to a liberal arts college in Colorado.

Graduation is not far away, and Sasha really wants to be a part of that
group. Since the school operates with an outcome-based mastery learning
education system, Sasha is allowed to retest and make up work until he
"masters" a particular outcome. He has worked hard to stay afloat but has
been playing catch-up since last year. Even if he completes all the requirements, where is he to go? He can't go back into his own country for he
is already in it even though he cannot recognize it. His English skills are
not to the level that would gain him admittance in any English-speaking
institution, and his knowledge of the subject areas in Russian institutions
of higher learning are different from what he has been learning. Add the
fact that since he has spent so much time on his English language writing
skills, his Russian writing skills haven't fully developed. Sasha is enigmatic
in a sense. He has become a foreigner in his own country, a square peg in
a round hole.

After British Literature and Creative Writing, I hop in the school van
with Genady, a local worker, and head to the fabric bazaar. The Commedia
dell' Arte Festival, fifteenth-century Italian improvisational theatre, which
I am directing, opens soon and I need to buy material for costumes. One
student's nanny is a seamstress by trade and has agreed to make the most
complicated pieces for the festival. Like many local professionals, this seamstress works a job outside of her trade. Since the fall of communism, many
professionals cannot afford to practice their craft and now rely on service-
type jobs with foreign embassies and companies. Doctors are housecleaners.
Electrical engineers are drivers. Because the foreign community pays in dollars, many locals make much more than they could if they stayed in their
own profession.

The fabric bazaar isn't far from the school, but the trip is always an
adventure. Most roads in Almaty are like the surface of the moon. Craters
are spread all over the streets, and drivers recklessly swerve without any
thought to the other cars on the road. There are no lines on most of the
streets, and what seems like a two-lane road can turn into a three- or four-
lane one depending on the traffic. Genady is quite adept at this race and
swerves and careens with the best of them. Genady and I make it safely to
the bazaar and begin to bargain for material.

One student actor that I must costume is Sasha. Sasha plays the fumbling
braggart soldier, Il Capitano. Where Sasha struggles in academics, he shines
in the theater. He loves the limelight and being encouraged to be bombastic
in front of an audience for the Commedia Festival is a dream come true.
He has embraced his comedic role and has had fun entertaining the rest of
the cast at rehearsal. It has been fun for me to watch Sasha in this environment. Many of our rehearsals are held after school, and Sasha seems to
be a different person. He doesn't feel inadequate or behind as he is in his

classes. Instead, he is a leader and one of the role models. Could this be Sasha's path?

Literature class rolls around after lunch, and we finish reading *A Midsummer Night's Dream*. Sasha reads for Oberon and then Lysander but admits to feeling closer to the mischievous Puck. Sasha struggled through parts of the play, but it is a play that he wouldn't have been able to understand at all a year ago. Many of the allusions and metaphors are lost on him, but at least he understands the main conflicts and personalities. He gives a Puckish grin and says that Oberon wouldn't be too bad of a guy to play since he is all-powerful and has relationships with both Titania and Hippolyta. Sasha has gradually improved in literature and has read more this year than ever before. Of course, he is interested in the Holden Caufields and other wayward characters, but whatever it takes to get him to read, I try to get that material to him.

In writing class the students break into their peer editing groups to share their latest drafts. Sasha throws his "Pop Music Sucks" essay into the fray, and it gets a good working over. The kids are very accepting. It is not a secret that Sasha is the weakest writer in the class, and consequently, the criticism is constructive and beneficial. However, the essay spawns a heated debate of what is worthy as music. Sasha the actor comes out and gives a spirited monologue on the merits of heavy metal music over pop. We tell him to write down what he just said, and Sasha's next draft is formed.

I pick up a note in my mailbox from the director of instruction wanting to know what outcomes any of the seniors need to make up. Sasha is on my list and we meet seventh period to prep him for a retest on poetry. I take the opportunity to talk with Sasha about his future. He is not very interested in going down that path and gives the standard "I don't know." I sit there for awhile and think about Sasha and how he got to this point. Is he one who has fallen through the cracks? He was definitely one who was passed on when he wasn't ready, and I had inherited Sasha and his lack of basic skills, but the cultural factors also come into play. Does Sasha have a fair shot as an ethnic Russian in a Kazakh society?

I gather myself and get ready for my final class-drama. Sasha is again in fine form and slays us all with his humorous stock speech on all the battles he (Il Capitano) has fought or at least is saying he fought. "I took out a whole army with one arm tied behind my back. No, it wasn't just one arm. It was two. Oh, and my legs too were tied." He writhes on the ground in battle and we soon join him on the floor laughing.

Eventually the bell rings and all the kids scurry out of the building and head home. I work at my desk for awhile and notice the note concerning makeup work for the seniors from earlier. I see Sasha's name and can't get him out of my mind. Has the system failed him? Is the deck stacked against him? Could I have done more after he stepped into my classroom? Will he become a leader in this rapidly changing country or an ethnic victim of shifting power? Even with all the questions I somehow feel that Sasha will survive. He has the instincts and the attitude to do so. He will run into difficulties from time to time, at first responding with the provocative Cobain quotation he used in our first meeting, but then with something more thoughtful. I stare out the window pondering all this complexity before gathering up my things to take home.

I put all the chairs on the tables and reattach a couple of posters whose corners have drooped since this morning. The sun is out and the afternoon rays heat up the room like a sauna. I re-imprison the CD player, hit all the lights, and pass through the cloakroom. I see the night cleaning lady coming down the hall getting ready to start on the first floor. We exchange greetings and I head out into the burning sun.

6

From the Midwest to the Middle East: Iowa to Abu Dhabi

Mike Kielkopf

In mid-October the daily high in Abu Dhabi, capital of the United Arab Emirates, was down about 15° F from the school-opening temperatures of late August. The days were finally struggling to hit 100°. The humidity was dropping too, but it was still powerful enough to leave you wondering why you'd bothered to shower if you had to trek from the computer lab to the cafeteria, perhaps a thirty-second journey. But inside Mr. Kiel's computer lab the Macs were humming happily at 60 MHz, and the Trane A/C units were in excellent form. It was finger-chillingly cool. My high school newspaper staff was working on the second issue of *The Quill* when the subject turned to the weekend volleyball matches at Dubai.

"Why don't they play the games on Thursday instead of Friday?" I wondered.

"Because they have school on Thursday," my Pakistani coeditor said.

"C'mon, I know I'm new here but even I know that the weekend is Thursday and Friday."

"Not in Dubai," Marya said. "Their weekend is Friday and Saturday."

I continued to protest. I suggested it wasn't nice to try to make a fool of the new teacher, that Iowans are a little more clever than they're sometimes given credit for, and that after six weeks at the American Community School of Abu Dhabi I figured I knew when the weekend was. But then the other editor, an Egyptian, chimed in: "She's not trying to fool you, Mr. Kielkopf. It's true," Barry said. "I'm tellin' ya, Dubai has a Friday-Saturday weekend. You mean you really didn't know that?"

"Nobody told you? There are different weekends all over the Arab world. Egypt has Friday-Saturday, like Dubai. And so does Pakistan. That's why all our sports events with Dubai have to be on Friday. That's the only common weekend we have. Really. Go ask Mr. Hackworth (high school principal)."

Of course, Barry and Marya were telling the truth, but no, no one had told me and everything I had read both in preparation for coming to the United Arab Emirates and since arriving had indicated that the country observed a Thursday-Friday weekend. The kids explained that since Dubai is the major business center of the UAE, it had adopted a different weekend than the seat of government, Abu Dhabi, so that it would have an extra day to do business with the West and its Saturday-Sunday weekend. This accomodation is, in a way, emblematic of not only the culture in Abu Dhabi, but also my family's unique experience here. The country, especially this city, is a fascinating combination of Muslim society and Western capitalism, which brings with it many cultural influences from all over the world, especially the United States.

These different forces coexist peacefully and successfully most of the time. In February of 1999, however, weekends became even more complicated and controversial. Without warning, government officials announced the weekend in Dubai—for all schools and government departments—would be altered to match Abu Dhabi's Thursday-Friday weekend, beginning in March. There were many protests from school officials and those working in private business. These protests pointed out that mandating the new school weekend would disrupt many families whose fathers work in private business and who would continue to have Friday-Saturday weekends. That would leave only one day—Friday—as a common weekend for such families. The objections centered around the UAE's constant championing of family values but those objections were ignored this time. The official weekend in Abu Dhabi and Dubai remains Thursday through Friday. And so it turns out I wasn't wrong back in 1994—I was just ahead of my time.

Weekends notwithstanding, teaching at the American Community School (ACS) of Abu Dhabi for five years has been one of the definitive experiences of our lives. That is why my wife and I decided to make 1999–2000 our sixth at ACS. And our son, who was a fourth-grader when we arrived here and is now a freshman in the high school, has been part of an international community that has surely shaped a worldview far different than what might have been expected had we remained in Iowa. Mary is founder and director of the Optimal Learning Program that serves elementary students with special needs. I teach senior and AP English and founded and advise both the student newspaper and literary magazine. Before our son was born, we had taught in South Africa. Then, we grew restless in Iowa despite teaching in excellent systems, and we decided to take our son and venture overseas. We have never regretted it.

But who would willingly go to the war-ravaged Middle East, home of Arab terrorists and Muslim extremists? Not us, we thought, until we traded our ignorance for information. The fact is that United Arab Emirates is as safe a place to live—even for Iowans—as the world has to offer. During the Gulf War, we were told, ACS closed for one day. After the conflict, it was school as usual. During the intervening years the various clashes between Iraq and the United Nations, the bombing of some U.S. embassies in Africa and other international incidents have impacted ACS only in canceling some team travel to Kuwait or Syria or Greece or other locations once or twice simply out of prudence. Other than that, neither the school nor we as individuals have been impacted. It is true that the school has adopted a more formal security plan since we arrived, but it is far less intrusive than the increasing number of U.S. schools in the United States that employ metal detectors, security officers in the halls, video surveillance of parking lots, restroom entrances, hallways, and other key locations. But what about those Muslim extremists and those Arab terrorists? They definitely exist, but not in the UAE. This country has no history of such activity and no reason to believe that record will be marred in the foreseeable future. Trying to label UAE nationals' views toward America is no easier than it was labeling the views of Americans toward Bill Clinton. The views fall all along the spectrum with the majority, in both cases, falling in the middle. Great support for many U.S. policies, for American business and for America in general, exists here, as the controversy of weekend days attests. The U.S. press often fails to reflect this support, thus creating an inaccurate, negative representation of Arab attitudes. Most Arabs are like most Americans: they simply want to live in peace and to see their children live long, happy, and successful lives. This observation signals another theme for my experience here. If international teaching is a journey, then culture and politics are eventually out-distanced by humanity—something we all share. On a personal level, most people we deal with in the UAE are friendly and helpful, and we have never felt threatened in any way.

And so the transition from the Midwest to the Middle East was only slightly more difficult, though far more engaging, than moving from Iowa to Arizona. Moving is moving: you have to pack, leave friends and family, and make adjustments. You have to unpack, find a grocery store, a doctor, and a dentist. Fortunately, there are people where you're moving to who have gone through the same thing, and most are happy to help. We felt comfortable in Abu Dhabi from the day we arrived. We had researched the country and the school exhaustively. (Of course, there were a few quirks you can only learn on site, such as the lowdown on weekends.) We had phoned teachers at the school and exchanged scores of faxes in the last days before the advent of e-mail. But one thing to remember is this: no matter where you go, there you are. This simple statement emphasizes a reality about moving into a new culture: enjoyment comes to people when they embrace their surroundings. And so there we were, smack dab in the middle of the Middle East, in an ancient Arab land that today is among the safest places on earth. Despite an occasional violent crime that reminds visitors that they are still on planet earth, the sense of personal safety is palpable as you stroll along Abu Dhabi's Corniche Road that borders the Arabian (don't call it Persian) Gulf much the way Chicago's Lake Shore Drive winds along Lake Michigan. And while sauntering around town on foot there are a variety of Kodak moments that illustrate the diverse scenes and often paradoxical nature of Abu Dhabi:

Fully veiled women driving with glasses on top of their veils and talking on mobile phones;

Almost everyone—kids, adults, men, women, Westerners, Muslims—talking on mobile phones;

Women wearing short shorts, short skirts, skin-tight pants, sleeveless blouses, or plunging necklines imperviously sharing the sidewalk with Muslim women in street-length black abaya, black gloves, and full veil in 114° heat and 91 percent humidity;

Construction workers on twenty-story buildings wearing sandals and turbans;

Mosques with minarets reaching three or four stories high dwarfed by twenty-story glass towers next door;

Pakistani taxi drivers' shacks slumping incongruously next to palatial single-family villas;

The towering minarets of the largest mosque in Abu Dhabi casting shadows over the neighboring St. Joseph's Catholic Church that is itself just down the street from the Christian Evangelical Community Church, a building that sits on land donated to its founders by the ruler of the UAE;

Nine young camels in a makeshift pen in the median of a residential street waiting to be slaughtered on site for a wedding feast;

A goat hanging from a tree by its hind hooves and being skinned and carved in the front yard of a beautiful three-story marble villa less than ten feet off the sidewalk;

Three- or four-year-old boys wearing their white dishdashas while riding bikes, playing soccer, rollerblading;

Teens and adults bowling or ice skating (at the Zayed Sports City Ice Rink) in dishdashas;

Hundreds of pairs of sandals outside the mosques during prayer call;

A Muslim on the side of the highway kneeling on his prayer rug and facing Mecca as he observes one of the five daily prayer calls while traffic and the rest of the world speed by obliviously;

Camels wandering the glistening dunes outside the cities the way cows roam the rolling hills of Iowa. Why, you can almost see Lawrence of Arabia there in the distance . . . ; and

Arabs in traditional dress driving Fords and Chevys as well as BMWs and Mercedes and eating at Burger King or Pizza Hut or Ponderosa.

Abu Dhabi is a fascinating pastiche of cultures, but as enjoyable as the sights of the city can be, the classroom draws the teacher to the real reason for his international journey. At ACS Abu Dhabi we have over 600 students in grades K–12 on a single campus. These students represent nearly fifty nationalities. This mix of general civility, intellectual curiosity, and international perspectives creates the special ambience of the overseas school. We have children of diplomats and business people, of teachers and doctors, of oil workers and military leaders. We have many students who speak two or three or more languages fluently and students who have lived in and traveled to most regions of the world. Cultural exchange in the classroom comes easily with class sizes from eight to 20 students. I usually have an average of 12–15 students in my high school English classes, which increases teacher time for each student and therefore helps manage student behavior. Discipline problems occur, but they are fewer and less serious than in many stateside schools. Chewing gum or being tardy are the most common transgressions. Things become even more teacher friendly when one considers the school faculty. We use the same English textbook series that I was using back in Iowa. We installed a media center full of green iMacs in June of 1999, and we have had school-wide Internet access since 1997. Our technology and materials are similar to that in the finest schools anywhere.

Since parents, or the companies they work for, pay a considerable sum for their kids to attend ACS, we try hard to maintain good relations and communications with them. Most of the time the effort succeeds, but just as teachers will be teachers and students will be students, parents will also be parents. We have open house early in the fall and teacher-parent conferences in mid-November for all grades, K–12. Most parents are understanding, supportive, and appreciative of the teachers and the school, but not all. Some parents pressure their children too much. In my second year at ACS I met with a career military man at conferences whose daughter, a freshman, was earning a C in my humanities class. I told him it was a tough class that included juniors and seniors and that Liz was working hard and, as far as I was concerned, doing her best. "I think you should be pleased with her effort. Earning a C in this class is very good," I said.

Liz's father sneered and squeezed the sides of the desk hard: "I should say it is NOT good enough. She has to be getting A's. Anything less simply is not acceptable." End of parent conference. The good news is that this attitude is uncommon. Whether in the United States or in the Middle East, some parents don't understand that young people who work hard and do their best will eventually outshine those who may earn higher grades. Both common sense and valid studies affirm this truth.

Some of our teachers enjoy proclaiming their determination to hold our students to "high standards." These teachers are ready to pounce on any student who dares to be one second late to class, who fails to meet assignment deadlines regardless of circumstances, or who fails to follow directions. Many of these same teachers, however, are the ones who are consistently late for professional meetings, who do not complete report cards and other assignments on time, and who often fail to meet other obligations. They always have good excuses, of course, but excuses they would never accept from students. The byword in recruiting international teachers is "flexibility," but many of us only laugh at that notion when we see that some of our colleagues are as flexible as a marble statue. Things are significantly better at ACS and many other international schools than in many stateside schools, but have no illusions. Again, I employ a phrase that has become a standard for me since we began teaching overseas: schools are still schools. This predictability, even in such a seemingly exotic and "un-American" place as the UAE is a strong antidote for any feelings of culture shock I may have had.

ACS is part of a growing trend in international schools in that a minority of our students are American citizens. Until about four years ago, the ACS student body was consistently about 60 percent American. Since then, the percentage of Americans enrolled has dropped below 40 percent. We like the mix because it adds to the international nature of this assignment. Many overseas schools, including the one up the road in Dubai, are so dominated by Americans that the experience can become one in which you may be overseas geographically, but you're really working in a stateside school environment.

My student rosters at ACS Abu Dhabi have included these names, representing every major continent: Stanimirovic, Mochizuki, Tokuda, Samara, Iskandar, El Gawly, Al Fahim, Amat y Leon, Das, Makriyianni, Mobassaleh, Shibli, D'Alessandro, Ahmed, Mushtaque, Deegudtum, Berezich, Al Askari, Bolanos, Syed, Patel, Zwets . . . I've even taught a Katharine Jones and a Steve Roberts.

Inside the classroom, education is a universal language; and kids, no matter where they're from and how you spell—or pronounce—their names, are kids. About 50 students graduate from eighth grade each spring. And every year 10–15 of them will attend new schools in other parts of the world for ninth grade. However, unlike schools in North America, people—students, teachers, administrators, and friends—are always coming and going, sometimes with as little as a few days notice. This constant change can be traumatic if you let it be, but it can also be invigorating. Transition becomes common, if never routine. At ACS Abu Dhabi, the student turnover is about 25 percent every year. The teacher turnover varies. Some years hardly anyone leaves. Other years it seems almost everyone does. Some teachers stay for the two-year minimum; most others plan to but somehow find they're still here eight, ten or even twenty years later.

Why do they stay? Why have we? There are as many reasons as there are teachers, but for us, besides the money, it is the relationships we have made.

About 7:30 on the evening of June 9, 1999, it is predictably hot and humid in Abu Dhabi. Both readings are in the upper 90s. Mary is uncomfortable even in her knee-length rose dress accented with a gold necklace that spells her name in Arabic. Matt and I are sweltering in our dark suits and ties as we walk quickly across the asphalt parking lot toward the entrance to the air-conditioned coolness of the Grand Ballroom at the Inter-Continental Hotel, a few blocks down Zayed the Second Street from campus. Just before we reach the door, a black stretch limousine glides to a halt about twenty feet away. Five of the evening's forty-seven members of the ACS Class of 1999 emerge wearing their kelly green caps and gowns. They all wave and Reem Al-Fahim beams when I flap my pig tie at her, the one that she had given me that afternoon. "See? I told ya I'd wear it," I yell.

Inside the Grand Ballroom it is clear that this celebration is much more than a high school gym or football field graduation. The intricate gold scrollwork on the walls and ceilings is illumined by majestic crystal chandeliers so magnificent that the Phantom of the Paris Opera House would feel right at home. In fact, this venue has hosted American presidents, British prime ministers, queens, kings, emirs, sheiks, and other leaders from around the world. And tonight it is hosting the largest graduating class in the history of ACS Abu Dhabi. Ladies from the subcontinent are wearing multicolored saaris and kamisas. African ladies flow down the thick, ornate carpeting wearing bright, flowing colors from home. Some Arab ladies wear the black abaya and some Arab men, including several officials from the Ministry of Education, wear the white dishdasha and the traditional gutra headpiece.

"I think there are twenty-one flags on stage. Is that what you get?" I ask Mary. She verifies my count. Every year at graduation a flag is displayed to represent the home country of every ACS graduate. Tonight we have flags from Japan, Palestine, Lebanon, Canada, Peru, India, Pakistan, Australia, the United Kingdom, and others alongside that of the U.S.A. I can't help but reflect how ACS represents the best of our American motto, "E pluribus unum."

"Excuse me, but aren't you Marwa Shuhaiber?" I say, thinking I recognize the young woman as a member of the class of '95, my first year at ACS. "Yes, it's me, Mr. Kielkopf. I just graduated from college and I'm back here looking for a job in Abu Dhabi. I have an interview scheduled already." And so we talk of the days in senior English and how the time has passed so quickly. Then the ACS band, including Matt on the trumpet, begins to play the processional. The international crowd rises and watches as the pairs of graduates make their way down the aisle to take their places on stage. Camera flashes fire from all over the ballroom. The dignitaries are introduced, including the U.S. ambassador to the UAE, and they are presented with flowers. Graduates Adam Hussein, Molly Goggin-Kehm, and Subhadra Das, valedictorian, give brief speeches focusing on various aspects of their class. Superintendent Dr. David Cramer offers a few remarks and then makes the surprise announcement that the ACS Service Award will be renamed for Mr. John Hackworth, the founder of the high school who was retiring after twelve years at ACS. After all the speeches are made and the awards presented, the Class of '99 files out, diplomas in hand as the band plays the recessional. Smiles and more than a few tears fill the crowd.

The overseas school community is special as it breeds special relationships, many of which will last a lifetime. During the year, of course, there are still the kids who don't pay attention, who don't do their homework on time, who don't seem interested in polynomials, participles, or even P.E. There are kids who are lazy and complacent. There are kids you love and want to adopt, and admittedly, there are kids you would consider abandoning on somebody's doorstep. There are colleagues with whom you would love to take a long vacation, and others you wish would just take a long vacation. There are grades to figure and computers to scream at and vendors to complain to when those books you ordered eighteen months ago still haven't arrived. I could at this point rely on that easy expression "school is school," but the international school defies such simplicity. The international teaching school is something more. I realized this special identity when on my desk I found a student-written note that reads: "Dear Mr. Kielkopf: Thanks for your advice on revising my college application essay. They told me it was one of the best they've ever had. So thanks for taking the time to help me. I'll never forget it."

Or consider a letter like this: "Dear Mr. Kielkopf: I just wanted you to know that you were right. I did cheat. I didn't think I would feel so terrible about it, but I do and I want you to know that I don't usually do that and that I plan to never do it again. I feel like I let you down and I let myself down. Please forgive me."

When we head back to the states each summer, the relationships we forged at our school allow us to make a special stop or two. Last June it was New York City to visit a member of the ACS class of '96. An Egyptian whose father is working in Saudi Arabia, Sherine is a senior in international relations at NYU now. And when we returned to Abu Dhabi in August, we stopped in London to visit a member of the ACS class of '98. Unna is studying at the London School of Economics.

Visiting such world-renowned cities in the West does not detract from our appreciation of Abu Dhabi. In addition to the cultural diversity of our school, we are always amazed at how cosmopolitan, modern, and green the city is. The infrastructure, although not perfect, is excellent. Water, electrical (240), and phone service are almost as reliable as in the United States, but unlike most U.S. cities, the roads in Abu Dhabi are virtually pothole free. Traffic downtown during business hours is daunting and drivers are unpredictable, except that you can predict that some drivers will try almost anything at almost any time. "Drive Defensively" isn't simply a slogan here, it's a survival strategy. Outside of the downtown area, driving is often pleasant on multilane thoroughfares lined with grass, flowers, shrubs, and trees. From daisies and petunias to a panoply of bougainvillea, from palm trees to weeping willows, it is immediately obvious why Abu Dhabi is "The Garden City of the Gulf." Literally millions of trees have been planted in the UAE over the last quarter century helping to transform the desert around the cities into huge oases.

Buses are present, but mass transit is still something that is praised rather than practiced. In addition to private cars, there are thousands of cheap taxis in the UAE. A trip across Abu Dhabi costs about $4. A ride to the airport, about twenty miles away, costs less than $10. The taxis are air conditioned and clean. Most of the drivers are accommodating, although many do not speak much English. But that's no problem. Drivers usually recognize place names such as "Hilton," and passengers can always pick up three key words: "yassar" (left); "cida" (straight); and "yameen" (right), to direct the driver. What you can't do, however, is give the driver an address. There are no street addresses, as Americans know them, in the UAE, although there is a plan in the works to develop them—someday.

Streets have names and numbers and buildings have names or numbers, but they are of little value. Individuals and businesses provide maps to help you find them. They'll direct you by saying something like this: "Go to the Falcon Tower building on Zayed the Second Street. We're two streets behind that building in the pink building with the Al Yousif Pharmacy on the ground floor." As a result, trying to find people, places, and things can be one of the most frustrating challenges in the country, and yet many stores deliver, including such fast-food outlets as KFC, Shakey's, Domino's, and Pizza Hut.

Americana, however, is not and should not be the essence of the overseas experiences. Almost any type of food you would like is available in Abu Dhabi. This city is a true crossroads of the world with people living and working here from virtually every corner of the globe. The major hotels (Hilton, Sheraton, Holiday Inn, and many more) reflect that variety in their restaurants: German, Russian, Italian, Mexican, Middle Eastern, Indian, Japanese, Chinese. There are dozens of food stands selling chicken and beef shwarmas with fries and other local favorites. And, thank goodness, you don't have to know Arabic to order food or do much of anything here. Even teachers who have been here for a decade or more know only a handful of Arabic words. English works here, although there are times when not knowing Arabic is intimidating, such as when you register your car and all the documents, including your driver's license, are written only in Arabic. Fortunately, however, the school employs someone to help with such things. Most of us would love to speak and read Arabic, but it is a difficult language and we simply do not need it to get along on a daily basis. There are times when I feel guilty about living in an Arab country and not knowing the language, but the reality is that most people who work here, not just Americans, do not learn Arabic unless their jobs demand that they do.

Consequently, many people rely on the postal system, and mail, in whatever language, is delivered quite reliably to post office boxes, although privacy is not guaranteed. There is no home delivery, and all mail for teachers goes to the school's post office box. A school worker picks up the mail every day and places it in teachers' boxes in the staff room. Postal rates may be a bit high, but mail is generally secure, unless of course you view state intervention as a breech of your security. The authorities can and do open some mail for inspection, and videotapes mailed into the UAE are always opened and viewed to make sure they do not contravene the country's censorship standards. We have had tapes of Disney's "Iron Will," various sports tapes and more opened and viewed. This inspection is no trivial matter, either. Bringing in banned items can get you thrown into jail, fined (or both), or even deported.

Despite this practice, which is disturbing for an American teacher, there are almost no limitations on the curriculum. I have never left something out of my instruction because I was ordered to or because I was afraid it could be offensive to Islam or the local Arab culture. A minor example related to English class is a movie poster advertising "Great Expectations" by Charles Dickens. The censor had drawn in the top portion of Estella's dress where no dress had gone before; although, ironically, the change probably would have met with Dickens' approval. Salmon Rushdie, the Booker Prize-winning author condemned by Muslim leaders, has come up for discussion, but we have not studied his writings. I am not aware of other teachers who feel there is any significant restriction on the curriculum. Within the school I don't see censorship as a problem, although it is important to remember that the American school in an international setting is not exactly the same as the host country. A difference exists which must not be forgotten.

Censorship is also applied to the Internet. The telecommunications industry in the UAE is run by a government monopoly, which is the only Internet service provider. As it sets the rates and the policies, meeting the demands is unavoidable. Every Internet user in the UAE accesses the Internet through a proxy, a government-run filter that blocks sites deemed offensive to the Islamic culture. Frankly, we kind of like the system, as it eliminates some concerns when students use the net. At school, the students and their parents must sign a form that says they agree to abide by the laws of the UAE and use the Internet appropriately at school. These kinds of measures may be appreciated in the United States.

For those North Americans who may become homesick, English television programming has improved considerably since our arrival here in 1994; then, we had virtually no access to English programming. Now we have access to a reasonable variety of American and British TV programming, including all newscasts from all major American networks. In addition to major international sports coverage provided primarily by the international version of ESPN, at the end of the 1990s shows such as *Friends*, *Ally McBeal*, and *Home Improvement* gave the homesick expatriate an oasis of North American culture.

While the extensive American programming makes living in the UAE much easier, it also complicates the cultural exchange that occurs in the expatriate environment. In 1997 a U.S. media educationist, Margaret Gordon, told the leading English language daily, *The Gulf News*, that much of the American television programming aired in the UAE and the Middle East is "sleazy" and presents an inaccurate picture of the United States and Americans. Gordon, who is Dean of the Graduate School of Public Affairs at the University of Washington, called for greater selectivity and more government regulation of American TV programming aired in the Middle East. We would have to concur.

"I was shocked by the type of shows that are being aired here," she told *The Gulf News*. "The programs show sleazily dressed women and give a distorted image of life in the U.S. People here probably think most U.S. women dress that way." She attacked the stereotypes of such programming and said that shows with significant violent or sexual content "create the basis for improper intercultural understanding and hamper international communication." We talked about this problem in my classes, but most of the kids know the states pretty well. Most have at least visited, if not lived there for awhile, so they are not too easily fooled. They understand that popular media is usually a dubious source for serious analysis of any culture—American, Arab, or otherwise.

The paradoxical nature of this cosmopolitan country creates, in Dubai especially, some mixed signals. While magazine covers fall prey to the ink of black markers and videos carried or mailed into the country are censored or confiscated, the state allows *Baywatch* and other "fleshy" programming to enter homes unimpeded; the government even permits U.S. and European-style nightclubs to operate openly. Moreover, alcohol and pork, while contrary to the lifestyle of devout Muslims, are sold in special sections of supermarkets. Ex-pats who wish to purchase alcohol must buy a government permit to do so, but no such permit is required for the purchase of pork.

Perhaps the most difficult aspect of the typical American high school experience to replicate is the interscholastic sports experience. Although volleyball, soccer, basketball, slow-pitch softball, tennis, badminton and swimming are all offered, schedule conflicts with other schools are endemic. Some students play squash, golf, tennis, and rugby for private clubs. An officially sanctioned Little League baseball program was started a few years ago by ACS parents but it is not associated with the school. An effort to expand baseball to teens was tried, but for a variety of reasons, failed. ACS does run an intramural program for kids in grades one through five in several sports, but there is no effective sports program for middle school athletes. Without American football or baseball beyond age twelve, the school's academic objective of providing an American education that would allow students to return to a U.S. school and fit in immediately is jeopardized. This fact creates a dilemma for our family, among others. Matt is a good athlete as well as an honor roll student, but he is missing opportunities to play football, baseball, and track completely and is missing a meaningful basketball experience (by U.S. standards) by attending an overseas school. Though sports opportunities may be limited, there are special opportunities that we've enjoyed here including hosting American servicemen when they visit the region. A few years ago, for example, we hosted two U.S. Navy men from the aircraft carrier Constellation. We provided dinner at our place, showed them around Abu Dhabi, and the next day they gave us a guided tour of the Constellation. It was our first opportunity to tour an aircraft carrier and is still one of the highlights of our Middle Eastern experience. In 1999 we also enjoyed the U.S. Marine Band that made ACS one of its stops as it toured the region. Other special visitors ACS has hosted over the years include *Roots* author Alex Haley, several astronauts, former CNN reporter and Pulitzer Prize-winner Peter Arnett, and Thor Heyerdahl.

Another perk of the overseas job that counter-acts the deficiency in school sports is the travel. Since signing on at ACS Abu Dhabi five years ago we have traveled to Greece, Egypt, Jordan, Israel, Hawaii, Washington, D.C., New York City, Great Britain, Japan, Hong Kong, Thailand, Holland, Italy, the Himalayas of Nepal, Turkey, India, and Singapore. We have other destinations we hope to add to the list before it's time to return to the states to stay.

It is hard to believe we are in our sixth year at ACS. Stepping off that plane at the Abu Dhabi International Airport and into the microwave that is August in the UAE seems mere moments ago. True, I have missed watching the Iowa Hawkeyes in person on the football field and the basketball court after having season tickets for about twenty-five years. I have missed seeing a lot of Chicago Cubs' games. It's true that we're away from family and friends except for our annual summer visits to Iowa. And it's true that some of the local laws and customs can be frustrating, but then we do have the Internet and e-mail, mobile phones, Big Macs, and Pepsi.

But there I go, lapsing into that trap of trying to recreate home when you're abroad. Ultimately, the overseas teaching experience never really is about things. Working in another country is not about television, concerts or amenities, as important as those things can be. Teaching in an international community is about people and relationships, and at the American Community School of Abu Dhabi, this lesson is especially true. Our now retired principal insightfully said, "Students don't care how much you know until they know how much you care." That attitude made Mr. Hackworth a great principal and, as long as that philosophy is practiced, it will continue to make ACS a great school.

Many exciting and important material improvements are being made at ACS, but when we leave we won't remember those things so much as we'll remember the eloquent speech that Unna Patel, senior class president, delivered at graduation. She named each individual member of her class and told a fitting anecdote about each one. I will remember the leadership of Marya Goga and Barry Kamar, first editors of our high school newspaper, and all the other editors who continue to work so hard to continue that tradition. I will remember George Antonios and Farah Syed, editors of the school's first literary magazine. I will remember the frequent after-class discussions about the Palestinians' plight with Reem Mobassaleh, now a student at Brown, and with Adib and Wasef Mattar, products of a mixed marriage. Their father is a Palestinian businessman working in Abu Dhabi and their mother an Indiana farm girl. I will remember Subhadra Das, Class of '99 valedictorian, who knows more English literature than anyone I've ever met. I'll remember Sherine Guirguis, who will graduate from NYU in the spring of 2000, as both a newspaper editor and one of the most powerful and assertive personalities I've come across in any classroom anywhere. I will probably remember them all, for we have all shared the intensity of the overseas school experience in one of the finest institutions, the American Community School of Abu Dhabi. It is an experience that, for us, has underscored the accuracy of Georg Lichtenberg's observation: "In each of us there is a little of all of us."

7

The Why of It—Lebanon and Egypt

Vernon K. Olson

Terror comes quickly when you are the only buffer between 40 eighth-grade students and bedlam. The feeling is exacerbated when you are new to teaching and your immediate supervisor has a reputation for lurking in hallways to uncover sloth and incompetence. Terror is complete when the class is out of control and you do not know why. The earlier glamour of the job was not mixing easily with reality for me. I was in trouble and painfully aware that I was not in an American classroom.

I didn't expect the raucous laughter. With conservative dress and academic ambitions, the students had been well-disciplined during the first two weeks of school. Diligence and courtesy had been the norm. Now control was slipping, and the neighboring classes were surely being disturbed.

Why were they laughing? We were exploring a grammar lesson that lacked excitement. Prepositions are not funny; spontaneous mirth is difficult to comprehend when the lesson for the moment involves explaining that a preposition can not be a preposition without an object. At first I considered one of the occupational hazards of teaching—that I neglected to do up the zipper on my pants. Surely this would not produce the explosive laughter that was occurring, though. A carelessly overlooked zipper would result in a rippled reaction with scattered muffled responses that might grow into something more audible in time. This outburst had been a full-blown chorus of uncontrolled laughter, instantly executed. Teaching was a new profession for me, but I could not recall any similar examples of this kind of classroom behavior when I was a student. All that I had said on that warm September day was, "The room is hot. Let's open up the windows and get some fresh air in here."

Finally, the class settled down again, and we continued to plod to the beat of the official lesson plan; although I was confounded, the class was in a more heightened state of alertness, thanks to the elixir of laughter. The incident was soon forgotten. After all, the class behaved beautifully, and most of the students appreciated having an American teacher, even one who might be confused on occasion. Glamorous movie stars and an effective foreign policy at that time had paved the way for a warm reception for any American willing to venture to the Middle East. The students also wanted to improve their English, and I was determined to be their enlightened guide. Having seen the movie *Blackboard Jungle*, I was convinced that some teachers spent much of their time struggling for control and for some semblance of self-respect, but I was in a quiet village in some beautiful mountains with polite students. They smiled warmly in the courtyard while passing, worked hard in the classroom, and addressed me as *Ustaz* (a title of respect in Arabic meaning "teacher"). Was this not an educator's nirvana?

Then, absurdity nearly struck again. Perhaps two weeks later we were experiencing another hot day, the classroom was stuffy, and I made the mistake of suggesting that we open the windows to get some fresh air. There was, once again, hearty laughter—even from a few students who were normally bewildered by much of what was happening in the class. Pausing again, but now not as intimidated by raucous behavior, I became, in fact, somewhat pleased as well as perplexed by my comic genius.

Later that day, Mohammed, a student in the class, had a confidential conversation with me. Over the several weeks that I had been teaching we had had several quiet discussions. Since he was trilingual, gentle, and imaginatively intelligent, it had been easy to talk with him. He did not run with the pack of other eighth graders and seemed to cherish a sense of tranquility. I trusted him. Furthermore, it was not necessary to restructure a conversation with him in order to be understood. Mohammed understood the first time. As the weeks passed, he was a reliable source of information about the intrigues of the school, too. The sheiks and princes of the area historically had their court conspiracies for amusement. The campus had its array of observers, too, noting and delighting in the peccadilloes of teachers and students alike. In this tightly knit, closed community, Mohammed became my eyes and ears. He did not miss much.

During our conversation after the second incident of laughter, Mohammed advised me not to use the phrase "fresh air" again. He told me that the word "air" in Arabic means the male sex organ. Consequently, when the room was uncomfortably hot and humid, I advised the students that they needed more oxygen, much to their disappointment. "Air" was more invigorating.

As days passed, other surprises followed within and outside the class-room. Teaching was definitely more interesting than my previous employment in social work, which lacked these spontaneous moments. Instead, there had been trying encounters with grinding difficulties, some of which could be corrected or lessened with money or counseling. The drudgery of that job, with its smoke-filled offices, depressing home visits, repetitive problems without repetitive solutions, and intense emotional expenditures made me beg for an escape.

In the classroom, however, one could witness the human condition in all of its shades—glorious times of magnanimity and poignancy, difficult periods when emotions were raw and sometimes unbridled, and treasured moments with spontaneous humor and unscripted fun. Similar to Ulysses' forays into the unexpected, it seemed that sailing along in this journey called life might be more adventurous in the classroom than anywhere else—especially the overseas classroom. And it continues to be.

In the autumn of 1990 there was a short article in an educational newsletter about the owner of a successful school in Kuwait. He was in the United States when his campus was invaded by Iraqi soldiers. At the request of some Kuwaiti parents, this educational entrepreneur flew to Cairo to establish a school for some of his displaced former students who had fled the conflict and for others who were interested in an American education. When I read about this school I never realized that within two months I would be teaching there.

Arab students seem like specks of humanity in an alien cosmos when considered from the shores of Cape Cod, but they quickly become very real when their eager faces are looking at you, their teacher. I was on a one-year leave-of-absence when hired in Egypt as a permanent substitute teacher. The times were unsettled. The bombing of Kuwait had just begun, and the administrators at the school did not know if many teachers would be evacuated from Egypt. Therefore, any passing teacher with experience was viewed as potentially helpful. In fact, shortly thereafter, when a Swiss teacher was ordered by her government to leave the Middle East, my long-term substitution assignment turned into a third-grade position.

I was not bothered by Westerners leaving the country and United Nations personnel discussing contingency evacuation to Cyprus should the Gulf War somehow extend to Egypt. My concerns were less global and more narrow. Would I survive third grade? I had just one experience in working with third graders. While visiting an English boarding school for a week in the 1970s, one teacher became ill. The headmaster asked me to substitute. Having had years of practice in dealing with fifth graders, I managed that class with ease. I left them feeling Napoleonically triumphant and marched into the next class, a third grade. After two hours with these students, even though English students have a reputation for being civil and disciplined (and they were), I realized I had met my Waterloo. The third graders enjoyed the experience, though; not many, I suspect, had had the opportunity to witness a grown man crumble into the early stages of a nervous breakdown right before their eyes. A serious lack of communication was the problem, which was not the fault of the students. There was no emergency lesson plan, either, so refuge could not be sought this way. The whole experience had been an ordeal, and now I was scheduled to encounter third graders again. This time, however, there would be no escape after one day. We would be in the same classroom for weeks or months or maybe the rest of the year.

Third graders from a distance probably appear benign and perhaps even cute. In a pack the pleasure of their company is more difficult to discern. Would there be any kind of communication? What do third graders know? I had no idea. What can they do? Do they spend much time studying new math, the one subject that was thoroughly confusing? Even though I was a certified elementary teacher, which meant that teaching math should be no different than other subjects, I had avoided this subject for over two decades, luckily for the students. Even when student teaching, the benevolent gods in the pedagogical universe had grieved for me—or my students.

When I was studying to be an elementary teacher, my college professors spent a fair amount of time developing strategies to encourage prospective teachers to initiate and sustain group discussions. This has never been a problem. In fact, just the opposite has been true. Students want to share their experiences, and the boys and girls in a third-grade class in Cairo were no exception.

A class discussion on March 7, 1991, was no different. Everyone was in class that day, and during our discussion of world news there were occasional diversions and unconnected meanderings. As most of the students in the class were studying English as a second language, discussions on anything provided helpful practice in speaking. There were occasional errors in the use of words. Hassan, a nine-year-old boy, in discussing his extended family in Kuwait, mistakenly referred to "my husband" rather than what he really meant, his cousin. Later, Amira, one of the few whose first language was English rather than Arabic, somehow connected our science work in classifying animal families with a hiking trip that she had taken with several other girls while visiting England. She nonchalantly mentioned that when the group was exploring the English woodland, it came across a cheetah. Everyone accepted this sighting without challenge. After all, Amira was the smartest student in the class.

The conversations then moved into the looting of Kuwait by Iraqi soldiers. Noha, a disorganized girl who was forever searching for notebooks or workbooks or pencils, mentioned, not in a condescending but in a matter-of-fact way, that her family had three cars while living in Kuwait. The nicest and newest, a Jaguar that belonged to her mother, had only been in the family garage for two days when the invasion occurred. She thought that the Iraqis had assumed that the car belonged to the royal El Sabah family as her house was next to one of the Emir's homes, and the license plate had only three numbers on it, often a badge of royalty. Abdullah then mentioned that his family had been luckier. Out of the nine cars at his home, only one had been stolen. The family driver had parked the automobiles so close to each other in the garage that it was impossible to get into them. In addition, the chauffeur had destroyed enough of the engine in each car so that temporary repairs were impossible. The cars could not be driven. The Gulf War for me, then, was not filtered by mass media and anchormen but by the perceptions of third graders.

Teaching these students for the first time in a new city and a new school, I found it difficult to respond to everyday happenings with the thought and understanding I expected of myself. Different questions or the same questions that I had successfully dealt with for many years came up, and my rote answers that had worked in the past seemed tepid and unworkable. Gamal, for example, during a morning break asked me what country I wanted to win—Egypt or England—during the 1967 war. My answer lacked integrity. I avoided it altogether by saying that I had not given much thought to that war; there had been so many.

In living in a Moslem country, the historical issues that I had considered and discussed on many occasions stateside required a shift in perspective or at least a heightened sensitivity. One morning a colorful book on castles, which was written and printed in England, was found in the library. I quickly checked it out for the daily ritual of reading to the class after the morning break, a technique that helped to settle down the group before more serious academic work was attempted. The first part of the book dealt with English fortifications in the British Isles. Without looking at the rest of the book, I thought that the class would be interested in such a topic. Unfortunately, as I began to read the text to the class, the focus of the book veered unexpectedly to the Christian crusaders of the eleventh century in the Near East. At this point I wished that there had been time to preview the book before publicly reading in front of the class. Where was the author taking us? Was he the type of writer who dreamed of the former glory of the empire? Once again I was upset for not previewing the book. After all, the students who were now completely engrossed in this story were followers of Islam, mainly. Their ancestors had been on the other side of the castle walls that the Christians besieged and attacked. Luckily, the biased historical descriptions that can be found in some earlier books were absent in this one. Feelings were not hurt that day, and I consequently scrutinized all books with greater care before their public presentations.

Before the regular teacher returned, the third grade had much to teach me in my two months as a substitute. The little girls and boys seen on the first day grew into personalities that transcended their physical size. Together we tried to make some sense out of what was happening to our world. Third graders no longer frighten me.

Another third grader gave me further insight into this country and its culture. The afternoon was warm but not hot. Egyptians were converging on one of the three bridges that span the Nile in the downtown area; they were headed for home, almost as a crowd converges on the entranceway of a sporting event. With the funneling effect the scene was full of life, as crammed buses and automobiles moved their cargoes homeward. Contrasting with this bustle, the Nile gently flowed north, carrying a few feluccas with it. I preferred to watch the therapeutic tranquility below to the chaos flowing just a few feet from me.

While standing on this bridge, watching two ancient sailboats glide under the bridge as they have done for centuries, there was a slight pull on my arm. Turning around, I noticed a small girl of about eight, clothed in a dirty and tattered hand-me-down dress, looking up at me with her imploring brown eyes. Her hand was outstretched in the universal begging posture, and she brought it forward to suggest that any coins put in it would go to feed her. Countless people are confronted with this dilemma daily, not only in the third world but on the streets of American and European cities, too. What to do? If there is a crowd of beggars, one can become besieged by an army of skinny outstretched hands, all wanting a share of the giver's generosity. In this case, the girl was alone, and she looked as if she could use some help. Better to err on her side.

I gave her a coin, and she quickly left. Almost immediately after, a man in his thirties came over to me and said in a serious and sincere voice, "I am sorry. I am so very sorry." His concern was acknowledged, but I did not recognize the depth of his feelings on this matter. I had politely responded with the popular Arabic word, *maalesh*, which means that's okay or it doesn't matter. With eyes cast down he left, and I continued to watch the end of the day approaching. Perhaps four or five minutes later, there was another pull on my arm. I looked down to find the same girl at my side. This time her hand was not outstretched to ask for money. Instead, she wanted to return the coin that I had given her. I looked around. I did not see the man who had apologized earlier, and I really did not want the money back. Yet, the girl was insistent, and I was concerned that she might be harassed if she failed in her mission. Reluctantly, I accepted the coin, and for a second time the girl disappeared into the crowd on the bridge.

I have wondered about this desire for dignity, no matter how poor or needy the recipient might be. This example contrasted sharply with another experience in the same city in the mid-1960s. The busload of tourists stopped, and we disembarked at some historical site, long since forgotten. Instantly, we tourists were surrounded by young, smiling children—perhaps twenty to thirty—all with arms outstretched and with one word on their lips, *baaksheesh*. The tour guide, with a small whip of about three feet, carved a passageway through this throng, and we ambled to the next appointment on the agenda for the afternoon. As he moved through the children, he swished his whip back and forth, without enthusiasm but with the intended result; we were able to get through. With a faint smile on his face, the guide, children, and tourists all played this game of charades well.

The earlier incident on the bridge was not a charade, though. The man had been deeply troubled by the little girl's request for money. Although there are certainly many poor people in Cairo, I was very seldom asked for money. There is an inherent need for self-esteem universally, no matter how poor the nation, and you do not nurture this feeling by throwing out alms randomly. Perhaps nations that are blessed with good fortunes need to develop ways of sharing these bounties without relegating the less fortunate country to the status of beggar-nation. In many cases the donations are not appreciated and at times even resented.

When people are poor enough to beg in a country where it's considered unusual, one can only hope the food nourishes them, but unless that girl's stomach was fortified with permanent Pepto Bismol lining, I'm doubtful she was always nourished by the food she found. Having suffered severe food poisoning in foreign countries and the resulting debilitating diarrhea on several occasions, I have developed a sincere respect for what unfriendly microbes can do to a host body; mischievous amoebas lurking in respectable-looking food are not especially discrete in their selections. My first serious case of food poisoning happened in the mountains of Lebanon. Being dangerously naive and hungry, I walked into a not-too-clean corner grocery store and immediately noticed the ice cream. Eating ice cream has always been a temptation for me. After timidly consuming locally prepared food, mystery meals that could not possibly excite any gastric juices, this ice cream was more than just an enticement. It gave me a profoundly new understanding of how Adam could have been tempted by a mere apple.

This gluttony did not go unpunished. Back at my small apartment at school, the pain would not subside. I felt as though an aggressive army of marauding microbes were making a special visit to every cell in my body. Sleep didn't help, and there was no medicine in Lebanon nor the world that could alleviate the discomfort, the agony. I only wanted to slip into the fetal position and find a sweet unconsciousness. Instead, I became an incapacitated host to neighboring visitors who had begun to arrive unannounced. Visiting the sick is the custom in that part of the world. These people, some of whom had never seen me before, would stand soberly by the door and gawk at me in bed. Because most of them could only speak Arabic, they could not express their sincere wishes for a recovery after a stupid binge which, I assumed, was their intention. Instead, they made their brief visit and left.

As this was happening, I could only think of a parallel experience that had happened earlier in the school year. At the morning assembly the school body was informed that a student at the school, a boy of about seventeen, had died and that the older students and faculty would walk to his village to pay our respects. When we got to his modest home, he was laid out on his bed with two wads of cotton stuffed in his nostrils. More touching than his unusual appearance was the placement of his few worldly possessions beside him on the bed. Some of his older female relatives and neighbors, dressed completely in black, were off in the background, wailing softly and not so softly. The students and teachers passed by his bed and then walked quietly back to school.

As I watched these visitors I could not help but recall this scene as I watched the visitors shuffle in and out of my room during my fall from Eden—all because of ice cream. The comparison was a morbid one—an uncomforting deja-vu. Naturally, these earlier experiences in Lebanon have made me somewhat cautious while eating in foreign countries.

The threat is real. I have met too many people who have suffered, sometimes with long-term effects. Jo's husband, a CARE worker who lived in the Sudan before Egypt, came down with hepatitis. He still can not drink an alcoholic beverage nor enjoy athletics on the same level of intensity as before. John, an international teacher who is truly dedicated to the spirit of teaching overseas and learning to appreciate what other cultures have to teach, suffered a similar fate. While teaching in Yemen, a country east of Saudi Arabia that can still provide the intrepid traveler with a window to the nineteenth century, he also got sick with hepatitis. With skin that developed a sickly tinge and a body that was seriously weakened, John was forced to return to the states to recuperate. This took half a year.

While eating in the third world, the threat is real, but precautions can be taken. Perhaps the odds are in your favor if you eat at the more expensive five-star restaurants or are very selective in the kinds of food that you eat. Green salads, because they are washed with local water, are a suspicious food. Well-cooked foods, on the other hand, usually cause few problems. Washing vegetables and some fruits, too, in special solutions of bleach or potassium permanganate—a reddish solution that looks like a strong dye—kills the germs but also usually weakens your appetite. With these kinds of discouragements, diets are not as difficult to enforce. The enticements are not as strong; the appetite ebbs when confronted with the real possibility of sickness or with the necessity of giving some of your food a bath in solutions, which could be used for tanning leather.

Why then, do some people travel to less developed countries to live? The advantages are not always so obvious. In fact, many people in North Africa and parts of the Middle East have the reciprocal dream—to live in the Western world.

There are increased risks in living in that part of the world. In Cairo visitors are informed that rabies is endemic among the homeless dogs that wander the streets. A marine biologist for the United Nations cited the statistic that 80 percent of these animals are infected. As a result, provident people do not befriend hungry animals. Instead, they monitor them from a distance and avoid their cute wares. In addition, other risks concern and frustrate the overseas teacher. How do you buy the things that you need? It is not easy to find sugar and flour in stores, and if you do, it is recommended that these staples be frozen for three weeks before they are used to kill any vermin that might have found a bountiful home amidst the food. Imported groceries are more expensive, of course, and some people have difficulty in just determining a price in a store when they shop, as the signs are often only in Arabic. Just telling a taxi driver where you want to go can be complicated if the passenger does not have a command of basic survival Arabic. Daily routines are no longer routine.

For some people, all these problems are viewed as challenges. These individuals are the international "outward bound" types, accepting difficulties not as moments of frustration but as times to experience new facets of the human condition.

One night after an evening class, four adult students climbed into Michael's car for the ride home. We were on a one-way street that had three lanes of traffic. The cars were not moving too quickly, though. A donkey cart in the right lane, double-parked taxis, and the absence of streetlights had all intermingled to slow the flow of traffic to a respectable speed. As we all sat wedged in the car, still numb after two hours of Arabic class, the newest arrival to Cairo, sitting in the backseat, broke down into uncontrolled laughter. "Did you see that?" David shouted. No one had, including the driver. David told us that a bus traveling without lights had just shot by us in the outside lane, going in the wrong direction. Strangely, the rest of us did not consider this unusual or even worthy of comment. The novelty of the locals' driving styles had already worn out for us. Only David, the newcomer, had the freshness to feel that a fast moving bus at night without lights, traveling the wrong way on a one-way street, had potential as a topic for conversation.

Despite these potentially deadly incidents, life abounds on the streets of Cairo. People, trucks, cars, and even herds of camels on their way to slaughterhouses or the camel market all vie for their legitimate use of the street. Considering the enormous problem, it is surprising that the mass actually moves, but it does, encouraged by the constant and incessant chorus of car horns and the occasional exhortations from upset drivers.

During the school year three boys of about ten in their school uniform of gray pants and blue sweaters walked each day for about two blocks to catch their school bus. One of the boys was always in the middle and was supported by the other two. The middle boy had the slow and awkward gait of an accident victim, his left foot not pointing straight ahead but extending at a left angle from the rest of his body. Slowly, he limped forward with the aid of his two friends. These two boys did not offer token assistance but definite support as they walked down the sidewalk.

The first part of the morning walk was slow, but at least it was not fraught with danger. That arose later when the three boys tried to cross a major road. Drivers expect pedestrians to scatter when their vehicles approach, which is especially true when they see young and agile children, but this boy could not run. He could barely walk with the help of his two friends. Yet his friends did not desert him at the approach of danger while in the middle of the expressway, waiting for their chance to limp off to safety. They could be seen on the road, these three musketeers, "all for one and one for all," waiting for a break in the flow of traffic, as forty-mile-per-hour buses nicked them on one side and menacing trucks with horns blasting taunted them from the back side—three small boys together dealing with the trials and tribulations of modern-day life.

These boys demonstrated the first law about crossing the street: the pedestrian needs to find others for group protection. Faced with a flock of people, most drivers, even if unwilling to stop, will at least slow down. Stationing oneself close to a not-too-agile lady, preferably a little on the heavy side so that she can not sprint suddenly to the other side of the street and leave one vulnerable, also works well. The lady and her entourage will then run a classic defensive football interference play. These are not chivalrous moves, and one should not be proud of such moments. They do get people across the street unscathed, however.

In Spain there is the annual running-of-the-bulls in the town of Pamplona. It is a media event worthy of notice with a very real element of danger. The narrow streets of this village funnel man and animal together into a passageway that is not always healthy for man.

In Cairo there is another kind of running—the daily running for the buses. This happens in Tahrir Square in the downtown area. To find a place on a bus or to even get on one, a spirit of aggressive determination is needed, especially during rush hour. In fact, buses can be seen on occasion that have become so crowded that some people hanging out the back door have literally no contact whatsoever with the vehicle. Their connections are other people who are also protruding from the rear exit; the sight is reminiscent of the 1960s college fad of stuffing as many people as possible into a Volkswagen. In Cairo, it seems that new records are achieved daily. The Volkswagens barely move, however; buses do and quickly. Hopping aboard while the bus is in motion before it stops at the main square to pick up passengers offers the best odds for finding a place. The best location for this feat is where the buses run, just before they jockey into their respective loading slots. If the expectant rider is lucky, there might be another bus in front of his, slowing down traffic to a manageable speed. With luck and stamina and a hand from others who are standing in the doorway, some people sprint energetically to earn their seats for the trip home.

Bus travel isn't completely chaotic, though; it was also on a bus that Gwenda, a fellow teacher, experienced intense regard for decorum and proper behavior. An English lady in her late 40s or early 50s, she married an Egyptian educator and was living in Cairo when it happened in 1987. While riding one of the crowded buses, and standing, as no seats were available, someone pinched her in the Italian manner. She immediately yelled out in English, "Who pinched my bottom?" After a quick translation by a passenger who knew English, the driver stopped his vehicle in the middle of the road. He turned off the engine, locked the doors, and right-eously proclaimed that the bus would not move nor would anyone be al-lowed to leave until the culprit confessed. After a pause to allow the passengers to reflect on the sincerity of the driver's threat, several men who had witnessed the sordid deed and who did not want to spend the next few hours on a hot bus, began pointing at one particular man. He was brought forth, made to apologize to Gwenda, and then thrown off the bus. To compensate for her emotional trauma, the driver cleared everyone from the front seat and insisted that she ride there for the rest of her trip. One pinch in the wrong location resulted literally in instant justice in the streets of Cairo. Of course, this would have never happened on the underground metro in Cairo or on the tram in Alexandria, as certain cars are reserved only for small children in tow.

Recalling Gwenda's story about what is appropriate reminded me of Abdul's "ejaculation question" in class one day. While working as a sub-stitute, I was assigned to take Jane's classes. She was a science teacher who would be out because of a sick child at home. Before school began I called her to review her lesson plans. The class that seemed to be the easiest on paper became the most complicated. The boys and girls were instructed to work on independent reading regarding sexual reproduction. It was a large class of tenth graders, and all of the seats were taken. The class settled down, and I began to prepare for another class. At that time an eleventh grader came into the room to pass out some letters that were to be taken home. There was a little chatter by the students, and then they were quiet once again. Five minutes later there was another knock on the door. Fuad and Leila, both third graders, asked if they could read a prepared speech to the class. They got the affirmative nod and began their recitation. "Some-one has taken two pictures from the third grade bulletin board. Please do not take any more and return the pictures if you have taken them. We are only third graders. If you ask, we might give you the photographs at the end of the year." Finally, they left after receiving nods of approval and encouragement. After some minor muttering, the class proceeded to work quietly again for about twenty minutes.

Then it happened. Without a raised hand or a warning the monastic silence was broken. Abdul, in a loud and clear voice asked, "What does ejaculate mean?" I did not know the student, and I did not know the class, but the mores, the civil niceties of the country, were well entrenched in my thinking. There is a Victorian-type sense of modesty that is much older than British colonization in Egypt. It is embedded in Islamic teaching that one is cautious when making sexual comments in front of female class-mates. Abdul's question was more than cavalier; it was incendiary. Only the week before in my outside adult Arabic language class, Maria, a United Nations worker from Europe, said that when she was in the women's bath-room at work that week, an older woman pointed at her short skirt and said, "In eleven days, no." That was the beginning of the religious holiday of Ramadan. Maria, in an understanding spirit but still exasperated said, "I only brought these kinds of dresses and skirts with me from France." Our teacher, Sherifia, offered to go out with her to buy some more "re-spectable" clothes before the holiday.

My initial reaction to Abdul was that he had violated the frontiers of classroom decency—had, in fact, intentionally embarrassed the girls under the pretense of a search for knowledge. In addition, he seemed to be taking advantage of an absence of his regular classroom teacher. Furthermore, why would he be asking this question while reading his American textbook that had both a glossary and an index for instant information? If we had been discussing the topic or if he had raised his hand for a quiet conference as had happened with several other students earlier, a more tempered re-action by me would have been appropriate, but Abdul, it seemed, was tinkering with the classroom atmosphere for his own amusement. All of these quick considerations encouraged me to invite him to leave the room. Interestingly, for all his efforts, Abdul received no snickering or support from any of his classmates, although they were fully bilingual and under-stood his question and probable intentions. Only one girl after class said to me as she was leaving the room, "Sir, Abdul is like that."

Later in the day while discussing the incident in the teachers' lounge, I discovered that there could have been a much more pleasant resolution. Gloria, a teacher who had had a Catholic school education in the states, suggested that I should have told him that ejaculation meant a short prayer. Gloria said that when she was a schoolgirl the nuns were always saying, "We must ejaculate now," and they would say, "My Lord and my God" or "Lord help us" or "My Jesus have mercy." For the next several days while passing Gloria between classes in the hallway, she would ejaculate with a "My Jesus mercy" or "My Lord and my God" or "Lord help us" to the puzzlement of the bilingual Moslem students next to her who thought that perhaps she had seen too much sun on her spring trip to Luxor.

While Gloria's behavior was a bit odd, even for religious students, it was not as surprising as the tidbits I read during homeroom from a book called

More Freaky Facts; it was great as a behavioral anesthetic before moving to the more traditional routines of the day. This practice was only done for three or four minutes, but it had a settling effect on the group. Because fifth and sixth graders enjoy hearing about that part of the world on the edge of believability, there was an instant cessation of socializing and a concentrated focus on the short pieces of information being read. "With the giant telescope at Mount Palomar in California, one can see a lit candle 40,000 miles away," is one example. Another short entry reads, "The Chinese stopped importing United States chewing gum when the wrappers were changed from green to purple. Because purple was the official mourning color, they believed that the gum was to be chewed at funerals only."

Living in some foreign countries offers daily exposures to a living edition of such a book. Perhaps the incidents were not literally "freaky" but were so alien from American cultural experiences that they broke from the mundane routines of normal teaching into the unusual or amusing or tantalizingly fresh.

Islam provides an example of a fresh change for the North American teacher. Many people at the school had mentioned the upcoming celebration of Ramadan, but what exactly would happen remained a mystery. At this time a Moslem devotes an entire month to fasting from dawn to sunset. This means that there is no eating or drinking or smoking for about twelve hours a day, a grueling experience, especially if the holiday falls during the summer and you are a farmer. On the first day of Ramadan in the middle of science class, Noha raised her hand. She had no question about the classification of plants and animals, but she said in a polite and matter-of-fact manner, "We must go to pray now." Everyone left, I waited, and they returned about ten minutes later. This happened in the afternoon, too. We had many days of Ramadan left. This moral obligation needed verification. When I asked several teachers about this commitment, they gave ambiguous responses. The students continued to say their prayers for a day or two. I made more inquiries. Some of the more serious Islamic teachers on the faculty suggested that children really did not participate in the strict requirements until about the age of eleven or twelve. The third graders were eight and nine. The next day when the announcement in homeroom was made that third graders would not be dismissed for prayers; there was only one reaction. Noha explained in a dignified and gracious way that she would really like to say her prayers. I felt uneasy, as it was difficult to tell whether she had deeply embedded religious feelings or just enjoyed taking a ten-minute break from class. She was asked one question. "Do you say your prayers when you are home around suppertime when there is another call-to-prayer?" She smiled and said nothing. That smile and that silence resolved the problem. I felt comfortable in not releasing the class for meditations.

There were almost daily excursions into the world of the unpredictable.

While waiting for a tutoring session to begin, several security men from the school rushed into the teachers' lounge to talk in their limited English to Carol. "Come quick! See the robot," they implored. Carol knew that the science department had a progressive program, but she had not heard about any robot. While Carol considered the invitation, the men, almost like shopkeepers hawking their wares, exhorted with even more enthusiasm and gesticulations. "Quick, quick, you will like the robot!" Off they went, down to the science room where Carol expected to see a remarkable class project. On arrival, she realized that there had been a slight pronunciation error. The robot lay dead, carefully opened to display its insides. Jane was dissecting a rabbit for her biology class.

Muddled pronunciation and vocabulary works both ways. An easy way to get an Egyptian to smile is to say a few words in Arabic. It is difficult to know if the smile is a result of a fractured accent or a sincere appreciation for any Westerner who has the audacity to work with this language. It is not an easy language to master. A bilingual driver from a travel agency who met me at the Cairo airport said that he had never met an American who had a good accent in Arabic. Later, upon reflection, he thought that his aunt who was born in the United States might qualify. When I asked a Lebanese man in Boston the same question, he just smiled.

These reactions did not force me to take a trip to a language school, but I was determined to learn some Arabic. After all, children throughout the Middle East seem to understand it; thousands of Arab students become proficient in English, and even Lawrence of Arabia was able to marshal legions in his successful battles against the Ottoman Empire, though it is said that his Arabic was not very good. Eventually being able to give directions in Arabic to a taxi driver without ending up in Alexandria seemed like a reasonable and obtainable goal. As I expected, however, the classes were frustrating.

The Arabic language to the untrained Western ear sounds threatening, even when pleasant courtesies are being extended. The thick consonants and the loud guttural sounds emanating from deep in the throat suggest sinister inclinations. The tendency to use gestures freely and to speak more emphatically also contributes to the expectation of ill will. In contrast, French, with its soft, sweet vowel sounds, is inviting and even seductive. To me, a criminal speaking French might be asking for your money or your life, but if you do not know the language, you may interpret such a demand as a polite pleasantry. The Arab, on the other hand, even though he might be poetically complimenting you on your exquisite taste and beautiful family does not communicate this feeling to someone unfamiliar with his language. The untrained Western ear interprets evil intent too often from this ancient tongue.

Other elements of communication can differ, too. While on one of our many walking tours around a small village with a group of teachers, the word "Johnny" (with a Swedish accent) kept slipping into the Arabic conversations. When asked for the meaning of "Johnny," there was no immediate reply. Essa was having some trouble in translating the word. This was unusual, as Essa was gifted in a number of languages. Finally he explained that this was the word that was used if you were pausing in your thoughts—it was a filler word while searching for others. In my provincial naiveté, I thought that the whole world used "aah" to fill in those silent moments.

Body language, too, has regional meanings. Americans shake their heads up and down to mean yes. The Middle Eastern head goes up, usually just once, but this means no. With this cranial ascension might go a quiet smacking/kissing sound. For heightened sophistication, an arched eyebrow can communicate the same message. Communication has many facets in the Middle East.

Even the sacred world of numbers holds some surprises. While in school, respectable math teachers constantly tell their students that we in the Western world use Arabic numbers. They lie. A few numbers are alike, but the Western zero, for example, is really the number five in Arabic. The Arabic zero is printed as a dot about halfway up from the baseline. Another example is the symbol that looks like the Roman numeral five (V). Seen on a sign in a shop window in Cairo, it means that you will be paying seven Egyptian pounds for the item. If it is flipped upside down (inverted), the cost escalates to eight pounds. What helps to stabilize this jungle of confusion is the desire of most people in this part of the world to communicate without pretense. With a combination of gestures, words from several languages, a history of accommodating an array of languages and dialects, and a general good-naturedness, most people seem to be more interested in understanding the message than in flaunting their perfect command of English or French or Arabic.

Unfortunately, the great diversity between Western and Middle Eastern languages has led to a separation rather than a sharing of thoughts. It has been said that Arabic offers a structure from which writers can soar as they explore the poetical bent of man. Khalil Gibran's writings in such books as *The Prophet* reflect this potential and give the occidental mind just a hint of these powerful traditions. Are there additional treasures to be discovered?

One form of language that definitely transcended the problems with words was humor, and a colleague named Dianne was a favorite with the students because of it. Students tended to stay in the classroom after the class was finished. Good-natured chatter and spirited laughter were often their reward. When it was absolutely necessary to vacate the room, there was sometimes a pleasant ritual that would be difficult to imagine in a school in the United States. Dianne, standing by the door as perhaps five or six students prepared to leave, would ask, "What do you have to say?"

The well-rehearsed response from these sixth and seventh graders, sounding like a disciplined choral group, was, "We love you, Miss Weber." Miss Weber, replying in a voice of unrestrained enthusiasm, would react by saying to any nearby adult who would listen, "Aren't they wonderful children," with the first syllable in the word "wonderful" crescendoing an octave or two. Six or eight or nine boys and girls would then file out, fortified with an emotional charge that would carry them through the day.

Egyptian people seem to be warmer in their personal relations than North Americans. This is seen with parents and children, friends meeting one another, and riders on crowded buses who extend a hand to strangers who are trying to hop aboard. Touching does not automatically result in derisive concerns of impure motives or hormonal problems. The contact seems spontaneous, warm, and human. An example of this openness, this freedom, happened spontaneously on the fourth day of teaching in Cairo. On that morning perhaps five or six sixth-grade boys and girls waited outside their classroom for the homeroom teacher to arrive. Miss Gloria, a late-middle-aged matronly-type teacher appeared suddenly. There was a cry of "Miss Gloria" from both the girls and boys and a spontaneous stampede to greet her. A prolonged and affectionate group hug followed for the next ten seconds or so with concomitant smiles of appreciation. It is difficult to imagine this happening in the hallways of an American school. If it did, perhaps the school counselor or principal would be summoned. In Cairo this seemed natural and wonderful. Starting the school day with a group hug beats a stiff and droning pledge of allegiance.

Hugs and loving words are definitely the order of the day in a mission that's tucked away inside Garbage City, an area where garbage is deposited and in some cases recycled on the edge of Cairo. Sponsored by Mother Teresa's organization, the mission is of modest size and appearance, and inside the walls are two generations at either end of life's continuum— babies and the old. All of these people are cared for by a few Sisters of Charity, women who have taken religious vows to help. Their lives have not been easy. Babies coming into this world and old folks on the verge of exiting demand more attention than most age groups, of course.

Yet, a quiet tranquility permeates the building. On the lower level is the older generation, and on second floor in three small rooms are the babies and toddlers, numbering from twenty to twenty-five and ranging in age from newborn to four or five. Some of these children are orphaned, abandoned, and handicapped. Some were left when parents could no longer care for them. There is some fluidity in this population, with children coming and going for many reasons.

Caring for these youngsters is not easy. When the suggestion was made that a washing machine would really help in keeping the clothes for both the young and old clean, it was pointed out that the young girls helping with some of the laundry are sometimes earning the only means of support for their families. If washing machines were purchased, they would not have jobs and their families would not have money for the basics.

Not too long ago the sisters began to get some help from another source—ladies and a few men in the community who donate their time and energies. The current coordinator, Pam, is a lady who could enjoy some of the luxuries of life as an ex-pat. She and her husband rent an impressive villa in a fashionable area of Heliopolis, and she has the necessary help to run such a household with a full-time gardener and other workers. Nonetheless, she volunteers in the mission to help with the pleasant and odious tasks such as playing with the babies or washing baby clothes. Early in her volunteer service, when diapers were washed by hand in cold water, Pam recognized the desirability of disposable diapers but also realized that they were too expensive. By contacting people she was finally able to arrange for diapers that were seconds, not good enough to sell but certainly good enough to do the intended job.

Perhaps the great achievement of this ad hoc group, though, has been to find additional volunteers to help in the feeding and coddling of these toddlers. Specialists who study early childhood development have recognized for some time the importance of social interaction for youngsters just starting out in life. These volunteers, recognizing that the sisters have many demands in just caring for the physical needs of these children, meet some of these emotional requirements. Healthy and smiling babies are their reward. The mission is a testament to what a multinational community can do.

It's hard not to be ambivalent about the reasons English-speaking teachers are desired and needed in places like the Middle East. Symptoms of a modern, post-colonial world of big business are ubiquitous: Gamal's question about who I favored in one of the past wars in his homeland, the young girl begging for a coin and later insisting I accept her repayment, the students crossing a dangerous street where the industrial revolution hurries noisily past them, and the city's time-honored camel markets. Empires have come and gone; now companies arrive, merge, and move, and in the midst of it all, are the expatriate teachers. They should always be aware of their remarkable opportunities, and in my experiences, they are. Overseas teachers engage with the full breadth of the human condition and drink from an elixir of personal growth. Like the children they teach, they are constantly maturing and learning. These thoughts inspire me to question the nature of civilization and recall a special moment I had while traveling in Egypt.

The pyramids awed the Greeks during Alexander's time and had their impact on the Romans as well. How could they not fail to impress, now as then? These monuments to engineering and determination reflect the historical continuity of man. What will our legacy be, as time nudges forward? Are we currently building anything that will be admired 3,500 years from now? These and other grand Egyptian sites are never overlooked by visitors.

I never expected to find a childlike delight in another Egyptian treasure, though. For one month I lived in a hotel in Zamalek, an island in the middle of the Nile River near downtown Cairo that was favored over the past century by wealthier foreigners and chosen by many governments as a site for their embassies. Some people have suggested that strategically the island offered these people the opportunity to be rescued by boat, should they suddenly find an inhospitable political climate.

The hotel room on the thirteenth floor had a small balcony, allowing for a view of the neighborhood and the Nile two blocks away. Even though the room was on the top floor of the hotel, clusters of small flying insects could be seen next to the balcony. This was the attraction, the bait. At sunset graceful swallows with dark upper bodies and bright mustard-colored bellies would swoop in for a final meal of the day. As a canvas awning blocked the view of their approach these birds shot by with no warning, only six to eight feet away from any bemused birdwatcher. Sometimes there would be dolphin-like motions with birds arching heavenward. The ballet would be choreographed to allow for the assent: a momentary stall at the crest of some unseen air current, and then the graceful dive. Swallows are delightful anyway, but to view these flashes of aeronautical poetry with the Nile as a backdrop was to nourish my aesthetic spirit with the essence of beauty. I was enveloped by a beautiful, childlike wonder. Perhaps those third graders taught me more than I thought.

PART IV

Latin America

8

From the Ground Up: Building a School with Cinder Blocks, Notebooks, and Friendships

John A. Hansen and Evan M. Smith

"It's still rainy season. I bet we'll get a run-in with some rain," the director said as we loaded our bags and equipment into the back of his sport utility vehicle, climbed in, and headed south for the small central Venezuelan town of El Tigre.

I had visited Escuela de las Americas once before. My first experience was in June, two months before school was scheduled to begin—a reconnaissance mission to see just what I was getting myself into. After registering with a search agency, and being contacted by phone, the school arranged an all-expense-paid, weekend visit, to meet the principal and get a feel for the school. I remember looking down as the airplane closed in on the red earth below, rich with iron deposits and oil reserves, and wondering why I was in this part of the globe looking for work. As a science teacher, there were alternatives much closer to home than this. I climbed down the stairs onto the runway in the blazing tropical sun, greeted by the short shrubs and tall grasses that grew among the cashew trees of the vast savannah. A strong wind tugged at the travelers' clothes and coaxed the light cumulus clouds across the tropical sky. With my only belongings tucked into a small backpack, I made my way past the armed natives in fatigues and across the worn pavement to the small group of waiting faces, hoping there was one for me.

That weekend I had a chance to see the town, try the food, meet another prospective teacher, Ruben, and of course, see the school. "There are two guard dogs here that are less than friendly so keep an eye out for them," remarked Carmel, the principal, as we drove down the long driveway to what looked to be an abandoned warehouse. The barred windows, chipped paint, and two dusty pickup trucks were not quite what I had expected for our school. Parking with the trucks, we scanned the perimeter for dogs, jumped out of the Jeep, and hurried into the building. The shade inside was cool. The sound of hammers and chisels breaking through concrete pierced the construction dust that hung in the air.

One of Carmel's first remarks was of assurance that the school, now nothing more than cinder brick walls under construction, would be ready in plenty of time for the first day of class that September. I had a feeling that perhaps she was assuring herself rather than the two prospective teachers that accompanied her as we toured the site. Our first stop, the soon-to-be library, was nice, spacious, and the biggest room in the school. We met her husband Ferdanando there, engaged in a spirited Spanish conversation with some of the workers. He was the operating engineer and foreman of this construction site. The science room was next. We made our way down the hall, gingerly stepping over the random cords, the bare wire from their stripped ends crammed into the outlets. "This is the science room," Carmel said as we entered the ceiling-less and door-less room. "It has access to water and gas." She pointed to the three rough pipes protruding from the far wall capped off in an "it will do" fashion.

"I'd like to stay here a while and think," I remarked. She nodded, smiled, and left with Ruben to continue the tour. There, in the science room, the sunlight poking through the few lapses of the corrugated steel roof, I thought, "Well, at least the room is big. I could get a science program going here." And then, without much more to see but a beat-up drill on the floor and a few screws and anchors to keep it company, I left to find Carmel and Ruben in the office. I prompted Carmel, "And you have science equipment?"

"Oh sure," she responded, pointing to two dusty, broken boxes resting in the corner of the office. I sat down on an old chair and began to sort through them. It didn't take me long before realizing that the frank answer to my question was "no."

"Now this will be a challenge," I thought. No equipment, and living in a small town with limited resources, obtainable only using my limited command of the Spanish language. Well, with a creative mind and some resourceful thinking I bet this first deficiency could be overcome. Then I saw the books. Some of the books were old and musty, some were new and musty. The tropical climate had a way of quickly decomposing any organic matter within its reach. I gave Carmel a look of despair. She responded that most of the science books were new and were going to be brought down by Dr. McWhorter, the director, when he arrived. "Okay, no science equipment, no books, yet, and many miles from the comforts of home." I told Carmel that I would have to think about this employment opportunity, and I sensed her despondency as the prospective science teacher was slipping away just as the tan lizards disappear between the mortar cracks of buildings planted here.

After lunch we stopped at the apartments where the teachers would be making their residence about two hundred meters from the school. We drove past more armed guards securing the entrance alongside the speed bumps or *policia acostado* (policeman lying down). On the third floor, the apartment did not appear overly accommodating, the only occupants being a sterile two-person table, chair, linen-less bed, and two sad-looking house-plants suffering in the stale muggy heat of the small space, whose air faintly smelled of bug spray. I sarcastically wondered if they had any problems with insects in these parts. I checked out the water pressure in the bathroom shower and was pleased to see a respectable flow after the coughs and spurts of rust and whatever else was hiding in the pipe percolated up. Carmel informed us that we might be sharing this very apartment together for "safety" reasons. My thoughts leapt ahead as to how to finagle getting the bigger of the two little rooms, though I knew I was already beat. Ruben, with his military experience, aggressive stance, and age, was far more dominant than me. We closed up the door, locked the many locks, and left another less than exciting factor of this employment equation. Ruben and I spent that night at the director's house still within the compound. Now this was what I wanted: three bedrooms, living area, receiving room all painted white and tastefully decorated with a Latin flavor. I lay down that night in a king-size bed listening to the tree frogs melodically singing outside, many thoughts on my mind: How was it that I am here, falling asleep comfortably, eight degrees north of the equator? How was it that I survived traveling through Caracas last night, an obvious traveler out of his element? How was it that I was beginning to feel comfortable with this idea of teaching here in El Tigre? And how was it that I was now developing a camaraderie with Ruben and my soon-to-be principal in a "We are all in this war together" type of fashion? That night I decided, "Count me in. This is worth a shot." I didn't give any thought to where it might go, or if it could be done. It just felt right. This opportunity was coming together cleanly and yet so strangely out of shape.

A few days after returning to the states, the director called. "Well, John, sorry I missed you. How did you like it?" I told him the opportunity looked interesting, but that I would need some money to purchase a variety of science materials I anticipated needing to outfit the school. "How much do you think?" he asked. Knowing that the first one to name an amount in any bargaining process always loses the most ground, I thought for a moment, and realizing that I would need about three thousand dollars, I said, "How does five grand sound?"

"John, you're going to put me in the poorhouse. How about I send you a check for twenty-five hundred," he replied. This guy was good. So, I

figured, take what you can get, and I began the process of requesting cat-
alogs and ordering equipment to outfit my new Venezuelan classroom.

Two weeks before school in El Tigre was to begin, I stood in the university Methods of Teaching Science classroom/laboratory, alone, in front
of a mountain of boxes piled high on two of the lab tables that at one time
provided the support for my notebook, as I prepared to be a science
teacher. I looked around the room at all the interesting science gadgets and
projects that decorated the shelves. I remembered why it was that I had
always wanted to be a science teacher—to explore and share the wonders
of the natural world. I took a deep breath and swallowed. "This is it,
Johnny," I thought. "Make it happen." That night I returned home to my
small college apartment, unloaded the science equipment, and waded
through the endless volume of starch-fiber packing peanuts that accompanied my order.

Off to Venezuela! It was one week before class was scheduled to com-
mence. My gear consisted of two hard-sided suitcases, one carry-on backpack, six-meter sticks, and a 250mL glass volumetric flask that I was
determined to carry in my hand, unbroken, from Chicago to El Tigre. I
met the director that afternoon in the Miami International Airport, and he
explained that he had arrived at seven that morning with a total of thirty-
four boxes of books and supplies. This was great to hear; he was indeed a
strong team member with whom to go into battle. We later met three other
teachers from various hometowns of the United States, and together flew
off for Caracas.

After a quick stop-over in the capital city, we took a short flight down
the coast, landing in Puerta la Cruz with only one leg of the trip ahead of
us—¡Adelante El Tigre! And down came the rain. One or two drops hit
the windshield at first, and then the sky opened up. "Welcome to rainy
season," the director chuckled to his SUV full of new teachers and gear
that bounced along the only road leading south to El Tigre. For the most
part this road was a good one. From time to time a few large dips that
could coax a fast car into the air would interject a "Keep your eyes on the
road!" warning, acting as constant reminder of one's speed. Por puestos,
the equivalent of a trans-city taxi, would zip past our Blazer in what seemed
like a race for life. These drivers made the trip from Puerto la Cruz to El
Tigre daily and knew this road by heart, the director explained. I watched
another one sail past in the rain, a dark-green 1970s LTD disappearing
around the turn ahead, flanked on either side by the never-ending sea of
tall waving grass.

We arrived in El Tigre about four o'clock that afternoon and unloaded
our gear into the director's house, our temporary residence until other accommodations within the neighborhood were available. An interesting law
in Venezuela is that one cannot evict a family or individual, even if the rent
has gone unpaid, until the evictee has found other accommodations. This

law is fully taken advantage of and is the reason for the small percentage of living accommodations that can actually be rented as opposed to being bought, further segregating the haves and have-nots of the country. It was comfortable being back in El Tigre, and I enjoyed the time getting to know my two new teacher-roommates in this new land.

And so, the games began! The first day of school arrived. Students filed past me as I greeted them at the door, all the stories of untamed Latino "kids" wildly dancing in my mind. I glanced into the room and noticed several of the first unnamed arrivals milling about my desk peering at the materials that I had carefully prepared to aid me. Knowing the student list, prepared by the principal, troublemakers' names circled, was on my desk, and not wanting the students to know that I had the jump on them, I barked, "Is that yours?" I was surprised at the large voice that emanated from my otherwise quiet mouth. They quickly retreated to safety and assumed seats in the sterile, white science room.

The school was now about 80 percent finished, and with the newly acquainted teachers, we kept the performance upbeat, and executed the first day flawlessly. Classes were small; the biggest, twelve, and the smallest, with one. One student! I can only remember my mind racing, as *she* entered the classroom, closed the door behind her, and took the desk directly in front of mine. All my method and preparation class rules—"Never be alone in a classroom with a student"—flashed red, and warning bells went off in my head. Tension was thick. The scare treatment of the United States' lawyer fantasyland and its omnipresent threat of, "You, the teacher, are guilty of everything," weighed on me. I was uncomfortable, though I had done nothing wrong. "Agostina," I said, in a loud voice that would have reached her had she been sitting in the back of the room, "Let's begin." I went through the same "business as usual" routine, and the tension began to fade and slip away like chalk dust under an eraser as we assumed our roles of teacher and student. We both had a job to do and were overly willing to get started with something that provided a familiar structure to this unfamiliar situation.

The day began with a homeroom of twelve middle school students. During my initial visit to the school, the principal had made the students out to be a disastrous mess, but I was pleasantly surprised. For the most part, they came from caring families of intelligent engineers or managers in the oil industry. The students reflected this intelligence, and as I paged through our 1988 physical science textbook, I wondered how to challenge them. Not only were these students above the expected curriculum level for grade seven and eight science, but I was also confounded with every daily written quiz I received—I had a room of ESL students and no ESL experience. And just to make it interesting, throw in two exceptionally bright, fluent English speakers. Group work, peer tutoring, and patience were my saving grace.

The beginning students did not fall behind, and the more advanced students had opportunities to lead, balancing the class nicely.

Science fair was an elective structured around competitions in which students, using the PIHEC method—Problem, Information, Hypothesis, Experiment, and Conclusion—would generate reports and build some type of project for the day. We raced balloons and talked about forces, calculated the volume of spheres, and made soap bubbles, giving my classroom the cleanest floor of the school. We built boats and met Archemedes. Students consistently tried to outdo each other with innovations and creativity. They were seeing, touching, and reasoning through real problems. And for the final project, students were required from day one to conduct and write a detailed report on an experiment they designed on their own. One group took advantage of our country location to purchase live chicken eggs and devise the ideal incubation environment, resulting in a few extra noise-makers in the back of the room.

In fifth and sixth grade general science, students were just as varied. I began class with our required book, and, to get a feel for the English proficiencies, we read around the room. To my dismay, what did I get? Yawns, restless feet, pencil-droppers. I quickly scanned the text for something exciting to capture the interest of the students and was dismayed at directionless lessons and realized I was going to be stuck that day. After school, I looked at the resources that I had flown down with me: *Project Wild*, Tik Liem's book of science demonstrations, and my own sixth grade reports from Mr. Gene Swager's science class that my mother sent with me at the last minute. I had an idea! I carried our science book up to the principal's office and inquired, "Carmel, I would like to put these science books aside. I read it, found it terribly boring, and I like science." And, just as if it was meant to happen, she said, "You're the professional, John, you're welcome to do as you wish, and as long as the students are learning science. . . ." I left her office that afternoon with a new sense of leadership. This was my program now. I drew up a brief outline that night with two objectives: 1. inspire wonder and appreciation of the natural world, and 2. learn how to organize information and generate a report starting from a rigid structure provided by me and ending with the student assessing and organizing what information they deemed important from the unit. We were set to light a fire that would fuel their interest in science class and the world.

I passed out the goggles, dimmed the lights, and ignited a large alcohol "spill" on the ceramic tile. We took notes and observed. Potassium permanganate and glycerin smoked and burst into blue flame with yellow cinders, as we took notes and observed. "What is fire?" was the question that we were set on answering. The tone had changed and students knew it. The books were shelved, the new program explained, and we set sail, not to read, but to discover the wonder.

Science class enjoyed and profited from the change. We began with fire, and moved to heat, light, electricity, and magnetism. The list grew as the students would mention their interests, and we would dig up the resources. I encouraged them to contribute to the new curriculum, and they were excited to help guide the class. "Plants are kind of neat. How do they work?" asked Cristina, providing the seed of an idea that sprouted into one of our most rewarding units. This class success constantly reminded me of Ruben's old army expression, "Adjust, adapt, and overcome."

I found myself relating to this saying on more than one occasion during the year. As I was getting the hang of being a teacher and living in a foreign town, a need for calcium carbide to fuel my miner's lamp sent me exploring the business district of El Tigre. This adventure turned out to be materially unsuccessful but culturally enlightening. My first stop, the *herramientaria* (hardware store), found this tall, lanky gringo in a mix of clumsy Spanish and charades trying to communicate about a rock-like substance, that, when mixed with water, creates a gas that can burn. Of course, then pantomiming a burning miner's lamp that fits on an imaginary hat that one wears as one creeps about in the dark—added to the absurdity of this theatrical production. After about five minutes of entertaining the group of hardware shop employees and local customers, one showed up that knew the material. *Carburo*, was the word. "Ahhh, *carburo*!" The bewildered looks on the faces of my audience grew into smiles and laughter with the success we shared bridging our communication gap. Unfortunately, the phrase *No hay aqui* (none here), followed.

In high school I used to work in a hardware store, and I knew and loved the kind of shoppers one would find there. And although El Tigre and Chicago were miles apart, the stereotypical characteristics held fast: do-it-yourselfers in discount pants and thin shirts, with scraps of paper bearing scribbled annotations of strange measurement systems which each of these guys had dreamed up and lived by, appeared to be the norm when visiting these shops—regardless of one's latitude.

"Welding," I thought. "Perhaps in this far away country it was still used." I dug out my dictionary, quickly looked up the word, and was pointed down the street. Sidestepping the brown stagnant puddles that collected in the broken sidewalks I jogged up the steep ramp used to dolly the many tanks of fuel gas and oxygen in and out of the welding shop. There I saw rough brown faces with black mustaches, speaking fast and drinking beer behind the counter. Free-spirited Latino music was spilling rhythmically out of the dusty old radio that sat next to the still-lit cigarette (safety standards were abundant here in the welding shop) smoldering casually in an orange, plastic cafeteria ashtray. I was able to catch the attention of one of the workers and asked for the all-elusive carbide. His answer reflected all the others: none to be found in El Tigre. Small setback, but a valuable lesson in how to find what you need in El Tigre—keep looking. Chemicals turned up at the Italian fine leather and crystal store. Dry ice came from the ice-cream man's cart.

But cultural surprises were not the only surprises to be found. "How would you feel about teaching physics instead of chemistry this year?" the director asked, as we sat in the principal's office three days before classes began. I thought back to my two overweight suitcases, full of chemistry equipment, and my thirty hours of chemistry background versus my ten in physics. And although I did not know it at the time, this question posed to me typified the experience of teaching overseas—expect nothing to go as planned. I looked at the comprehensive physics book and the class list of four students and concurred; at the very least we could work together through the book and teach each other—which turned out to be a wonderful approach. A fellow teacher once commented that students can relate to their own kind better than to an adult figure, and these students not only enjoyed teaching each other, but they were good at it! Laboratory experiences were fewer than I would have liked, but we had our stopwatches, a few carts, and the water tower, from which we could drop objects from seven and four-tenths of a meter above the waving grasses and scrub trees as far as the eye could see.

The school celebrated American holidays, as we were trying to uphold these aspects of American culture. Students enjoyed the new experiences and traditions of Halloween and Thanksgiving with the student council preparing activities and fund-raising events. Mothers would bake and fathers, who worked as engineers in the day, would sell ice cream at night, pushing the rented ice-cream cart amongst the tables in the gymnasium during the dances and parties. One of the more surprising aspects of teaching in a foreign school occurred at the teachers' meeting before the party. The principal's concern was: "Will alcohol be available for the parents?" This was a bit of a shocker as she presented the issue in a very matter-of-fact way. The Latin American culture here was very pro-drinking. Having a good time at a party was the norm, and school parties were no exception. Being my first year teaching, and new to all this, I voted to keep our party dry, as did just over half of the other teachers. The decision was an unusual resolution for this side of the globe, and perhaps the reason for the low parental turnout at the Halloween dance.

Two short months later, the Christmas holiday arrived. Students exchanged gifts and had a small pageant with traditional songs and stories and food. When the midday bell rang, the students all hugged each other good-bye, piled onto buses, and went home. Elated at the idea of returning to the United States for a wonderful three weeks' vacation, I cleaned up my desk, packed my bags full of clothes and gifts, and flew, in one day, from the culture of El Tigre, to Puerto la Cruz, to Caracas, to Miami, and then, finally, to the culture of Chicago and our English-speaking ethnic melting pot. I always liked the stop in Miami, as it is a buffer in going from one culture to the next—plenty of Spanish and Latin Americans, as well as plenty of the signs that one is home. I became all choked up and quite emotional when we landed there, and the very first plane seen taxiing had "American" painted in red and blue on its white side. Walking up to one of the internationally recognized images of our country—the tall, over-weight, white customs officer—the pride welled up in me as he asked, "United States citizen?" in a burly voice with a touch of down-home South-ern accent. "You bet, sir," I replied, blue passport in hand, ever happy to be secure, safe, and home on American soil.

The first year passed with many trials and triumphs. And as an educator, fascinated by growth, I looked forward to an opportunity to continue watching my students mature. I signed up for a second round at Escuela de las Americas and was excited by the chance to have another year of new experiences and friendships, one of which would be with the new English teacher across the hall.

"Good morning, everyone. I'm your new English teacher," I said to the grade 9/10 class of about fifteen students. Marina, Agostina, Antonio, and the others smiled back, ready to break out in nervous laughter, but I wasn't sure why. This class was the first of my teaching career. I considered rea-sons for this atmosphere: Matias, the reigning class and school clown hadn't arrived yet, but his absence didn't seem to make a difference to his classmates. Smirks were quivering, waiting to crack wide open. We all needed something to break the nervous tension, and I unwittingly gave it to them. As I offered my biography to facilitate a warm interaction, I suavely sat on one of the empty desks in the front row. But suave I wasn't. The desk tipped, I slipped off, and the clatter of metal and wood on the polished concrete floor was followed by peals of laughter. Christianne's brown Mexican skin went red—she couldn't stop giggling.

The rest of the class, comprised of Argentines, Ecuadorians, Venezuelans, Canadians, and an American, who had been with the school since its in-ception three years before, had seen their share of new North American teachers and first-day antics. Eventually, their laughter settled, in addition to my own, and an incredible and unforgettable year began.

"Was that ever embarrassing," said I with a laugh to the teacher beside me. "And then there was that time a few weeks later . . ." The stories about my first weeks at Escuela de Las Americas in El Tigre bubbled like a spring. I continued recalling the first semester as I pushed a seashell through the hot sand in front of my beach towel. It was January first, and I had just returned from Christmas break in Canada. Organizing the flight from El Tigre shortly after my arrival had been a nightmare, as everything to Miami had already been booked since August. I ended up buying two return flights with a charter company, four flights in total, and only using two of them. Being back on the beach for two days before classes resumed provided an important though awkward buffer, a middle space between being responsible for the education of young minds, and being buffeted in the turbulance of rapid international travel and culture shock. I wanted to consider how I could improve my teaching, but I was mired in a strange mental and emotional space pondering the time I had just spent with family and a serious girlfriend now five thousand kilometres away. The shell in my hand reflected these feelings; it was coursing through the sand as my skis had done in the snow only two days before. "That's weird!" I exclaimed. "What?" the math teacher asked as she applied more sunscreen, "s.p.f. forty," to her white skin. "This is. Laying here on this beach, so familiar to us now, after being back home for two weeks. It's such a strange experience—hard to describe."

This new friend, with whom I would eventually collaborate on a project for the grade five students, demonstrated her professionalism: "You should get the kids to write about it in creative writing." It was a good idea, especially since I was about to take on the reluctant grade nine/ten class for the compulsory second English class of the day, fulfilling the school requirement of each teacher leading one elective class. Most of the students were expatriates as well, and they would want, perhaps even need, to tell their stories and express their feelings. I became excited to continue the school year. Not only could I tackle my classroom challenges with fresh and more seasoned resolve, but I would soon serve on two committees for our school's stateside accreditation process, attend a professional development weekend, and bring a new repertoire to the school's choirs.

The proximity of the Caribbean coast to our school also enticed me back after that Christmas break. Two hours north of the apartments and houses in which all of the teachers lived was one of my favorite beaches: a small island cove surrounded by cactus plants and rocks facing the green coastal mountains of South America. Now that it was winter in Canada, living in a tropical country had even greater appeal. As I heated up for my next swim, I continued to recall the first four months at Escuela de las Americas.

"We're really excited about this year," said the director at our first in-service meeting, several days before my embarrassing introduction to the grade nine/ten class. He continued: "This is the biggest staff we've had yet. We now have 120 students enrolled from Junior Kindergarten to grade twelve. And this year we're all going to be involved in a self-study. You're going to try your hands at being administrators." Though quite surprised by this added source of anxiety, I did like being named both the chair of the English committee and a member of the editing committee; I was excited, and apart from a pesty abdominal disorder that I was hoping was merely a symptom of my nerves, I was incredibly motivated. My new administrative titles meant meeting with the elementary representative and submitting a report about our methodologies and application of the curriculum. Our section would then be added to the other departments in the school to be collated into a book for SACS, the Southern Association of

Colleges and Schools. "And I know all of you are dying to get some SACS," quipped the director to lighten the mood. A few more sacs/sex jokes in addition to a deadline five months away eased tension with the teachers already shouldering their new teaching assignments in this foreign country.

After the meeting, the director's wife, ostensibly the codirector, grabbed me by the wrist and led me to the book room which was full of new or recent texts from the United States. "Now don't worry about your SACS report right now. We have to get your classroom organized," she explained. In theory, and in the director's policies, split grades should be taught as one grade, advice that was contested by the principal. As I brought the mostly new textbooks to my classroom, a spacious air-conditioned room, she clarified my job: "In teaching the seven/eights, for example, you should use the grade eight book one year and the grade seven one the following year. There's not a large difference between the two texts, no students will read the same thing twice, and you can do a better job."

Later, the principal, promoted from her previous role of English teacher, stopped by. Her ideas differed from the director's. "There's no way some of your grade nine students can read that grade ten book." Theory confronted practice. Experience collided with inexperience. While the directors deserved respect, the Principal would be my sergeant major on the front lines. Ultimately, the school was hers, as the Directors' appearances would only be intermittent at best; they would be concerned with the development of a new sister school in the coastal city where we would spend many weekends. Consequently, my lesson plans on Frost and Longfellow, Wordsworth and Langston Hughes, would only work for half of the class. Thus, while I only had to teach five of seven periods in a day that ran from eight to three o'clock, those five really became ten or more, depending on the ESL contingent in the class.

The social studies teacher exacerbated my growing concerns about the students' language abilities by pressuring me about my role in the school. "The parents are going to come to you first at parent's night," he said. "They want their kids to be perfect English speakers."

"You mean they're not already?" I naively asked. He snorted. I grew worried. The school had an English as a Second Language teacher, a woman from Guayana to whom I would send the students who were more than two levels behind their peers. All new students to E.L.A. take reading comprehension and vocabulary placement tests. As much as possible, students were placed according to their age and grade levels. Teaching split grades became even more challenging, therefore, as at the grade seven level and up, students could be as many as two grades behind the class, constituting a third group in the same classroom.

A second reason that more students were kept in my class instead of going to ESL instruction was because the school is private, not funded by the large oil corporations. Those schools, richer and larger than our independent one, set strict standards which ensured that their classrooms are no different than those in an average North American school. At E.L.A., language ability standards were lowered to keep enrollment high enough to run the school and pay the salaries. A more intense and multilevel ESL program was the school's biggest improvement while I was there, but before that change, the broad range of English abilities in my classes forced me to be organized and versatile, ready to accommodate the needs of these exceptional students. My preparation periods were essential for taking a breath from the downhill slalom course of each period: constant turns and bounces from one group of students to the next. At times the runs were smooth, allowing me to carve graceful turns through the curriculum, and at other times the run was covered with icy bumps, knocking me off course. At those times, students were left rolling around in the snow of grammar, spelling, or comprehension questions.

Recalling some of the more difficult classes of my first four months made me squirm on my towel, which was now twisted and filled with sand. It was time to swim and snorkel with my fellow teachers, my new friends. "The amazing thing about diving under while you're snorkeling," said the science teacher, "is that you suddenly exist in, and move through, three dimensions. It blows me away!" His enthusiasm for the natural world was a nice match for my love of expressing its delights with words. Our little vacations to the coast invigorated our teaching. While the PE teacher scaled the cliffs above us, the science teacher pointed out underwater rock formations, and I waxed poetically about the whole experience. Together we combed the bottom of the Caribbean Sea. These vacations offered more to us than just fun. They are integral to the professional as well as personal development of an overseas teacher. We all returned to our classes the following Monday relating our stories to our students and incorporating them into class. Our excitement inspired students, and new ideas for extracurricular activities from choir to chess were born of this excitement and adventure.

Extracurricular activities were crucial in providing a complete self-study for SACS, but ironically, the start of the school chorus in November only delayed my SACS duties. Chorus practice was one day a week for each group, juniors and seniors. My acoustic guitar and repertoire of contemporary rock and folk music were ideal for the non-musically trained students. And though my formal training was weak, I was hailed as a pioneer of the school's music program. Despite the lure of intramurals provided by our dedicated PE instructor, the chorus season ended strongly. With a couple of enthusiastic tone-deaf students in the senior chorus and a grade five student with Attention Deficit Disorder in the junior chorus clobbering others with his voracious animal movements during the song "The Unicorn," the choral part of the Christmas program went well.

The school's Christmas program was well-attended by mostly Latin

American parents who couldn't understand but seemed very proud to see their children on stage engaging in this cultural mosaic, speaking the preferred language of the business world. Quite a few of the fathers earned their engineering degrees in the United States and realized the value of speaking English. Foreign companies, many of which are from the United States, are contracted by Venezuela's national company to service the many different facets of the oil industry. I learned a lot from Mr. Gomez, the father of one of my students, who I tutored for extra money twice a week. "You see, I am in the cement services," he explained. "We, um, um, how do you say, pour? Yes, pour different mixtures down the well at different times. Is that correct? You must tell me." I was nodding my head vigorously as he continued to ask questions about his performance as he spoke. Our conversations led us through the process of tequila production in Mexico, Mexican traditions, and of course, one of the favorite pastimes of many Latinos, soccer.

Soccer was our trump card among the five American schools in our state, Anzoatagui. With the PE teacher I began to draw plays and drills in the sand as we geared up for the winter/spring sports season. Although he had spent Christmas break in Margarita Island while some of us returned to the North, we met at the beach. Perhaps to compensate for missing winter, he also had some hockey planned: "I'm hoping you can referee the roller hockey tournament. You can use my blades while I coach our team," he said excitedly. All of this depended on the workmens' progress on the *cancha* (an outdoor gym) that was under construction while we were gone on Christmas break. And here's where our story gets a bit difficult. Enter the most pervasive attitude in Latin American culture, encapsulated in two words: "*tranquilo*" and "*mañana.*"

In December, after two and a half months of chasing not only promised donations from an oil company, but also workers, the *cancha* was started; it was not, however, a smooth process. Realizing that he was finishing his last field activity and in need of a gym by the start of January's classes, our P.E. teacher grew more and more frustrated with each two-hour siesta the *cancha* workmen would take. His fuse had burnt, and when the workers started to break up a section of the new gym floor right before the Christmas holidays, he blew up. Struggling with his Spanish he angrily asked, "*¿por que?*" and shouted, "*No hay tiempo!* There's no time!" He was answered predictably with "*tranquilo!*" Take it easy. Relax.

Naturally, with this kind of philosophy, time changes from a measure of industry and success to an elastic measure of relaxation—a rubber band stretched around a beer can, shot around a gathering of friends for a while, until it settles in the shallows of the sea. Sharing a couple of cold beers for an hour after work stretches into a few more beers for a few more hours. A seven o'clock meeting time stretches to encompass any point within the whole hour of seven. Among Latinos, a time to leave for the beach is rarely set. We get there when we get there.

School, however, worked like clockwork—a North American clock, that is. Christmas holidays were over and six more months of classes would resume the next day. The strangeness of being amidst snow, home, and family one day and grains of tropical sand the next had to be dealt with. Pushing that awkward goodbye with my girlfriend into a corner of my heart, I realigned my thoughts and feelings: time for school. Time for work. Like my friend and colleague, I wase anxious to see if the gym floor was ready. The memories of the four months before Christmas were about to be replaced by six months of new experiences. We packed up our beach stuff and headed to the jetty where the *piñeros* (small fishing boats) picked the people up. The Venezuelans carried their trashed beer cans and pop bottles, an act that seemed reserved only for the national park beaches. They carried their large coolers to the dock, laughing and cheering for no discernable reason on the way. Our boats passed the oil tankers anchored in the bay at Puerto la Cruz, waiting to moor at the dock where oil flowed by pipeline from many of the country's reserves. Just beyond, one could see a bright steel vein arching over the coastal mountains.

Following that pipe was our route home: the plains of East and Central Venezuela where wells and rigs surround El Tigre. We traveled to those wells and our school via a two-hour drive straight south at a mere 4,000 Bolivares, eight U.S. dollars (1997) in gas. We could sign out the school Jeep for weekends at the cost of fifteen dollars a day. Poor roads and sewers make such vehicles essential. During rainy season, which runs from June to October, many small cars stall in puddles three feet deep and forty meters long. Although these problems are ubiquitous in Venezuela, El Tigre still seemed more deprived of aesthetic urban planning than anywhere else in Venezuela. It is neither interesting or attractive, charming or exciting. While Puerto la Cruz boasts fancy hotels, quaint villages, mountains, and beaches, Ciudad Bolivar, two hours south, lies beside the impressive Orinoco River separating the Amazon watershed from the rest of Venezuela. This historic site was where we went for colonial charm, museums, and galleries. Compared to these two cities, El Tigre did at least have the advantage of being central, equidistant between the two, but even that advantage diminished for us when we made a professional development trip to Valencia, in the West of the country

"We're all going to be taking a plane trip together to the VANAS conference in Valencia," announced our fatherly director at our first meeting in January. "That's the Venezuelan Association of North American Schools. It'll be a professional development weekend, all expenses paid. We'll have to close the school that Monday." Excited glances and smiles flashed around the table of nine teachers. What an opportunity! Those three weeks of classes went quickly, and with the *cancha* finished for our basketball and roller hockey teams, the tempo of that first six-week grading period in the new year was intense.

Intensity was redefined me, however, at that conference; there, my overseas journey reached a summit, an epiphany. After a welcome assembly comprised of almost four hundred teachers and administrators from the United States, Canada, Britain, Ireland, the West Indies, Latin America, New Zealand, and Australia, my senses were heightened; being with such an eclectic group of educators was thrilling. That afternoon, I climbed the hill to the school's upper campus where there was an incredible view of the city and the rest of the cordillera stretching north, toward Caracas. Those dusty-green hills could be seen from the classroom where I was the only teacher in a workshop on rubric making. At least twenty workshops had been offered for this last period of the day, and I had the pleasure of matching my untempered enthusiasm and inexperienced idealism with a committed, veteran educator at the end of her career. She was from Louisiana, and her professionalism and dedication to education were moving.

Feeling humbled and inspired, I left her room and was at once transformed: in a moment in time that was as small as a single grain of sand on one of Venezuela's beaches, my spine shivered with Latin rhythms and soared over the mountains to the sea. Needing to express the intensity, I shouted something in the beautiful new language I was learning: "*Se me pone la piel de gallina*" (I have goosebumps). That's what Leo, one of my two grade twelve students, taught me to say when we were discussing the kind of intense experiences that inspire poets. Somehow, capping that incredible feeling with something that a student had taught me seemed right. Regaining my composure and beaming with delight from seeing my overseas journey through one delicious million-volt shock, I descended the steep path to join the other teachers for refreshments at the end of the day social With each successive beer, teachers broke free of their shells. Energy flowed amongst the young group as they planned parties, exchanged numbers, and said good-bye with Latin kisses.

When we returned from the professional development weekend, extracurricular sports were in full swing, classes were going well, and we began to plan our vacations for the last three breaks. Carnival was first. As *tranquilo* as we had learned to become about many things in Latin America, our plane tickets became the source of comments like "never again" and "I want to go home!" The secretary of our English-speaking travel agent drove them to the door of the airport ten minutes before departure. On board, people had already begun opening cold cans of beer. My colleagues and I started to relax, but the days and minutes preceding that moment caused us to suffer enough hardship to fill up one hundred Lents.

I had just finished explaining to my students that Carnival and Lent commemorated Christ's sacrifices while in the desert, which I thought was acceptable lesson material in a nonreligious school since so many of them had no idea why they threw balloons, dressed up, and paraded down the streets on the weekend before the sacrifices begin. I stopped myself short of scolding them for not knowing this part of the culture as I recalled my own ignorance about Halloween—the other occasion for costumes and pageantry. Since they don't really celebrate it in South America, I thought I'd first educate them on its history. It took me a visit to our spacious library to discover that it was rooted in pagan Ireland. No wonder Latinos don't celebrate it. Another occasion for costume and drama brings this story to our next holiday.

Semana Santa means holy week and it leads up to Easter weekend, which the science teacher and I spent in Merida, a colonial university city in the Andes. Easter passion performances in the plazas (town squares) complete with Roman soldiers, fake blood, and strobe lights, are the focal point of the week in many towns and cities. I enjoyed the spectacle, complete with vendors selling edible Virgin Marys, but the high point of our week was trekking to the bottom of a glacier some 4,000 meters, roughly 16,000 feet above sea level. Somehow, being at my personal highest point on the earth's surface seemed an appropriate time to take stock of my life. I had definitely had a honeymoon with Venezuela, definitely had some low points, and definitely evened out into a great friendship.

The good-byes I exchanged with the students and parents at our graduation ceremony amplified that friendship, a friendship that extended beyond. Venezuela, down to Argentina, over to Ecuador, up to Chicago and Calgary, and across to Boston. With all these places represented in my E.L.A. yearbook, including two in Europe and Asia, I knew I had become a citizen of the Americas. My contribution? My grade seven/eight class's performance of Shakespeare's "Pyramus and Thisbe" seemed to sum it all up. Not only did they all smile and finally get the jokes, but also Andrea, one of the quiet ESL students who made my lessons so challenging, finally projected, and in Shakespearean English no less, with confidence. Following the ceremony, the directors gave us one last dinner out and implored us to stay even though they had already organized the next year's line-up of staff. Leaving was not easy.

Despite being incredibly anxious to return home, I made the compulsory trip to the breathtaking Angel Falls and cosmopolitan Caracas before I reached Miami, that buffer in going from one culture to another. I became quite emotional when I saw a jet on the runway with a large maple leaf on its tail. One more three-hour trip and I approached the customs desk in Toronto, contentment and joy welling up in me. Leafing through my passport, the officer noticed the year-long work visa stamped inside. "You've been down in Venezuela, eh?" he said. And beaming with pride, I replied, "You bet, sir."

9

Teaching a Future President

Shirley Hooper

It wasn't quite one year after the *"Offensiva"* when we arrived in San Salvador, El Salvador. The *"Offensiva"* (Offensive), or first real push in the civil war, was when the war came into the capital city and became known around the world. We had applied for the job change in February when the official civil war in El Salvador was still only a few months old, but since we were coming from Colombia, it was rather like changing one war zone for another. At the time, the war in Colombia was being felt more and more in the capital city, Bogota, where we had been teaching for ten years. Car or truck bombs were being left in places in and around our neighborhood and the government offices where we foreigners had to go for official transactions. A truck loaded with dynamite had blown up the government building where we had to register, make address changes, or notify the authorities that we were leaving the country. The explosion took place before first period on a school day. There were a few students in the classroom when we heard not only the roar of the dynamite, but also the sound of the classroom windows rattling in their frames even though the school was miles away and high on the mountainside away from the explosion itself. A few weeks later my sons and I walked fifteen blocks from our home to see the hole left by an explosion we had heard the night before. A tourist agency no longer existed at that location.

Considering this alarming event, El Salvador seemed quite tame by Colombian standards. After the *Offensiva* there was little to no fighting in the capital city, San Salvador, and other than telephone and electrical outages (the rebels liked to blow up the poles leading into the city) and travel prohibitions, my family and I could get along quite well. It is amazing how something that worries your family back home, as they see the news program dwelling on the terrible upheavals in your host country, really aren't bothering you much at all. Also, you must keep in mind that most news stories will be datelined from the capital city so the fighting between the police and rebels which is causing your relatives to place panicked phone calls to you may well be happening hundreds of miles away and in another region from where you're living. There were little problems such as not being able to make a call until another night or not counting on showing a video in a class because the electricity will probably be cut, but you would be pleasantly surprised at how quickly such things become no more than minor irritants. I was more bothered by the fact that milk would be spoiled by the time you got it up to the cash register so I went over to powdered. The ability to adjust and the cultivation of patience can become very important in an international teaching position.

I love teaching in international schools and living in foreign climes; I've been at it for over twenty-five years now. All of my teaching experience has been in Latin America: Peru, Chile, Brazil, Colombia, El Salvador, and, at present, Mexico. Generally, I teach high school English, and teaching it in this part of the world is a fun adventure. On the whole, students in American schools in Latin America are very friendly and intelligent. After all, these are private schools and are able to set their own admission standards. But for all their intelligence and good, supportive family backgrounds, they do have some traits in the classroom that can drive you up a wall.

One such trait is the felt need of students to talk virtually all the time, appropriately or not. Latin students are a sociable lot, and would seem to have emerged from the womb with all their verbal capacities fully matured. Talking is probably the number one discipline problem in the classroom as given the least opportunity students will be chatting away. If you turn your back, take too long of a moment to think about the next word, drop the chalk, or have one of those numerous administrative interruptions, the class will quickly begin pattering in groups. Once their attention is brought back, they are most apologetic, but do not be deceived, they have their conversation topic held at the ready in the forefront of their minds, and they will be off again at the slightest opportunity. As I mentioned, the students are quick to apologize; they do not talk out of maliciousness, nor are they out to destroy your class—they just can't help themselves. Self-control does not seem to be a Latin trait. To combat this problem, I have asked classes to picture a large foul-smelling, drooling, alien creature with an enormous mouth and lightning-quick reflexes who lines up all the school children in front of him on the soccer field. This creature would command in a riveting tone that everyone be quiet, or they would be eaten.

Along with the chattiness goes the inability to listen. I've read that listening is a faculty being used less and less in stateside schools also. To demonstrate the importance of listening, I once brought a rock into my seventh grade classroom and introduced it as a new student. I suggested that it (the rock) would probably get the same grades as they did because it had an equal capacity to listen to instructions and follow discussions as the rest of the class. "Rocky" became the subject of a good creative writing project and was even invited to a sleep-over. In another strategy I once made one of my students the "page-repeater" of the class. She was so interminably slow about getting her book from the rack under her desk to the writing surface on top of the desk that she could never hear to what page number I had asked the students to open their books. It became her duty to repeat whatever page number I had said as many times as asked. At first the students had a lot of fun with this as the girl was self-confident enough to think the whole thing quite funny, but after a time they ceased to ask her to repeat because she could always do it. Somehow, her book flew to the top of the desk, and the students could see it opened to the correct page. When I had the same group of students a few years later as juniors, no one ever asked me to repeat the page number, least of all the former official page-repeater.

Latinos also have a different idea of space and taking turns. I've had students shove their papers on top of the one I have in my hand and am discussing with the writer. Students will be just plain rude by North American cultural standards. They stand extremely close, interrupt, and never wait for you to finish what you're doing for someone else. If you remain adamant, never wavering, you can get the behavior you desire. Most students just don't understand that your standards are different until you take the time to explain the things that really bother you. Don't get carried away and expect students to be able to tackle your ten pet peeves all at once: one at a time will get you better results. The flip side of this behavior is that students don't think anything of a friendly touch, will kiss a female teacher on the cheek when they see her in public, and are not above giving you a kindly hug. Many small reassuring behaviors are expected and given here.

Another, more serious discipline problem that seems to be ubiquitous to Latin schools is cheating: a problem that is present at some time in nearly all classes. When teachers claim that no one cheats in their classes, I think they are probably unaware or lying. Few teachers I have known actually try to give a grade for homework as it is assumed that a great deal of copying has gone on. Teachers usually give students credit for having completed the homework or use the completed homework as a requirement for taking a quiz or doing some other class work. Students will copy on any assignment they can. At the first of the year, as I was checking what would become a routine, weekly dictionary assignment to look up words used on the SAT exams, I accused the students in my twelfth grade class of being ridiculously poor copiers. They retorted with "We never copy," which is always worth a general laugh, and then they asked how I knew.

At this point, all the teacher needs is one example. At least half the class had the definition of "languorous" as "characterized by." "But, but," they remonstrated "that is exactly what the dictionary said." "Of course," I replied that that probably was exactly what the dictionary said on the first line of the definition, but whoever the kind soul was who had let his/her notebook be copied had neglected to finish the whole definition: "languorous—characterized by physical weakness or faintness," and everyone copied a partial definition without thinking. I then suggested that from now on they copy only from someone who knows how to properly read the dictionary, which brought on another general laugh.

More serious, of course, is the copying that goes on during quizzes and exams. Students have to be continually watched in any exam situation because they are amazingly well-practiced at seeking a peek or whispering an answer. Besides being watchful, it helps to move desks into a special exam arrangement so students can not easily see another's paper or talk to a neighboring student. No matter how good a student you think you are working with, he will cheat if it means helping a friend, even if it will lower his own grade. Every school I've worked in on this continent has very strict rules about cheating and yet at least four or five cases of serious cheating will come up every year. There have been instances when whole classes have schemed to steal a test from a teacher's locked closet or file cabinet. I have heard of students who claimed they really didn't steal the exam because they only photographed the pages so the exam itself never really left the room. Cheating is almost a pastime and many students do not feel that cheating is bad; the only "bad" thing is getting caught.

Another form of cheating, plagiarism, is very difficult to fight against. Doing battle with the students who plagiarize on research projects always has me saying, "Never again." To counter this type of cheating a friend of mine who teaches American history requires that the students turn in a photocopy of their resource material. Students are to highlight those lines from which they selected their material. When another friend, who works with middle-schoolers, spots too-perfect construction or four or five words in the first pages that she feels the students wouldn't be able to use or know, she asks the student to explain the meaning in other words; when he/she can't, she knows she is looking at plagiarism and so does the student. Because I ask for specific, original work in the introduction and conclusion of a research paper, my clue is the difference in writing style and word usage between these two sections and the body or middle of the paper. A couple of questions usually make it apparent that there is plagiarism. It is best to have your consequences for plagiarism written on the assignment sheet or schedule that you give to students. When I have given a zero on a long assignment for plagiarism and tell the student that a rewrite will automatically receive no more than a passing grade, I have often had to meet with parents who believe from their child that I never explained the assignment or consequences fully. Written instructions with a clear time-line, due dates, and consequences for missed work or plagiarism are inval-uable when you're faced with irate parents.

Teachers who believe that they can give the same test to every class period seem to be surprised by how much better the afternoon classes do than the morning classes. Any major break in the schedule such as lunch will mean that students have plenty of time to exchange information. There is nothing more honest to a student than swapping chemistry test infor-mation for history test information. To stay ahead make out different quiz-zes or tests changing enough items that students realize after a time or two that passing on test information is of little to no value. I would rather make cheating as difficult as possible than have to cope with an eighteen-year-old boy who has tears in his eyes and is begging on his knees for me to change his zero for cheating on a major exam because he will not pass the course.

Admittedly, these are not the only problems you may have in a Latin American classroom. There are students with personal and emotional prob-lems, problems in dealing with authority, peer problems, etc., just as there would be back home. On the whole, the degree of most discipline or class-room management problems seems to be less than you might be used to in public schools in North America. A teacher can really spend a minimal amount of time disciplining and a maximum amount of time teaching. Remember these students have been selected even if the only selection cri-teria you're aware of is that their parents graduated from the school or an uncle is on the board. Even though your students may chat a bit too much or be quick to take advantage, they are lively discussers and fun creative thinkers. Their parents are interested in their progress and, in most in-stances, are paying a good deal of money to give their children the advan-tage of learning English in an American school. Parents tend to be supportive and respond well when I ask what I can do at school to help their child so they can more effectively help him/her at home. The initial costs of placing a child in one of these schools means that the parents have monetary means either of their own or from the company for which they work. The children are likely to come from a home with many resources and to have traveled, often extensively. But for all their money, they are still kids and respond to the things that most kids do.

Latin students are generally very friendly and genuinely seem to like teachers. You are not considered an enemy, but someone whom they trust to help them learn. Elementary teachers, especially, are appreciated by their students and parents. These teachers receive gifts not only at Christmas, but also on Teachers' Day and at the end of the year. At Christmas they are often so loaded down that they have to take things home on consecutive days unless they have transport. Elementary teachers are invited to attend birthday parties, join in family meals, or enjoy an outing with a family. You might get an invitation to spend a few days at the family's beach house or visit Aunt Edna in a neighboring country. It is not uncommon to form friendships with families, which last for the years spent at the school and beyond.

High school teachers don't get quite the same perks. The teenage code doesn't allow for open admissions of admiration of teachers, which is really all right with most high school teachers. If you're a high school teacher, you have undoubtedly worked out why it is that you like working with this age group. The rewards may be more subtle, but they are definitely there, and here in Latin America, they are even more apparent. I have received gifts at Christmas, although not many and only before classes begin in the morning, but the less tangible rewards are the most heartfelt. Students from years ago will hang out of car windows to shout, "Hi, Miss, how are you?" as they drive past. You'll see friendly smiles and receive greetings in the grocery store or at the movie theater.

Not long ago, while I was walking my dog in the park near my home, a former student spotted me, stopped his car, leapt out, and came to ask me how things were going and talk about how he was doing in college. Another time, while walking home from some late function at school, I was in a dark area of the street feeling a bit nervous when a large, shadowy form coming toward me said, "Gee, Miss, you're still here. That's great!" I instantly relaxed and fell into conversation with a former student who was finishing his university studies. He walked me the two blocks home, and I heard how things were going with him. Students here rarely ignore teachers and will happily introduce you to their boyfriend or girlfriend even if they are just passing by in their cars. Of course, this friendly exposure can be a drawback. On our first date, the man who was to become my husband and I were spotted together in Maracana Stadium (Rio de Janeiro, Brazil), which has still got to be one of the largest in the world, and became the topic of student prognostications on Monday morning.

In another time when I could have done without being introduced to a junior student's mother, I had nothing in my shopping cart but five bottles of tequila. Because I had a car, I had told my friend I would pick up the drinks for the party that night, but somehow I felt it was awkward to make excuses to my student's mother—which would probably draw more attention to my purchase than I wanted. She either thought I had a well-hidden drinking problem, or, I hope, she thought I was buying for friends. For teachers who taught students in middle school or the early years of high school, it is often hard to recognize them later because of their physical growth. I usually respond a certain way: "Wow, you've become so pretty— or handsome . . . I'm sorry your name has slipped my memory." If the student seems upset that I have forgotten, I add, "I'm just the same but older so, naturally, I'm easy to remember, but you have changed so much." The comment is always sincere, too. Of course, there are some students, no matter how much they have grown, that a teacher can always recognize: the student who always came in a bit before class started to chat, the one you saw dance in the ballet recital, or the one who seemed to willingly take all your advice and ended up winning the speech contest.

The experiences and memories involved in teaching in an international community are wonderful indeed, and they do etch indelible marks on your life. As I mentioned, I've been in Latin America for some twenty-five years and several of those in virtual war zones. I have had a couple of cheap watches taken off my wrist in Bogota, and the car was broken into three times in Central America. I no longer bother with a car radio or tape deck since I travel with my dog who I truly believe has grown fond of hearing me sing "Oh, Danny Boy" and "Look for the Silver Lining." She's not quite so keen on "Yesterday," but maybe I don't do it justice yet. I'll have to get in some more practice on my next trip up to El Paso. You do need to be careful, but probably the same rule applies back in the states. I never pull out a lot of cash, I drive an ordinary car, I watch my luggage (especially in the Miami airport), and I realize there is some risk involved in any venture. On the plus side, my two sons had the benefit of excellent educations and they speak, read, and write Spanish well after ten years in Spanish classes with native speakers. I have known and worked with really good teachers and students, I have friends in many parts of the world, and I have seen many natural wonders.

Above all, I've had the chance to work with young people who will be leaders in their countries, and I let them know that I'm just waiting for one of them to be president someday and really do something for their country by giving it honest leadership. I feel that I have not only taught them something about the English language but also helped them to think more deeply and more democratically. I am a widow now, my sons have finished college and taken up their adult lives, and I'm wondering where I should head next.

PART V

The West: Austria and Australia

10

The Kaiser's Mélange: A Year of Teaching in Vienna

Karen L. Newman

"Just don't tell me when it's your last day! Come in, sit at the usual booth, read the day's *Herald Tribune* and take your *Mélange* as always!" ordered Herr Jahn, my favorite tuxedo-clad waiter at Café Diglas. And who was I to say no? In Vienna, a city that prides itself on its historical association with coffee, a city that is famous for unique cafés filled with marble tables, bentwood chairs, plush velvet booths, rich desserts, and quirky waiters, I was more than happy to oblige in what had become a daily ritual for me, as it was for many Viennese: the trip to a beloved café. The trip must include a *Mélange*, Vienna's version of cappuccino, a leisurely read of the latest local and international newspapers, and, as the Viennese aphorism goes, the opportunity to be alone in public. As I approached the end of the school year and my stay in Austria, I saw my daily *Mélange* as symbolic not only of my fond attachment to this Viennese ritual, but also of my deeper understanding of the pleasant mélange of traditional and modern elements that coexist in the "K. u. K. Hauptstadt," or Imperial and Royal Capital City of Vienna. I could hardly have imagined, though, that my introduction to this city would have come about through my role of ambassador of American English to students in a Viennese high school. Prior to my year in Vienna, I had extensive overseas experience, having grown up outside of the United States as the child of U.S. government employees. I studied for four years in Germany, and it seemed natural to me that I would eventually seek employment overseas. Fortunately, my advisors at the doctoral program to which I had just been accepted were eager to see their students develop their scholarly, pedagogical, and personal goals.

Since I had heard of a program that placed American students as English teaching assistants throughout Austria, I decided to apply and request a leave of absence from my program.

My eventual placement as a teaching assistant for the Austrian Ministry of Education in the 1997–1998 school year was facilitated by the Fulbright/Austrian American Educational Commission in Vienna. One benefit of teaching overseas with an established program is that few of the technical aspects of travel, training, and placement are left to chance. However, no amount of previous overseas experience or program participation can shield one from occasional frustration, isolation, or loneliness; particularly when another language is concerned, the potential for frustration is all the more. Since I was fluent in German and had previously lived in Germany, I had not anticipated difficulties with linguistic or cultural adjustment, as Austria and Germany share a common language. But these two countries have much less in common than I initially realized, and my preconceptions about Austria, which had been influenced by its larger geographic neighbor, were subject to constant revision. I soon discovered that Austrian German offers many a linguistic surprise; even a simple Austrian café menu contains words unrecognizable to a German *Bundesdeutsch* speaker. As my pocket notepad grew with scribbled memos of Austrian equivalents for familiar words, so too did my appreciation for the intricacies and humor of the Viennese dialect and for my understanding of the city's unique history.

For me, the mélange that is Vienna was soon becoming evident. Although the empire may be long gone, I could sense a musty tradition, embodied in the ubiquitous images of the fatherly Kaiser Franz Joseph and his fashionable, melancholy wife Empress Elisabeth, coexisting with sophistication and modernity. Add to this mix a dash of the neurosis made famous by Vienna's own Sigmund Freud, and you have a fascinating place for a new American teacher.

The modern side of this mix took precedence at a "crash course" in language pedagogy in late September, which was sponsored by the Austrian Ministry of Education. The course was the start of the school year for all 200-odd new English language teaching assistants assigned to Austria's schools. All assistants gathered at a sports conference and training facility in Hollabrunn, a small town north of Vienna, and we were housed in dorm rooms for a two-day teaching seminar. The premise of the seminar was to clarify the tasks and duties of the teaching assistant in the Austrian school system, and to give those of us who had never taught before, the opportunity to learn and practice communicative teaching methods in a supportive environment. Small-group discussions were led by practicing language teachers, all of whom were up-to-date with the latest literature and pedagogical theories of second language teaching and learning. This seminar also provided teaching assistants the opportunity to bond with fellow English speakers and establish contacts that would prove of immeasurable support during the year in Austria. The Ministry offered a follow-up meeting three months later for Viennese teaching assistants to touch base and discuss experiences, but our guidance and mentoring was the ultimate responsibility of English teachers in our respective schools.

I was assigned to a newly-built *Gymnasium* in the southernmost, 23rd district of Vienna, a growing suburban area dominated by a mix of bland and architecturally novel high-rise apartment buildings as well as expensive villas nestled near hilly vineyards. The Austrian secondary education system tracks students according to their elementary school performance, and the *Gymnasium*, or high school where I taught, encompassed grades five through twelve and served to prepare students for the university track. The school was excited to have a native English-speaking teaching assistant, as they had not been assigned one in the previous school year. Since most of the school's nine hundred students were studying English, the overworked staff of twenty-one full- and part-time English teachers was anxious for the assistance of a native speaker who could prepare culturally relevant and linguistically authentic materials. Upon my arrival at the school, I was warmly received and offered an apartment on the spot by one of my friendly colleagues; fellow teaching assistants at other schools found themselves scrambling for housing, as the Ministry did not assist in finding accommodations for teaching assistants. I must concede from the outset that many of the hardships experienced by my fellow contributors in this anthology, such as cramped accommodations or schools with inadequate books and materials, were fully absent from my teaching experience in Vienna. I was truly in a privileged environment.

Combined with this environment, I had expected to find the Germanic cliché of order, exactitude, and precision. I assumed that this severity would permeate the halls of Austrian education, that teachers might maintain a stern distance from students. Eager to fit in and look the part of "teacher," I even purchased a new suit before leaving the states. To my simultaneous joy and displeasure, I soon found that some of my assumptions were more myth than reality. My suit went unworn, save for a night in standing room at the Vienna *Staatsoper*, as the dress code for teachers is decidedly more relaxed than in American schools.

In my experience, collegial respect and support characterized teacher-student interactions; nevertheless, formality is still an important part of life in Austria, again reflecting this *mélange* of traditional and modern elements. Titles become part of one's legal name and signature, and teachers are always addressed as "Frau Professor" or "Herr Professor." The symbols of history and tradition were evident everywhere, as each classroom had at the front a framed print of the Austrian eagle (minus its former double head, an updated symbol of the once-dual monarchy of Austria-Hungary), and a small wooden Catholic cross, reflective of the country's dominant religion.

In spite of this tradition of formality, a benevolent chaos, and a live-and-let-live attitude characterized the learning environment at my school. By this, I do not imply a laxness toward standards or student performance, since these were taken quite seriously by the principal, the teaching staff, and by parents and students at my school. I can't help but think that perhaps the school's *laissez-faire* atmosphere was a reflection of Vienna's history as a once-bustling center of a multiethnic and linguistically diverse empire, a center that is tempered by memory of Austria's complicity with and scars from the events of World War II. The students I taught demonstrated an admirable respect for other students, for their teachers, and for the enterprise of learning, one that I have often felt lacking in my teaching experiences in the United States. In turn, teachers were extremely supportive of their students and of me throughout my year at the school.

My official status was *Lehrassistentin*, or teaching assistant, and, because I was not a certified Austrian teacher, I was not permitted to remain unsupervised in the classroom and was not accorded a full load of teaching duties: my employment was part-time, I was not assigned my own classes, and I did not administer exams. On a typical school day, I accompanied five different teachers to their regularly scheduled, fifty-minute English classes. However, when it was learned that I had prior teaching experience at the university level, I was given increasingly more teaching responsibility, and colleagues came to value my contributions to the positive language learning environment in the school. For me, an experienced teacher, my status of assistant and accompanist was one of the most perplexing aspects of my stay. I was at once a low-ranking person on the official totem pole, and, because I was the only native English speaker in a school with mandatory English requirements, I was also a minor celebrity. This dual status lent my English lessons the air of a circus sideshow, and it often caused an enthusiastic commotion during my classroom appearances.

Admittedly, I found this chaos to be a bit disconcerting, as I value a certain amount of orderliness to classroom lessons and activities. However, my status had a clear benefit: it helped me to foster positive working relationships with my students. I was caught somewhere in the middle; I was neither one of them, since I was older than they were, nor a full-fledged member of the regular teaching staff. Nonetheless, because of my nebulous age and rank, many students tended to view me as a friend and ally. Two of the best-kept secrets in the school were my age, and that I actually could speak fluent German, and students attempted any number of playful ways to ferret out one or the other "secrets." One particularly enthusiastic class of sixth graders often followed me through the halls between classes, shouting, "Frau Professor, Frau Professor," or patiently waited outside the teachers' room for a chance to chat between classes (showing off their outstanding English, I might add) and ask me questions about the latest American film or boy band. At the time, *Titanic* and the Backstreet Boys were all the rage. While British English is emphasized in Austrian schools, students' interests rest squarely with American pop culture and fashion. Jansport backpacks, Converse high-tops, and Levi's jeans are very much at home alongside the Tyrolean *Dirndl* or *Kneebundhose* (knee britches), further examples of the *mélange* of styles in Vienna.

Benevolent chaos came in many guises and often offered a glimpse into that strange duality that defines Austrian culture. Students came up with any number of innocent pranks to effectively disrupt the flow of lessons, and I found them more humorous than anything. Two of the most popular pranks included fountain pen "accidents," which would cause a fresh ink puddle and require immediate cleanup, and the mysterious "disappearance" of chalk and erasers. Often, I would enter a classroom to find the blackboard covered with the previous teacher's lesson. While this barely merits discussion for most teachers, who would simply erase the board, I immediately discovered that to do so would violate an implicit code of teacher and student roles. I was bumping up against a solid embodiment of tradition, a leftover from public education in the Kaiser's time, as each class elects members to perform certain respectful, almost subservient, duties for the teacher, including the erasing of the board. Because teachers don't erase boards, and the chalk used in Austrian classrooms is quite thick, requiring a thorough washing down with a wet sponge to remove it, a typical start of class involved determining who was the board-washer and inducing him or her to perform his or her elected duty. By the time the sponge was "found" in a neighboring classroom, and the board was washed and allowed sufficient time to dry, ten minutes could easily elapse.

Another prank and window to the past involved the retrieval of the *Klassenbuch*, or class roster. Not the slim computer-generated sheet a North American teacher might expect, this roster was an amusingly oversized, hardbound book, which duly records attendance and general classroom goings-on in exquisite Austrian script—another artifact from the Kaiser's time. The elected student would "forget" to retrieve the book, and, when finally prompted by the teacher, would walk downstairs (at a snail's pace, of course!) to find it and bring it back to class. The days of this tradition are bound to be numbered, though, as my school's *Klassenbücher* were openly stored in the hallway next to the teachers' room, and one book had disappeared altogether. I soon realized that the best way to approach these class-stalling attempts was to establish clear expectations from students for my "visits," and students were typically happy to oblige their guest teacher's requests.

Within my first week, I was instructed of the importance to taking a glance at the *Lehrer-Lehrer-Laufer*, or the handwritten teacher-to-teacher log, to check for sudden schedule changes and updates. Any school day or meticulously planned lesson could be set into utter upheaval by one classes' two-hour test, *Schulausflug* (field trip), or ski trip, for the ripple effects would be felt by other classes whose teachers would not appear as scheduled or whose classmates would be missing and otherwise occupied. To prepare for the inevitability of such occurrences, each teacher maintains a daily, state-mandated "substitution hour," as Austria does not have a standing army of substitute teachers waiting at home for the early-morning call to duty. A positive result of this is that students eventually get to know all of the teaching staff through such substitutions, and tricky issues of unfamiliar faces in front of the class, official working hours, and overtime pay are circumvented. Nevertheless, the potential for disorder always loomed large. Resorting to cultural stereotype, one of my fellow Viennese teaching assistants humorously described Austria as follows: "Imagine that German institutions were run by the Italians." At my school, the only thing I could realistically do was to maintain a flexible attitude, and accept that advance planning, while a necessary part of teaching, was not as important as a willingness to make exceptions for sudden changes in the teaching day.

Some school situations, however, seem common to the teaching profession worldwide. As in other teaching situations I have experienced, teachers in my school in Vienna also struggled with a shortage of space. In Austria, it is more common for teachers, rather than students, to move from classroom to classroom, because students are grouped into permanent "homeroom" cohorts and separate only occasionally for language or special-interest classes. Thus, teachers do not have a homeroom, and all of the school's sixty part- and full-time teachers vied for limited desk space in the cramped teachers' room. As a teaching assistant, I shared whatever limited space was available on a given day.

Another universal in the life of a teacher is a mediocre salary and an unsympathetic public. Austrian schools have recently experienced a wave of governmental budget cuts for education, and, as a result, class sizes have increased, and teachers are now expected to put in more hours for the same pay. I was surprised to learn that Austrian teachers are not paid as highly as teachers in Germany, although both countries require public school-teachers to have the equivalent of Master's degrees in two subject areas. After substantial taxes are deducted from teachers' paychecks, Austrian teachers with average seniority take home the equivalent of about U.S. $1,600 a month. Historically, the status of teachers in Austria was high, and the profession of teaching was one that afforded great respect. However, the current public perception of teachers, fueled by the boulevard press, is that they complain about their pay, often threaten to strike, receive more vacation time than the average citizen, and are generally lazy. Such reports ignore the reality of teachers' low paychecks, the additional hours they put in at home to correct students' homework and prepare classes, added responsibilities, and the general stress level associated with teaching.

In addition to the insights I share above, a few additional points stand out from my teaching experience in Vienna. These had little to do with the classroom, but everything to do with my well-being in a country far from home. Thanks to the trial-and-error of my previous overseas experiences, I knew of the importance of forging immediate contacts with people and institutions beyond the confines of work. Shortly after my arrival, I was lured by a friendly advertisement that boasted "no experience necessary" to join the university choir. I also enrolled in a dance class, and later a beginning Italian class at a district *Volkshochschule* (the equivalent of an adult night school offering noncredit courses).

These activities provided me with immediate outlets for meeting Austrians and making new friends. I also made a conscious decision not to "go native," which, admittedly, can be quite rewarding for those who wish to fully immerse themselves in a new language and culture. My decision was based upon linguistic and social factors: I already spoke fluent German, my *raison d'etre* in Austria was to teach and speak English, and I maintained supportive friendships with fellow English teaching assistants at other Viennese schools. These activities provided me with a solid social network that reached beyond the confines of the classroom and ensured that, although I lived alone, I was not socially isolated from Austrians or fellow English speakers. Thanks to these contacts, I was rarely at a loss for company; I frequently went to musical and theater performances (standing room tickets were cheaper than a *Mélange*!), or spent a lively evening with friends at one of the many Viennese cafés. A last point in relation to my teaching bears mention: In the years since my teaching experience in Vienna, I have, thanks to e-mail, maintained this contact with friends, students, and former colleagues from my school. English teaching assistants come and go in Vienna, but sadly, few bother to keep ties to their schools. I recently returned to Vienna for a brief visit and spent a few days with former students and colleagues at my school. As a professional courtesy, I've given teachers at my school a standing offer to provide them with authentic English materials for use in their classrooms, and they greatly appreciated the thirty pounds of American books, magazines, and games that I left with them.

On one of the last evenings of my year in Vienna, a fellow teaching assistant and I made our way to "my" café to partake one last time in our favorite Viennese ritual. We arrived to find the café particularly full, and patrons were crowding the doorway, anxiously waiting for a table to come available. As soon as we entered, my waiter recognized me. In one swift motion, he removed the permanent *Reserviert* sign from the prime table, and, with an expressionless nod, indicated that we were to be seated. My friend and I looked at each other, smiled, and realized that the meaning of this gesture couldn't have been more significant. We were experiencing a privilege reserved for the select few, a reminder of the long tradition of the public and private, the new and old elements that blend together in the Viennese coffeehouse. We had crossed that invisible barrier between cultural "outsiders" and "insiders," and had just been afforded the status of "regulars." And we knew that a *Mélange* was on its way.

11

A Canuck Down Under:
Reflections of a Canadian Teacher
on Exchange in Western Australia

Ross Laing

Excitement was mixed with brief pangs of trepidation as I surveyed the city from the air. The Quantas jet banked steeply before its final approach. Perth, Western Australia, sprawled down below. The city of Perth runs north-south for miles and miles, parallel to a glinting Indian Ocean on the west and corralled by the Darling Range escarpment to the east. Home to more than one million inhabitants, the city is built on a giant sand dune and is the most remote large city in the world. This would be home for the ensuing year. I would learn much about myself as a teacher.

Just days before, my wife and I had waved good-bye to the teacher, and his wife, who had been paired with me for an international teaching exchange between Canada and Australia. It's a slightly unnerving, very surreal experience to have relative strangers bidding you farewell from your own doorstep. Our consolation was that we were also waving good-bye to minus twenty degree centigrade temperatures and mountains of snow.

We were greeted at the Perth airport by Ivan Jacobsen, who we came to know and love as "Jacko." We didn't have trouble finding him at the airport. We'd seen his picture, and he was unmistakable. Big head, cropped beard, robust in girth, loud in voice, and legs like the native karri trees—he was an imposing figure! You wouldn't want to mess with him. Ivan was approaching the second half of his 50s, and the deputy principal at a high school in Perth. His heart was huge. He became a close friend, and, along with his girlfriend Fiona, they became like surrogate parents to my wife and me.

With tsunami-like force, a wave of heat blasted us upon leaving the comfort of the airport's air conditioning. It was the afternoon of a typical midsummer's day in Perth, over forty degrees centigrade. Ivan ushered us to his car and suggested that before doing anything else, we should visit my new school, Morley Senior High School, as it was the last Friday before the school year was to begin, and it might be a good opportunity to meet the principal and get a copy of my teaching schedule. Afterwards, he suggested we should go for cappuccinos—did I mention that it was forty-two degrees centigrade? My wife, huddled in the backseat and surrounded by suitcases, later noted that West Australians rarely put the auto air-conditioning fan above level "1," no matter how hot it is, and Ivan was no exception.

Intending to prod a particularly slow driver ahead of us as we left the parking lot of the airport, Ivan bellowed what has since become a favourite Aussie expression: "C'mon mate, RATTLE YOUR DAGS!" In a voice several decibels lower, with a glint in his eye, Ivan followed his expletive with "D' ya know what 'dags' are?" He seemed impressed when I told him they are the dried dirty bits, which dangle from the tails of sheep. Like many Aussie expressions, there is a hint of the profane accompanied by vivid imagery.

Getting out of Ivan's car, I surveyed my new school. The hot dry air released an aromatic scent from the numerous eucalyptus trees. We were given a gracious welcome by the principal Gavin Smyth, who towers at about six feet four inches and has an authority in his voice that commands attention. He invited us to wander around the school. To tour the facility was to work up a sweat. One of the first things I saw was a large circular sign with a series of "M's" in red, white, and blue, proclaiming the school motto: "Together We Achieve."

Morley Senior High School is an extensive series of buildings, typical in design to many public high schools in Perth built in the 1970s. The school is situated on a piece of high ground surrounded by expansive lawns, tended gardens, and sports fields. A series of covered walkways connects separate buildings that house individual subject areas. For example, there is a separate science building, social studies buildings, the administration offices, the library, etc.—all brick with metal roofs. The tin roofs acted as conductors of heat in the summer and during the rainstorms of the spring-time in September and October, teaching would often have to be suspended because of the incessant din from rain pellets hammering on the roofs. Only the administration area and the library are air conditioned. Most class-rooms have large sliding windows in order to catch the "Fremantle Doc-tor," which is the nickname for the sea breezes which roll in about mid-afternoon to cool the city down. Architecturally, the buildings are pleasing to the eye. Many of the buildings are two stories high and exca-vated in such a way as to create numerous levels. A student in a wheelchair would have a tough time with the various banks of stairs. Most classrooms have carpeted floors, some have skylights, and most connect to teacher preparation areas through interior corridors. Each classroom is equipped with a heater as well as an oscillating pedestal fan. There are also "geographical" distinctions between upper school and lower school areas. Upper school students are those in Year 11 and 12; lower school is comprised of students in Year 8 to 10. As most physical education activities take place outside year round, the gym is small—minute by North American standards. A fifty-five-gallon drum with a plunger pump stands by the door to dispense sunscreen. A large open area, which resembles a cloistered courtyard at the centre of the campus, serves many purposes, from the school cafeteria to an outdoor stage for dramatic performances. I was struck by the openness and sense of freedom in the entire physical layout. I realized how weather has a dramatic impact upon the nature of education. In contrast to the openness of Morley and the West Australian schools I would visit, weather dictates that Canadian schools are closed and confining, crammed inside with students and walls lined with rows of lockers.

Morley prides itself with several specialized programs including its computer facilities, its aeronautics course, visual arts technology, and a media production course. There is also a Training For Employment (TFE) section of the school, which accommodates nonacademic students who will be leaving school early to enter work placements and low-skill employment. The school also owns a large recreational camp facility about two hours' drive south of Perth where large groups of students attend a week at a time during the school terms. Morley is also twined with a Japanese school and reciprocal student exchanges took place. The school has an enrollment of over 1,400, which exceeds the capacity of the buildings, so several "prefabs" or portable classrooms, dot the property. The school population comes from mostly middle-class homes, with a large number coming from Mediterranean and Asian backgrounds. About two-thirds of the high school age student population in Perth attend public schools like Morley; the other one-third attend either "high fee" or "low fee" private schools, most with religious affiliations. Unlike Canadian schools, nearly all schools in Perth have some sort of identifiable uniform.

The night before my first day at Morley, I realized I didn't know the dress protocol for teachers. To beat the heat, I opted for "comfortable" clothes. To my students, I must have appeared as the stereotype of the American tourist in Hawaii. Bright, loud-coloured shirt, beige shorts, deck shoes, and eyes wide open, taking everything in. The only thing missing was a camera draped around my neck! That first day at Morley, I was fascinated by the number of male teachers who wore khaki shorts with knee-length socks and pressed white shirts and ties. One of the deputy principals barked commands at both teachers and students, and the perverse thought occurred to me that he was like a drill sergeant on safari. I truly was in a different world. It was exhilarating.

It was also a very memorable day. My first day as a "chalkie" in Australia was only my fifth day in Perth. Arriving at the school early, I watched the staff arrive and was struck by their laid back attitude and apparent lack of anxiety. In Canada, in most schools, the first day is frenetic, with teachers lining up to use the photocopier or wrestling to obtain the least dilapidated copies of texts from the book room. I was relieved to see the pace at Morley was pretty civilized. This relaxed attitude was evident to me amongst both staff and students, and is typified in common Aussie sayings such as "No worries" or "She'll be right, mate." It's far more sensible, but I must admit my heart was racing at an unhealthy rate that morning.

In passing one teacher in an outdoor courtyard before the first bell, she said, "How ya' goin?" I innocently replied, "I'm heading for the library," when I should have said, "I'm Okay. How are you?"—just one faux pas of the many I would make that day. I recall having to ask a student to repeat his name several times as I hadn't tuned my ears to the Aussie lingo.

In spite of computer technology, where class lists could have been printed and posted on accessible places such as doors or walls, large groups of students were ordered via the PA system to assemble at various locations throughout the campus. For example, all the Year 8 students were gathered in front of the lower school English building. Then, a Head of Department (a "HOD") stood in the middle of the group of students to shout out the names of each student and inform him or her who the student's tutorial (homeroom) teacher was going to be. This process took a good part of the morning; it didn't seem to be either too efficient or effective. I had to wonder if the exercise was a discrete way for the teaching staff, who dutifully stood quietly at the perimeter of the group of students, to "suss out" the troublemakers as well as gauge the listening skills of their new students.

My tutorial class consisted of students enrolled in a Year 12 Senior English class. They arrived that first morning in the school uniform which was as liberal as school uniforms get, in that students had to wear dark trousers or a skirt and wear a polo-style shirt of either red, white, or blue. Jeans fit the criterion of dark trousers. My students had not had stunning academic success through school, nor were they particularly motivated, but they were very personable and did give me a pleasant welcome in spite of my "Yank" voice and "foreigner" ways. During that first class, I recall opening the top drawer of my desk, only to be confronted by a stray cockroach as big as my thumb. I visibly flinched in a simultaneous reaction of horror and awe; graciously, my students soon forgave my innate deference to bugs. Soon I would be able to handle strange bugs, lizards, and snakes with relative ease.

Later that morning I was introduced to a remarkable institution that was common to every West Australian workplace: morning tea. For twenty minutes each morning the entire school stopped for a break. The teachers retreated to the staff room to serve themselves tea or coffee (I had become so used to instant coffee by the end of my teaching year that I almost thought it was real coffee!) along with scones and biscuits, which had been prepared by another workplace institution, the tea lady. She was hired by the staff to prepare the morning refreshments. Meanwhile, the students lined up at the outdoor cafeteria for hot meat pies to sustain them for the rest of the morning.

After morning tea I met my other morning class, which consisted of a Year 12 English Tertiary Entrance Exam (TEE) class, comprised of students who aspired to sit the rigorous statewide examinations which would determine if they would gain entrance to "Uni." Only two of every five students who apply are accepted at university. These students were more anxious about being assigned a Canadian teacher; understandably, since I was likely to have a significant impact upon their future prospects for university acceptance.

That afternoon I met the most exciting class of my teaching career. I was assigned a group of about thirty Year 10 English students who were bright, enthusiastic and fun from the first second in class. Even though the lower school students (Years 8–10) were ostensibly destreamed, there was actually a perceptible streaming process, and I had been given the academic high-flyers. Throughout the entire year this class lived up to its initial promise, keeping me both on my toes and in fits of laughter. Their range of interests, level of intelligence, and sincere joy in learning was inspirational.

My last class that first day consisted of Year 11 English students and they were a night and day contrast to my previous class. The novelty of the first day of classes had already worn off on this crew. Given a small classroom in the direct glare of the sun during the hottest part of the day, we stared at each others' red and perspiring faces. The novelty of a Canadian teacher did not seem to excite them in that oppressive heat. The students couldn't learn anything in the heat, but it certainly kept the class quiet! My wife had tuned into the weather reports; it was forty-three degrees that day in Perth. I arrived home to a bath of cold water, with ice cubes for extra measure! I am forever in debt to her thoughtfulness.

I felt a disconcerting wave of overwhelming panic only once during my entire teaching exchange and it came toward the end of that first day. The principal had instructed each teacher to provide an outline of the term and major assignments to each student on the second day of classes. In general, the course content of the curriculum was very prescriptive by Canadian standards, but little direction was available for evaluation and assessment. This was especially true for the lower school grades, of which my wonderful Year 10 class was one. I was bombarded with the immensity of the challenges in front of me. Self-doubts abounded: Could I really do this? Would I last the year? Had I made a terrible mistake? Why hadn't I taken more teaching resources with me? After a few minutes of angst, I managed to cast aside my "deer caught in the headlight" fears. I stayed up very late that night scouring through curriculum guidelines and resources and eventually arrived at what I thought was a reasonable outline for each of the classes I taught. My anxiety passed. I had made it through day one.

I truly felt "down under" at times—or perhaps "upside down" is a better way of describing my mix of emotions and reactions. In a totally new environment, I couldn't help but make comparisons to life and to teaching in Canada. There were the anticipated changes like a different house and driving on the other side of the road, the hot weather. But there wasn't any warning of the wild possum that lived in the roof and scratched incessantly on the ceiling above the bed each night. Or the way I had to suddenly jump the curb of a road median with my car because a huntsman spider as big as the palm of my hand crawled out of the defrost vent. I had not been forewarned of the archaic banking system or the high crime rate. In those first few weeks, I was deeply worried about my wife's homesickness. And in the early days, I continually swore at the horrible heat rash breaking out all over my arms and legs, which forced me into long sleeves and long trousers.

While there were times when packing up and heading home to Canada skirted the edge of my consciousness, there were many times when the only thing to do was laugh. Once again, strange creepy crawlies made idiots of us; the smaller the bug the more lethal it seemed. For example, the mail was delivered by a young fellow on motorbike who drove up on the front lawn (when visiting friends in Western Australia you just park on their lawn rather than the street!) and deposited the mail in a slot on the street side of the mailbox. For some inexplicable reason, a slot on the other side of the mailbox is used for retrieving the mail. During the first few months my wife would don yellow rubber gloves to fetch the mail and I wouldn't dare open the latch of the garden gate without my pair of yellow gloves, all out of fear of the dreaded red back spider and its venomous bite. We certainly must have given the neighbours something to talk about.

On the other hand, there was pure exhilaration in the experience of just being somewhere very different. We lived beside a swamp and on my first walk on the afternoon of our arrival I discovered black swans with striking red bills and legs. I ran home to tell my wife about my "rare" discovery, only to subsequently learn that the birds were everywhere in Western Australia. I relished the daily pleasure of driving down North Beach Road, climbing up the ridge near the end of the road, reaching the top of the hill, being briefly blinded by sunlight, and then seeing the Indian Ocean sprawl vastly before me in all its winking iridescence. And while I wasn't as naive as to think a class system did not exist, I loved how people in Western Australia were not as quick to "label" a person by job or income. I enjoyed the opportunity for my wife and I to connect as just us, without the obligatory commitments to family and friends, as much as we missed their company so many thousands of miles away. And I was pleasantly surprised by the liberal drinking laws that allowed BYOB at restaurants to make dining out affordable. As in any significant change in one's life, there are pluses and minuses. Though I rarely verbalized my criticisms, in adjusting to down under, I tended to see differences first and was often critical of the Australian way of doing things in comparison to the way things were done back in Canada.

In coping with the essential routines of daily life and my eventual acceptance of the ways of my host country, gradually, with time, I came to understand and usually accept the ways of the educational system too. Many aspects were radically different, some not so. Some aspects were better, some were worse, but overall, the educational system was just different.

The structure of the school and its curriculum was worlds apart what I was used to in Canada. In Western Australian schools, it was night and day between the lower school (Years 8–10) and upper school (Years 11–12). The lower school grades were supposedly destreamed, but I was aware of at least four levels of difficulty. One unit of study was assigned for each of the four terms in the school year; therefore, a lower school student between Year 8 and Year 10 completed sixteen units before progressing to the upper school and the Year 11 course. It was a "connect the dots" kind of curriculum, and each class completed a different picture in its meandering course through lower school.

The units for my subject area of English were clearly distinct and covered a wide array of specialized language and literary topics, from fictional analysis to magazine layout, children's literature, and project-based summative activities. There were lots of different texts tuned to students' interests and abilities. Texts ranged from classics of American and British literature, with about one-half of the resources being Australian in origin. Each class, based on its perceived academic ability, was assigned a specific sequence of units. Some of the units provided remedial work. Students traveled as a group and there were almost no failures since the pass mark was 30 percent. Each class arrived at a different spot by the end of Year 10. This approach was vastly different from the curriculum I was used to in Canada where there was an attempt to get students to the same point at the end of a certain grade.

The focus of the curriculum in the upper school Years 11 and 12 was on preparations for the dreaded Tertiary Entrance Examinations (TEE). There was a huge jump in the level of expectations in Year 11, and many students appeared to flounder at this stage. While the lower school program allowed for a diverse curriculum, many students reached Year 11 with no uniform program of studies and the fact that there were no exams in the lower school tended to produce a lack of accountability. My Year 11 students were in the mid-level of a three-level stream and for the most part were not keen students, and only could be motivated to do the bare minimum. The curriculum used a wide variety of resources that had been selected from a list of resources specified by the Ministry of Education. For example, at Morley all of the Year 11 English teachers taught the American classic *To Kill a Mockingbird* and *My Place*, an autobiographical novel by Sally Morgan, a West Australian aboriginal writer. The Ministry of Education also provided very useful study guides for each of the approved texts. Since the key texts were similar to all the teachers of a specific stream who taught the same texts simultaneously, there was a meaningful sharing of materials amongst the teachers of the course.

Consistency in marking and standards was developed through Across The Board (ATB) marking, whereby one specific essay question was assigned as an in-class test by all teachers of a specific course on the same day, and then the essays were distributed amongst those teachers for marking. Eventually, the essays were returned to the students who were aware that another teacher may have marked his or her paper. If a teacher saw a large discrepancy between the ATB marks and his or her own, then some soul searching might be necessary. This was an excellent and simple method for ensuring more consistency.

Another method of ensuring consistency, though strange and disconcerting, came in the form of a spinsterish-looking lady (think Lilith Crane from the sitcoms *Cheers* and *Frasier*) from the Ministry of Education. The Year 12 TEE course at our school was being audited by this woman, and as I had a Year 12 TEE English class, I was required to submit samples of my students' assignments along with my marks for the selected assignments. Each of the teachers in the English department who taught Year 12 TEE was required to do the same. She arrived, took our folders to the upper school English office, and marked. I felt as though a black cloud of obscurity and judgment enveloped that office, as teachers were not permitted to talk to her apart from saying "hello." No chance of currying her favour with my quaint foreign accent. Then, at the end of the day, my students' folders were returned to me and I was required to raise or lower my marks based upon her assessments. No dialogue. No conferencing. No explanation required. Unfortunately, the informal atmosphere of a bar where "everybody knows your name" never arrived to soften this woman's stern appearance or the ominous insensitivity of her task. It was very clear that I was not in an American sitcom. I was in a different country, and I felt violated; I felt eviscerated; I felt totally undermined by the experience. There was little integrity in this form of bureaucratic bullying.

The TEE examination dictated the upper school curriculum, especially for the Year 12 students. The exam consisted of four parts, one of which involved an essay response that required students to synthesize documentary film with fiction and nonfiction sources. The TEE lasted three hours and imposed a great deal of stress upon both students and teachers. The exam results were combined with a standardized test score and term marks to produce a number that would determine acceptance or rejection at a university. The teachers were under pressure, too, because results were published in the press, and the school results were of great concern to administrators. A school's reputation was at stake.

There were many features of the school system that I found most interesting. The weekly school assembly was an eye-opener. It was part pep rally, and part forum for the administration to lecture all in attendance, including the staff. Just before lunch on most Wednesdays, an announcement would beckon the staff and students to assemble on the sprawling front lawns. A microphone and a podium stood at the far end, along with a row of seats for those who were to speak at the assembly. Often there were guest speakers who spoke about community involvement and issues related to health and lifestyle. The principal ably used assemblies as an opportunity to foster school morale through the presentation of a staggering number of awards and kudos. An example was made of those who succeeded. The assembly was also an opportunity to reinforce school rules and many of the assemblies were pedantic lectures. While I didn't always agree with the principal's style, I respected him for the strength of his convictions and his sincere wish that the philosophy of the school and its motto, "Together We Achieve," be evident in every endeavour related to the school. Students rarely had an opportunity to speak at these assemblies. As part of my teaching duties, I taught an interest course in guitar and requested that my music students perform at an assembly. We had the student body mesmerized with our musical debut; following the performance I received mixed reviews from the principal for our "rock concert"!

Discipline at the school was strict. I saw little evidence of any serious problems with discipline or violence. I didn't hear one student swear at a teacher (though teachers yelling at students was common). Homework was usually done. Students rarely had part-time jobs after school. No smoking was permitted. Students did not drive their own cars to school. Parents were generally supportive of the school (and there usually was a parent at home when a phone call had to be made). Attendance was excellent. All in contrast to my teaching experience in Canada in recent years.

At Morley there were the usual high school sanctions, such as after-school detentions for students who did not comply with the dress code. An interesting disciplinary technique was SCAB (I'm not certain if it's an actual acronym) duty for students who had committed minor infractions of school rules. Each teacher was issued a booklet of tickets at the beginning of the term that could be used to assign students to complete various tasks around the school property. The teacher, like a traffic officer, issued a SCAB ticket for, say, twenty minutes of clean-up duty at lunch to the offending student. Copies of the ticket went to the student, a deputy principal responsible for that grade level, and one copy was retained by the teacher. The student went to a supervising teacher during the lunch period on the date assigned, and had his ticket initialed at the start of the clean-up duty and again after the twenty minutes were completed. It was an effective system.

There was the school year itself. The school year consisted of four terms of about ten weeks of classes each followed by a two-week break. A longer break of six weeks took place during the third week in December and ran until the beginning of February. I was overwhelmed by how much healthier both students and staff were because of the shorter terms, in comparison to the usual North American model of grueling marathon terms of up to seventeen weeks back-to-back before a long summer hiatus. Again, weather may dictate more about education than we think.

For those expecting more alternative pedagogical styles by going to the land down under, such as those practiced by wacky "Crocodile Dundee" type characters, that visceral hands-on style of teaching, there was the staff room. There, and at staff parties, stories about teaching in the outback abound in Western Australia most new teachers have to work in the outback, or at least, in a rural area of the state. While Perth has a population of about one million, the next largest center, Bunbury, consists of approximately 25,000. Most towns are small. Some postings were at an intersection in the middle of nowhere. All teachers are assigned their positions centrally by the Ministry of Education. Listening to stories of teaching experiences in the remote outback schools was fascinating. During morning recess students would barbeque lizards as a snack. There were anecdotes of teachers, along with nurses, in these small communities spending Friday nights cruising the main roads on the edge of town to save drunken Aborigines, drawn from the cold desert to sleep it off on the warm tarmac, from being run over by multi-trailer "road train" trucks that didn't stop for anything, or anyone. The usual stay for the teachers is about two years before the inevitable gravitational pull of "civilization" lures most back toward the more urban centres. When a teacher seeks a promotion, it usually involves another stint in the outback. Understandably, this process is disruptive to the families of those teachers who choose to advance their career. Interestingly, the teachers who seem overly ambitious are considered "tall poppies" and are considered a bit full of themselves by less ambitious colleagues.

Because Morley Senior High School was a large school, there was a teaching staff of almost ninety. In common with any large institution, there were varying levels of commitment to the profession, but I was often struck at how teaching for some was "just a job" and not a vocation. For many, teaching was not considered a lifelong career. Many teachers were undoubtedly demoralized by a "top-down" chain of command that begins at the Ministry of Education and extends to the school's administrative structure. I sensed that many staff members felt they didn't have much of a voice. Most of the staff left the building within thirty minutes of the dismissal of the day's last class. There was little incentive to upgrade qualifications. Teachers were paid extra to attend professional development activities after school hours. Union membership was voluntary. In comparison to most Canadian teachers, benefits were not as generous and salaries were significantly lower, but teachers appeared to have a comparable standard of living to their Canadian counterparts. A full-time teacher in Western Australia had a manageable number of five classes (not seven, as is common in many parts of Canada), the capping of senior level class sizes was respected, and teachers seemed less stressed because they did not have to deal with as many issues related to school violence and social problems. In spite of some contradictions inherent within my general observations, most of the Australian teachers I met were committed, caring individuals who were concerned about the education and well-being of their students.

There are many other facets to my story; there is so much I have omitted. For me, the teaching exchange was an affirming experience in every respect. I went with three books: a general composition text, a general handbook on teaching language arts, and a text published by my local school board entitled *On Your Marks*. I did not have all of the resources I was accustomed to—no computer flat screen projectors, writing labs, e-mail networks, etc. I succeeded with my own teaching skills and instincts. I tried to be an ambassador. I gave numerous presentations and workshops to several schools and colleges on topics ranging from "Life as a Teacher in Canada" to "Small Group Learning" to "Creating and Effective Computer Writing Lab"—all of which were well received. Unencumbered by the responsibilities of being a department head, I found time to focus exclusively on lesson planning. I even found time to sit on the back patio and read books by Australian writers in the evening while the bamboo plant and lemon tree in our yard swayed in the breezes behind me, the bird of paradise plants looked on, and the galahs, cockatoos, and kookaburras noisily returned from their daily excursions to their nests in the nearby swamp. The resident blue-tongued skink or "bobbie"—a foot-long lizard that kept the property free of snake eggs—was out there somewhere in the yard keeping me company too! Not a bad life.

Throughout the teaching exchange, I made some wonderful lifelong friends. The role of the Exchange Teachers' Club warrants mention as it allowed a group of about sixty teachers from all over the world to share their experiences and it provided numerous opportunities to travel and explore together. Some did not have as pleasurable a teaching experience as I did. While I did have the opportunity to meet many Australians from different backgrounds, most of my contacts were with fellow teachers. My wife and I spent many joyous hours hosting and being hosted by warm, outgoing, vivacious, and vigourous people—many of them genuine characters. We were a bit of a novelty too; all welcomed us and treated us as honoured guests, inviting us to experience new adventures unique to a Canadian. Also, we were constantly amazed by the amount of time and the effort so many people went to on our behalf. In particular, the Bowering family adopted us as their own and gave us every opportunity to live like locals. Fortunately, we have been able to return the hospitality as several friends from the exchange have visited us in Canada since then.

Each and every day I felt truly alive. Earlier I wrote of my process of adapting, of starting out by making constant comparisons to things "back home" and gradually coming to some understanding and acceptance of my new world. I succeeded and overcame the self-doubts that plagued me that first day of classes. I proved myself as a competent teacher outside of my usual environment. I learned something new every day from my colleagues and students, and I felt I had something of value to offer them in return. The experience made me stronger.

Just before Christmas, on the last day of school, during the speeches at the year-end staff luncheon, the principal claimed that he had never encountered an exchange teacher adapt so readily—I was a "'ridgy didge' Aussie chalkie" in his estimation. I truly felt at home as a teacher at Morley, and in Western Australia. Being from the northern hemisphere, I was coerced into playing Santa Claus at the luncheon, and after performing my duties distributing the gifts, and hoarse from "Ho! Ho! Ho!-ing," I escaped from my warm white beard and red suit to catch a breath of fresh air in the parking lot. It was as hot out there as the day I had arrived in Perth just short of a year ago. The sun was high. In a couple of days I would be following that same sun home to Canada. I felt both an emptiness and a wholeness. I knew that I would miss the city of Perth, my students, my new friends and teaching colleagues immensely; I am restless to return.

PART VI

Versatility

12

Having It All: How to Teach Overseas and Keep Your Public School Job in the United States

Deborah M. Boucher

Teaching overseas, a dream for many U.S. teachers, all too often remains just that—a dream deemed too daunting to achieve and too impractical to execute. As teaching couples and singles explore the possibility of living and working overseas, the logistical problems may seem insurmountable. What about my extended family and my aging parents? What about the house that I own? What about my ongoing financial responsibilities in the states? What about my tenured public school job? Is it really worth the time, energy, and trouble to go abroad for a few years if I don't plan to stay overseas for the rest of my career? The answer is definitely yes. My husband and I have built satisfying careers as teachers who are based out of the California public schools but take jobs overseas periodically by securing leaves of absence from our stateside employers. In this manner, we have managed to keep our tenure while relishing the adventures and professional opportunities offered to us by teaching abroad, often enjoying classroom experiences we could never have in our home school district.

The surprise is that there are so few teachers in international school settings who choose to go back and forth between public school and overseas teaching positions. The vast majority of teachers we have encountered during our time spent working at three international schools seem to have made the decision to remain overseas permanently. Even if they have only been living and working for a brief time abroad, they often express the sentiment that they are happy to be out of the U.S. public schools, and would not consider going back for a variety of reasons; yet, in contrast, each time we have been ready to take a leave of absence from our public school jobs in California, our colleagues there have expressed surprise that we would want to live and work abroad. While they might admire our sense of adventure, their comments and questions communicated clearly that this lifestyle is not for them. They see too many obstacles to leaving: "what about my house, my dog, my teenaged children?" they wonder. "It's fine for you," they say, "but we would find the move much too difficult to arrange."

The truth about living and working abroad and stateside lies somewhere between these extreme points of view. It is definitely worthwhile and not as difficult as one might imagine. At our encouragement, a few of our California colleagues have taken the plunge and become overseas teachers. None of them have stayed out of the country permanently, and all of them have been challenged and enriched by their overseas experiences. My husband and I are currently enjoying our third tour of duty overseas. We plan on returning to our jobs in Mammoth Lakes, California, after two or three years, and are already thinking about teaching somewhere else abroad before we retire. It is just too much fun.

Make no mistake. It takes organization and planning to have the best of both worlds by going back and forth between an overseas job and a stateside position. That is why I would recommend that if you decide to try it for the first time, you commit to two years. Many overseas schools will not hire you unless you are willing to sign a two-year contract, and frankly, it may not be worth the time and energy on everyone's part to be away for just one year. For the faint of heart who feel that a two-year commitment seems like an eternity, don't despair. There are schools that will hire you for a one-year contract, renewable by mutual agreement. That is exactly what we did our first time out. Why? We wanted leaves of absence from our San Francisco area districts and could only get one year. Nevertheless, we found an overseas school—Colegio Nueva Granada in Bogotá, Colombia—willing to hire us. It was a "hardship" post, a place many would never consider going, yet we had a fabulous time living and working there. Some of the classroom benefits afforded us by both being sixth grade teachers for a year at this school included: team-teaching a core curriculum that blended American history and language arts; Spanish lessons provided by the school to the U.S. teachers free of charge; cultural and travel opportunities organized by the school for any of the teachers and their family members who wished to participate; a chance to be a part of a truly bilingual bicultural program; and of course, a love for Colombia: a country of unsurpassed beauty in spite of its negative image in the world due to its drug-related problems.

After living and teaching in Colombia for one year, our feet were wet and we were changed forever. Never again would we be satisfied with just teaching in our public school positions in California. The world was at our doorstep through teaching overseas, and we were ready to return in the not too distant future. The year in Bogotá had provided us with a rich experience. Professionally, I discovered that the integration of language arts and social studies at the middle school level made perfect sense. My Spanish improved tremendously, affording me meaningful contact with Colombians. We made friends, both within the school setting and in our neighborhood, which allowed us to experience the culture. We traveled throughout Colombia and marveled at the incredible geography and rich history. At the end of our year teaching in Bogotá, we took a six-week trip through most of the other countries in South America: an experience of a lifetime. We bid adios to that continent thinking that we would definitely teach abroad in the future, but probably do it in a different region of the world.

Eight long years passed before we were able to leave California again. Why? Life. During that time, I had a second child. My oldest daughter accompanied us during our year in Bogotá, but having two children changed my focus. I actually cut back to part-time teaching in order to give my girls the attention they both deserved. My husband decided to pursue a master's degree in administration, which took several years to complete during the evenings and summers. He then pursued a career as an administrator that necessitated a move on our part. When we went to Colombia, we had been teaching in different school districts in the San Francisco Bay Area. My husband's first administrative position took our family to Mammoth Lakes, California, a ski resort located on the eastern side of the Sierra Nevada Mountains. Once again, we were new teachers: without tenure, without security, but challenged and invigorated by our move from large suburban districts to a small, rural district in an isolated setting. This move required that we become generalists more than specialists due to the wide variety of needs and the few hardy professionals who literally had to "do it all." My husband wore many hats during our first five years in Mammoth Lakes. He worked at a 7–12 high school as the teaching vice principal. He taught science and social studies, directed student activities, directed athletic events, and helped the principal with discipline and attendance. My position was at the K–6 elementary school as a reading and math specialist, plus an English as a Second Language (ESL) instructor. My Spanish is what landed me my job in a district in which it was notoriously difficult to get hired. After five years of working in the Mammoth Unified School District, we were tenured and ready once again to explore employment possibilities overseas.

One of the biggest changes we encountered in the seven years since we had first gone out was the advent of the mega-recruitment fair. In the early 80s, International School Services (ISS) was the only overseas placement agency, and recruiters went to several university campuses or large cities around the country conducting low-key interviews. By 1990, all that had changed: the recruitment fair was an essential stepping-stone to securing an overseas teaching position. Hundreds of teachers were flocking to these fairs that took place in several locations scattered across the country in search of the ideal position teaching abroad.

Our job search the second time began with the purchase of the ISS Overseas School Directory. We then wrote letters to schools on every continent that sounded interesting, hoping that this would secure interviews at the regional recruitment fair. We signed up to attend the fair being held closest to our home in California. Imagine our surprise when the phone rang one evening and the superintendent of Escuelas Lincoln, in Buenos Aires, Argentina, called offering my husband and me positions, sight unseen! I would be the head of the ESL department at the bilingual school—a dream-come-true position for me. The catch? We had to commit to two years or the school would attend the recruiting fairs and hire someone else. We went to our local school board and gulped as we asked for a two-year leave of absence, something that had never been granted to anyone in our district before. We laid out the advantages to our public school district upon our return: fluency in Spanish; a chance to work in a truly bilingual setting; plus intercultural and professional stimulation. The school board said yes, and we were on our way.

This second time out was more complicated and required more planning on our part. We were going for two years instead of one. We were a family of four instead of three. One of our daughters was approaching high school age and was more reluctant to go. We had pets. We owned a house, but none of these things proved insurmountable. We were able to arrange everything to our family's satisfaction. Luckily, we were not in debt (other than our house payments) and we had learned a few things from our first time abroad that helped us with our second stint as overseas teachers. First, we learned that you need to have a property manager to oversee the rental of your home if you plan to keep it. We did not do this the first time out, and our in-laws were burdened by tenants who had to be evicted. Our second time as absentee landlords went much more smoothly because of the indispensable property manager. The additional expense was worth it to have a professional to take care of minor repairs to the house, collect the rent, deposit it, and then run an ad in the newspaper when our first set of tenants opted not to renew their one-year lease. The property manager wrote out a new lease, did the background check, and visited our home periodically to make sure everything was all right. This is essential if you plan to keep your house stateside.

We also knew to set aside some money from what we had saved overseas to allow for our stateside readjustment. In most locations around the world, teachers will save money due to living expenses subsidized by their employers. What they do with that money is up to them. We knew that we would have expenses when we returned to California, so we planned accordingly. We used some of the money we saved in Argentina (which was considerable) to travel and explore South America, but we also earmarked money for refurbishing our house after two years of tenants, and for making a down payment on a new car upon our return.

We asked a relative to help us with our financial responsibilities while we were out of the country working. This included paying property taxes, receiving and storing documents for tax purposes, writing checks and depositing money into our stateside account since many schools pay you partially or entirely in dollars. It is easy to set up automatic payments for many ongoing expenses, but you will still need a trusted person to be in charge of your finances at home.

We also knew that we would return to the states at the end of the first year in Argentina to visit family and friends. It's amazing how much this will do to help your loved ones support your decision to live and work overseas if they know they will see you and your children for an extended visit each North American summer. Some schools pay for this after the first year. Most pay for yearly visits, but only after the first two years. We budgeted money to return between our first and second year. We also used this journey back and forth from Argentina to California to travel to other parts of South America along the way; this plan was a real money saver for a family of four and an enriching experience as well.

Professionally, teaching at Escuelas Lincoln, in Buenos Aires, Argentina, was a rewarding experience. We had visited Buenos Aires during our six-week trip after our year of teaching in Colombia. I had fallen in love with this European-style city and was delighted to have the opportunity to live and work there. As head of the grades 2–8 ESL department at Escuelas Lincoln, I worked daily with an Argentine staff that included many wonderful teachers. Coming from a school in California with a growing bilingual population, I brought my experience of teaching English Language Development (meaning teaching English in English) to this new setting. The difference? I now taught students from over twenty different countries. I could no longer rely on them knowing Spanish to communicate if something was not understood. Escuelas Lincoln had a large population of Asian students who were under the gun to learn both English and Spanish simultaneously in order to stay in this bilingual school. They were given two years of ESL classes, and then were expected to transition completely to the regular classroom. It was challenging. It was incredible. During my years at Escuelas Lincoln, all my students (except two) made the transition successfully. I also worked with the outstanding Spanish as a Second Language (SSL) department at that school. We shared methodologies with each other and we learned so much together. Although pull-out models are currently out of vogue, both stateside and in many international schools, we conducted a pull-out program that worked. The results spoke for themselves. The students, their parents, the regular classroom teachers, and the administration were all totally satisfied with the dual ESL/SSL program. It is only now, years later that I realize what a unique situation that was for me. I'm not sure I will ever get to teach in that way again, let alone head up a department. This is why you teach abroad: You can't afford to pass up such enriching professional experiences.

My husband was a middle school math teacher at Escuelas Lincoln, a welcome break from his administrative routine in Mammoth, and one that he thoroughly enjoyed. We used our two years in Buenos Aires to work on our Spanish and to visit new parts of South America that we had not seen before. Some travel highlights for our family included: Iguazu Falls; the Galapagos; Southern Chile with its lake district and fjords as seen from a small cruise ship; Patagonia in Argentina with its gorgeous mountains and desert-like shoreline teeming with whales, penguins, sea lions, guanacos, and many other unusual animals. Once again, we remembered what we loved about this continent. Every country is unique, but the language is the same: Spanish. Even in Brazil, my Spanish came in handy. Living in Buenos Aires was a cosmopolitan affair, offering us the chance to take in concerts, theater, opera, museums—something difficult to do in Mammoth Lakes due to its rural, isolated nature. Because I worked with a mostly Argentine staff, I made some wonderful friendships. These Argentine teachers included me and my family in their lives and gave us a more intimate glimpse of the culture. The other huge plus of living and working in Argentina was the safety. My teenaged daughter was able to use the cheap public transportation in Buenos Aires to visit friends or go out to the movies and dinner, without us being overly preoccupied. I'm not sure we would have allowed her the same freedoms in a U.S. city of ten million.

After two delightful years of teaching in Argentina, we returned home once again in order to keep our public school positions in Mammoth Lakes, California. We had been tempted not to go back. Our public school retirement system figured hugely in our decision to return. While many overseas schools now offer some type of retirement reimbursement or system membership, California has a good package and we were not prepared to give that up. We knew that we could continue to work in the Mammoth Unified School District, then ask for periodic leaves of absence. We would still remain members of our state system, and upon our return to the California public schools, we would accrue years of service credit along with higher salaries that would all figure into the benefits we would eventually receive upon our retirement. We were blessed with colleagues and a superintendent who saw the advantages of having teachers like us who would bring a world perspective to our classrooms. The interchange of ideas, the ones we took with us from California to our overseas schools in both Colombia and Argentina, plus the new ideas we carried back to our public school, made it worthwhile for everyone involved. A teacher who has been out of the United States and teaching overseas for many years may not be in touch with current trends in the U.S. public schools—unless they have gone out of their way to attend stateside workshops—a difficult, often impossible thing for them to do. Likewise, a teacher who has remained in the same public school system for many years may be totally unaware of another way of doing things. A truly multicultural perspective was perhaps the richest reward we brought back when we returned stateside after two leaves of absence to teach abroad.

We live in a day and age where "multicultural education" is a hot topic. What better way to experience this than to teach in an overseas setting? Not only are you living and working in a foreign country, you are facing a classroom of multinational children whose parents comprise the diplomatic, religious, and business leaders who make up the international community. These parents choose to send their children to an American school in the country where they work because they know it is the one worldwide school system they can count on, whether they will be sent next to Switzerland or Swaziland. When public school teachers are given leaves of absence to teach in overseas settings, they are being given a real multicultural experience that they can bring back to their school in the states.

The vast majority of my students in California are from Mexico, but the Mammoth Unified School District has students whose families come from Chile, Argentina, Colombia, Honduras, El Salvador, and Nicaragua. Each of these countries share a common language—Spanish—but their cultures and histories vary greatly. By living and working in Colombia and Argentina, I was able to broaden my perspective of Latin America. I was exposed to new worldviews, authors, traditions, dances, artwork, food, and holidays. It was interesting to compare and contrast the many countries; it was fascinating to see what is similar and what is different. People in the United States tend to lump Spanish-speakers into a category labeled "Hispanics," which while convenient, is unrealistic in that it gives the impression that everyone south of our border eats tacos and dances La Raspa. If anything, my experience teaching in South America has shown me how unique the country of Mexico is, and what a rich diversity of culture is contained in that huge continent called South America. It is difficult to bring this multicultural awareness to life if you have only attended workshops and conferences stateside. It is even difficult to experience it if you travel in Central or South America, or do a summer of language and cultural study. Living and teaching in a Latin American country, for several years, is what makes it come alive.

Conversely, when the international school is willing to hire the stateside-based teacher on leave for several years, and welcome that professional into their unique community, it is receiving the benefit of a teacher who is usually up-to-date on the latest stateside methodology. In Colombia, we were allowed to test out the concept of team-teaching a core class of literature that complimented the study of U.S. history. In Argentina, I was allowed to watch second (and often third or fourth) language acquisition take place with an international student body. My ESL students learned foreign languages (English, and in some cases, Spanish as well) under intense conditions that called for fluency in a relatively short amount of time. My two years at Escuelas Lincoln convinced me that intensive English works. The exchange of ideas and culture that went on inside and outside the classroom has made me the teacher I am today. The benefits to the public school that grants the teacher a leave of absence, and to the international school that willingly hires that temporary teacher, are multiplied because the teacher is truly part of both worlds.

During our years after returning from Argentina, we knew that we would go overseas again, so we planned accordingly. We wanted to make the most of our time back in California. I got my master's degree. While it is not necessary in California due to frequent in-servicing and salary rewards for additional units from taking educational classes, it is essential in the overseas market where the schools tend to pay significantly more for professionals with higher degrees. It also makes you more attractive and competitive when seeking certain positions at the highest paid overseas schools. Our oldest daughter completed high school in Mammoth Lakes during this period—something important to her—and then entered the University of California, one of the finest public universities in the country and a real bargain economically. It was definitely to our advantage to be California residents during that period of time. If we had remained overseas for our entire teaching careers we could have lost that financial advantage. My husband and I also received more training to obtain additional credentials as bilingual and English Language Development teachers. The training was a positive way for us to advance our professional development and would have been difficult to accomplish from South America. Ironically, it also could not have happened without our experiences teaching in Colombia and Argentina, proving once again that going back and forth between the overseas school and the U.S. public schools can be the best of both worlds.

Something else happened rather unexpectedly that put our plan to return overseas on hold for several more years. I was diagnosed with breast cancer. As depressing and frightening as that was, one of the saddest aspects of dealing with this chronic disease was my fear that I would never be able to work overseas again. This, too, has proved to be untrue. I am writing this essay while serving in my third position abroad, happy and healthy, firmly in remission. My desire to live and work overseas helped me mentally in my battle with cancer. I knew that I had to get the cancer into remission or I wasn't going anywhere. Luckily, after two surgeries, six months of chemotherapy, and two months of daily radiation therapy, my cancer has remained in remission for three years and I have enjoyed a good quality of life. The illness did mean that I had to carefully consider health insurance policies offered by prospective schools abroad. I also felt I needed to disclose this situation to any future employer, which did eliminate one possible position in Europe due to the country's nationalized health care system. Although the school was willing to hire me, the government had the ultimate say. We all feared that I would be rejected as a bad health risk. I still got a job, not in Europe, but in a part of the world that I love: South America. I opted to continue my stateside insurance for the first year overseas as my new school's insurer had a preexisting clause that would not have covered a reoccurrence. I completed my first year at the American Cooperative School in La Paz, Bolivia, and received a clean bill of health from my stateside oncologist during my summer visit home. This allowed me to drop my double coverage—a huge savings. When I return to the California public schools, my former insurer cannot reject me or exercise a preexisting clause. This will save us a lot of money upon my return as well, but my health and insurance problems were not enough to keep me from living and working overseas once again. God forbid that my cancer reoccurs while I am here. I can be back in California within one day. It really is a small, small world. Life is too short to not enjoy the experiences that La Paz, Bolivia, has offered to me and my family.

We currently find ourselves looking at one or possibly two more years of leave from our home district to finish up our current teaching assignments in Bolivia—my husband is teaching sixth grade while I am teaching fourth grade. It's amazing to think that we could conceivably ask for and receive a total of three years leave without forfeiting our public school positions—something unheard of in California twenty years ago. The option of remaining here for a third year would allow our youngest daughter—now a high school junior—to graduate from the American Cooperative School of La Paz, Bolivia, with her new friends if that is what she chooses to do. Or we could return to California for her senior year, allowing her to graduate with her Mammoth Lakes friends with whom she has remained in touch through the wonders of e-mail. In any case, our lives have once again been enriched by our living and working in Bolivia, the country in South America most populated by indigenous people. We have appreciated the Quechua people's way of life as we get to know the mountains and *altiplano* that serviced their rich ancestral history, the Inca empire. Our travel in Bolivia has also allowed us to get to know the neighboring jungles of the Amazon Basin, and constantly, our Spanish language abilities improve. Ironically, I am hired here to instruct in English in a regular classroom—something I would not be able to do in Mammoth Unified School District. During the intervening six years between teaching in Argentina and Bolivia, I instructed mostly in Spanish, as a teacher in our bilingual program. I helped my school with parent meetings, conferences, and translation of everything from newsletter to Individual Education Plans in Spanish. For Mammoth Unified, it really was the best of both worlds. When my husband and I return, the district will once again enjoy the services of two fluent Spanish-speakers who will help to serve the ever-increasing numbers of Latino students in our small, rural school district.

There is one catch to this mobility. Upon our return to the Mammoth Unified School District, we are placed where we are needed, not according to our preferences. But that's the trade-off for our adventures overseas. Still, imagine our surprise after teaching two years in Argentina when I returned to bilingual kindergarten, and my husband—who had never taught below sixth grade—was assigned to a bilingual third grade class! The new assignments were challenging in the beginning, but they became great labors of love. We both enjoyed our time as primary teachers and felt the joy of giving back to our community the language skills so desperately needed in our culturally diverse state. We have also had the pleasure of mentoring several colleagues from our California district as they enter the world of overseas teaching, following in our footsteps, knowing that they, too, can enjoy the best of both worlds. As I complete my twenty-fifth year in this profession, and look forward to my second year teaching and living in La Paz, Bolivia, I know that my career has been enriched by my time spent teaching abroad. I know that my career is enriched each time I apply my new skills to my stateside position upon return. I would not have done anything differently. I would encourage all teachers to consider doing the same.

13

Globe Trotting: Teaching Around the World for Volunteer Organizations and Private Schools

Victoria Egan

I have been teaching overseas for sixteen years in nine countries on four continents and have thoroughly enjoyed every minute of it—almost. My experiences have been challenging, often entertaining, at times frustrating but never boring. Over the course of these years I have come to realize that I am a survivor. I have endured a Nigerian coup where I had a machine gun pointed at my head, the big earthquake in Mexico, and a hurricane in Bermuda. I have endured being lost in a Borneo jungle during a typhoon on Christmas Day, being robbed five times (once in Nigeria where everything I owned was stolen, right down to dirty laundry), and having a very angry student bring a loaded gun to school. I was struck by lightning, and I have even survived malaria and the sinking of a cruise ship—these things happen!

I am a Canadian, but other than brief stints teaching at two Ontario colleges and some supply teaching while home in Sarnia, I haven't taught in the Canadian system. Right after teachers' college I traveled to Nigeria as a C.U.S.O. (Canadian Universities Services Overseas) volunteer. If I could write the rules, I would deem it mandatory for all teachers (everyone for that matter) to work in a developing country earning the local wage and living as the locals do. As naive as this may sound, I truly believe that there would be far fewer wars if this were the case. There is more to the adage "If you could walk a mile in my shoes" than many realize. Of all the countries I've worked in, Nigeria will always hold a special place in my heart, even though they have all been fascinating, unique, and exceptional in various ways. Living in Kutigi was like being in another world. I had no running water, no electricity, and, at one point, I had to teach seventy-eight students in a class with no desks, no chairs, and no books.

My students often perched on the half-built walls of the "new building" (giving literal meaning to the expression "climbing the walls") or brought rocks to sit on when I held classes in my garage. A piece of board was painted black and hung on my garage wall, but the blackboard wasn't much use as there was rarely any chalk. One day, classes were temporarily suspended when a black spitting cobra took up residence in my garage. The experience was less traumatic for the villagers than the first time they saw me, though. Many of my students cried on the first day of school as they had never seen a *nesara* (Caucasian) before. I could relate to their fear though, as when I was four years old I had a black nurse during a hospital stay and was terrified of her (Southwestern Ontario was not very multi-cultural in those days). I remember how my parents had tried to get me to say good-bye to her but I would only cower behind them. This all came flooding back to me the first time I walked down our village road, while children shrieked and ran at the sight of me. The difference in skin colour can be quite striking when you're not used to it. Eventually, however, I felt completely at home as the only *nesara*. I remember months later traveling to Kaduna, a large city an eight-hour drive to the north. I was walking down the street there and was approached by a large group of Caucasians. I remember thinking how white and sickly they all looked simply because I'd gone many months without seeing a group of white people. Realizing the changes in my perception of things was a very strange experience.

I wasn't the only white teacher in an all-African village though. I knew many C.U.S.O. and VSO (Voluntary Services Overseas) volunteers in Nigeria. Situations between posts varied, at times significantly. There were, though, some commonalties. Teachers with C.U.S.O. and VSO get paid enough to cover living expenses with a little left over for pocket money. Few would go into debt to teach in a developing country and no one was there to make a buck or take advantage of the indigenous peoples. (Nigeria has over two hundred languages and even more dialects.) While all volunteers seem to be very accepting of their situations, financing problems did cause some big bumps in the road. We often went months without pay and would spend hours at the bank trying to withdraw naira. There were times when I had no food or money, yet I never worried; time and money took on a whole new dimension and it was all part of the experience. At one point all teachers in my state were ordered to the capital where we spent three days in the hot sun waiting for our names to be called. The exercise was dubbed, "weeding out the ghost workers." Apparently many people were collecting paycheques when they either weren't teachers or weren't teaching. I remember feeling as though I was a guest on "The Price is Right," awaiting the words, "Vici Egan, come on down." Unfortunately it wasn't that simple. Names were being called from three different windows simultaneously without a sound system and our names weren't being pronounced in a recognizable way. After three days, when a colleague informed me that my name had been called, I went up to the window and proceeded to collect my paycheck and a friend's. She had returned to Canada ill and was, in effect, one of these ghost workers. No papers were required and the paychecks were handed over, no questions asked!

Nigerians love pomp and ceremony even if they fail to produce the desired results. At one point the military government promoted a massive campaign entitled "W.A.I." (war against indiscipline). I remember coming home after being away and finding that all the corrugated tin shacks, which were homes and food kiosks for many, had been knocked down. Apparently they were indisciplined. It appeared though that the campaign was unsuccessful as weeks later it was replaced by "T.W.A.I." (total war against indiscipline)!

While recently reading over my Nigerian journals, I was struck by an entry: "I've been here a year and a half and I still love it. Every day is a new adventure and I can't imagine ever tiring of it." One of the reasons for that captivation was the people. Neighbours would provide food when necessary and the favour would be returned another day. Friendships formed quickly and bonds were strong. Conversation seemed more meaningful; people really talked to each other instead of sitting in front of a television set.

This cordial custom is important; it's difficult for me to put into words just how much I learned from my students, their families, and my colleagues. People who had very little were willing and happy to share what they did have. I don't know how reciprocal our exchange of learning was, as large class sizes, lack of resources, and my inexperience made teaching quite challenging. I was contemplating extending my contract to a third year when, tragically, I was forced to endure something that put my assortment of traumatic experiences into new perspective. In the first-world comfort of Canada my younger sister died in a house fire. I never returned to Nigeria. By the time I was able to contact my Field Staff Officer, weeks later, there were already ten people living in my house.

A few months later, perhaps needing to be distracted from this tragedy, I found a book that listed schools all over the world, the E.C.I.S. International Schools Directory. I started sending off letters in search of employment and was offered a job at an American school in Mexico. I accepted and a week later I received another job offer from a school in Bursa, Turkey. I wrote and told them that I had already agreed to a job for the coming academic year and they sent me a contract for the following year. My next two overseas posts were lined up!

The year in Mexico was a difficult one professionally. In retrospect, I think it was too soon emotionally for me to leave my parents and remaining eight siblings after the death of my sister, with whom I was very close.

Because of my experiences in Nigeria, in Mexico I was given the "difficult class" of thirty-eight grade three students. They were very wealthy, spoiled, and far more trying than seventy-eight Nigerians who had desperately wanted to learn. In Mexico, the students I had were quite wild. I had never heard of A.D.D. (attention deficit disorder) or A.D.H.D. (attention deficit hyper-active disorder) but I think that many of my students would have fit into one of those categories. Their parents, however, weren't exactly paragons of model behaviour. I remember my first PTA meeting where our principal tried to establish order for at least twenty minutes before he was able to begin his talk. Throughout the meeting, parents spoke unabashedly amongst themselves so that it was next to impossible to hear the person who held the floor, even with a microphone. All of a sudden my students' behaviours made sense. I found the work very challenging.

Discipline followed a North American code, which was very unlike the Nigerian one. There, I would never send a student out of the room for misbehaving. The school sergeant would round up any delinquent students and punish them by making them kneel in the hot sun with arms extended and whipping them if they faltered. There were other equally cruel methods of punishment, all of which involved being exposed to the midday African sun. Sometimes students were made to balance on one foot, holding large buckets of water. While I didn't, and don't, follow these draconian practices, I must admit that I did appreciate the support. The school in Mexico didn't offer me much of a support system. The school was fairly new and was experiencing growing pains, but I loved Mexico, the people and the Latin *joie de vivre*. If I hadn't already accepted the job in Turkey, I probably would not have agreed to teach wealthy, private students again. I was glad though, later, that I'd accepted the job at the private *lisei* (this was not a French college, but what schools in Turkey are called). There the students were rich, but they were not spoiled and they behaved very well.

An amusing aspect of teaching in an international school surfaced during my time in this position. I taught several levels of ESL but I suppose the *hazerliks* (total beginners at eleven years of age) were the most memorable. I remember thinking that I was making no progress for months when all of a sudden it was as though a light went on and they were off and running. I shared this group with a teacher from England and with one from Texas. We tried to cover some of the same material simultaneously and were working on "can" and "can't." One day, Ufuk, one of my *hazerliks*, approached me. "Ms. Egan, why is it that you say 'can,' Mr. Hinton says 'con,' and Ms. Cecile says 'caaan'?" I thought it was quite perceptive of Ufuk and explained to him that even though we all spoke English as a first language, we did indeed sound different, particularly with certain vowels. Another of my *hazerliks* didn't fare so well in the mastery of the English tongue. Poor Yilmaz. He was very tiny and regardless of how hard we tried, Yilmaz seemed immune to learning. At the end of the year concert though, we were so proud of his dancing. He was remarkable as a junior whirling dervish! It was comforting to see that Yilmaz could succeed at something.

I enjoyed my year in Turkey, teaching in Bursa and traveling in the country during vacations. It did seem rather odd teaching on Christmas Day, but Turkey is a Muslim country and Christmas is not a holiday. There was so much to see and learn in Turkey, and the people were very warm. I loved the food, the markets, and could never tire of a minaret-dotted skyline.

From Byzantine beauty I moved to cosmopolitan Europe. In London, England, I began teaching at a private language school. I taught business people from around the world, one to one. It was a great job, especially since the school paid for me to take the clients out to lunch. I taught at three different central London locations and also spent a week teaching at a lovely resort they had in Winchester. Unfortunately, the school went through a very quiet period and since I was the most recent hire, I was laid off. Looking for work, I accepted a temporary teaching position at an inner-city school, and was shortly extended a contract for the remainder of the year.

I didn't really know what I was getting myself into when I accepted that position. England was in the midst of bringing in "The National Curriculum." This was a mammoth undertaking and while it was very much needed, it was being implemented far too rapidly. As a result, teachers were openly disgruntled and morale was low. This was all too evident in the school where I was employed. I was hired as a full-time supply teacher for six months. The administration must have been anticipating a lot of sick calls and they were right! I filled in for different teachers almost every day. If I arrived at school and wasn't needed as a supply teacher, which was rare, I taught ESL instead. When teachers knew they were going to be absent, I asked what they wanted me to do with their classes. Invariably my questions were met with indifference. I was told to do whatever I wanted. This freedom was a very different experience from supply teaching in Sarnia, Canada, where everything had always been laid out. In addition to having no plans in this same role in England, I didn't have any luck locating books—texts or notebooks. I wasn't very impressed with my limited experience with the English educational system and can only hope that things have improved now that the National Curriculum has been up and running for many years.

Then, when that contract finished, I interviewed in London for a job in the land of olives and wine. A school in Arta, Greece, had advertised the position of English teacher. When I arrived in Greece I soon found that the things I had been assured of were not forthcoming. Instead of my own apartment, I was living in a room in my employer's house, sharing a bathroom with her elderly parents who were staying in the room next to me.

My immediate reaction was to leave, but upon meeting a few other teachers at different local language schools, or *frontisterias*, as they were known, I decided to stay. I taught Greek students who ranged in age from four to eighteen. They were great and I loved teaching them. Because the students attended regular Greek school, they came to us in shifts. Therefore, sometimes I worked mornings and sometimes evenings and other times I would have a full afternoon or morning off. The variety of working hours was very enjoyable. I love Greece and can envisage returning there to retire and write one day.

Nonetheless, still restless after one year in Greece, I left and signed on as the coordinator of the Intensive English Department at the Canadian International school in Singapore. Singapore is a very easy place to live and for the first time in my nine years of teaching I was making a decent salary; up to that point in time, I had been making local wages. Breaking my pattern of one- and two-year stays in a country, I stayed in Singapore for five years.

This was my first job at an official international school. Instead of teaching strictly locals, I taught students from over forty nationalities. The experience was great as I grew professionally as a teacher and an administrator. As the latter, I was thrown in at the deep end with a department of twelve to manage and no prior experience. It was definitely a case of baptism by fire! As a teacher, I had spent nine years in small local schools and had received no professional development since the ESL course I enrolled in after teachers' college. And the course hadn't really even begun to prepare me for that challenge! While in Singapore, however, I attended four different annual S.E.A.T.C.O. (South East Asian Teacher's Conferences) in Bangkok, Kuala Lumpur, Jakarta, and Singapore. It was wonderful to return recharged with lots of great ideas to try. I realized after the first conference that this professional development was one of the most important elements I had been missing in my teaching career. I felt as though I had been working in a vacuum during my previous teaching assignments.

In my second year, the elementary section grew significantly and they built a new building on the current site. I had been teaching in the high school. There was a need for an ESL teacher in the elementary school so I decided to step down from the coordinator position after two years and move to the elementary panel—just for a change. Yes, another change. I enjoyed it and remained for three years. I've heard Singapore called "Singabore" or referred to as "Disney World with the death penalty," but I found it to be a pretty enjoyable place to live. One of the nicest things was its central location as far as traveling. Because we had Chinese, Malay, Indian, and Canadian holidays, I was able to do a fair bit of traveling during five years of vacations.

The other real bonus was that at that time I paid into C.P.F. (Central

Provident Fund). The government took 40 percent of our salary and we didn't see it until we left the country. The fund became an enforced savings plan and I was able, in effect, to compensate for all the years that I had worked for a pittance. (Don't get me wrong. I don't regret those years at all but it certainly was nice to see some real cash for a change.) After a pretty hefty shopping spree, I handed most of the remains over to a financial advisor with the instructions, "Make me rich, please. I want to be comfortable during my golden years." Central Provident Fund is no longer taken off ex-pats' salaries but it certainly worked well for me. Singapore can be a very expensive country to live in and I found that the more I earned, the more I spent. There are two ways to live there: one way is like a local where you eat local food at hawker stalls for very little money, drink there, and shop at the markets. The second way is to eat and drink at restaurants and shop at Cold Storage or Sogo, the expensive grocery stores that carry very expensive imported foods. Unfortunately, I chose the latter option. This choice led to a financial squeeze which, coupled with school a policy of unsubsidized housing, led me to search for something new.

I applied to a couple of other international schools in town, and after having an interview with one of them, I was offered a job at its sister school in Beijing. I wasn't sure if I could go back to teaching in a developing country after being spoiled by five years in Singapore but what attracted me was the fact that it was a one-year contract. I figured that you could put up with pretty much anything for a year and I'd always wanted to see "The Wall."

China is a very interesting place to be and the turn of the new millennium is a very exciting time to be there. Things are changing so fast, even in the two years that I have been here. I look at the little old men and women on the street and am astounded by the chaotic changes they have seen in their lives, having lived through the birth of communism, the upheavals of the cultural revolution, protests in Tiananmen Square, and the slow but inevitable demise of communism.

The people here are incredibly resourceful and one person in particular provided me with the most unusual and amusing sight I can recall. I live in a serviced apartment which means that an *ayi* (auntie) comes in daily for light housekeeping. Once, my *ayi* had asked me to supply her with a spray bottle for ironing. The request was simple enough, but I forgot about it, even after I began to hear strange sounds coming from the living room. Then, one day I was sitting at my computer while my *ayi* was ironing with her back to me. She picked up a large water bottle, filled her mouth with water and proceeded to spurt forth an amazingly well-aimed fountain spray of water all over my dress! Totally gobsmacked and with my mouth agape, I picked up a pen and wrote in large letters, "buy a spray bottle!" I could hardly fault her for lack of ingenuity! She is one of the many little things about my travels that sticks up like a sign post in a journey that still has no discernable end.

My plan is to teach for two more years in Beijing and then take a year off, traveling around the world, writing, and visiting friends. There are still many places in the world where I would like to teach, as after teaching in such a variety of countries, the desire to experience other cultures definitely gets in your blood. When I pick up a copy of the *The International Educator*, the definitive guide to overseas teaching positions, I hear myself thinking aloud, "That job sounds interesting."

With all the errors and unexpected experiences included, overseas teaching has become a way of life for me. My experiences have been rich, varied, exciting, and highly rewarding, but teachers considering overseas teaching for the first time should not feel they have to follow in my many footsteps; they should not feel they have to spend nineteen years teaching in nine countries. I certainly didn't. Experiencing life in different cultures is an incredible opportunity that I would highly recommend, whether you are about to graduate or are a veteran teacher ready for a change in lifestyle.

14

International Teaching—A Welcome

David Reid

What is it like to teach in a foreign school? In an international school, you are hired precisely because you do come with teaching methods of your home country, and these ideas are not to be discarded; they are to be adapted, though, to the culture you find yourself in. International teaching, however, is not limited to international schools as many teachers end up teaching in local schools in various countries. (I have spent much of my time alternating between international schools, local schools—and just traveling.) There, ideas from your home country are appreciated, but you must judge the proper balance. For example, the Ivory Coast (Cote d'Ivoire, West Africa, formerly a French colony), where I taught physical and natural sciences, still has extremely close ties with France. Science textbooks were imported from France with many examples in the books taken from daily life in Paris. I looked around at the jungle surrounding the village, with its pythons and papayas, and at my pupils, and I realized these students do not know what a sewer system is. The examples were worthless. I used examples from *their* lives. Because the book was so far from their experiences, they were just memorizing out of the book or the teacher's notes. They were surprised when I told them that I would give no credit for anything either memorized or for an explanation that I could not give to a younger child. The book, as a crutch, went out the window. Radical, but accepted, this new policy produced good results.

Whether teaching at an international school with either an American or International Baccalaureate program or at a local school with a local curriculum, the expatriate teacher may confront restrictions upon him. Within my subjects, mathematics and physics, there is constant change, and the skills of scientific thought and rational thinking are much more valuable than whichever curriculum is being taught. For example, in Colombia, I taught an eighth grade physics class with a Colombian colleague, alongside a somewhat more traditional eighth grade physics teacher. The next year, when a new colleague, a Dutchman, came in and taught ninth grade physics, he said that he could tell which students had been taught by me, and which ones by my Colombian colleague. When the Dutch physics teacher explained the goal of an experiment, those who had studied with me were quickly up and scurrying about to organize the experiment. The ones who had learned under the Colombian continued to sit in their seats, waiting for more specific instructions (which the Dutch colleague had not intended to give). Same curriculum, different styles. This story illustrates what international teachers are hired to do; they must make a difference in the way the students think, whatever the subjects are that they teach.

The question as to how far they can go in their creative interpretation of curriculum is one that each one of them—and you—must resolve once you are in the country. On one side, you are there to bring a certain amount of your foreign expertise; on the other hand, you are not there as a colonial master. Thus you must appraise what values are really worthwhile to introduce, and do it "through the back door." For example, in mathematics one handles concepts of "less than," "greater than," "equal," "equivalent," "noncomparable," and the like. One should always give examples from real life. In Colombia this gave me the perfect forum for discussing the comparison of the sexes. It was not hard to create interest in a macho society when one talks about the ways in which females are superior to males. The ensuing discussion led to some thoughtful faces, and discussions in the corridors—and never any problems with the parents. School pupils are more open to challenging the notions that they inherited from their parents. This application of mathematics was perhaps the most useful that most of them will ever encounter. Therefore, I covered the usual program while making a difference in the pupils' culture—and thus the future culture of the country. Well, one can hope.

As for tailoring your curriculum and relating to the local community as a teacher, generalizations about students generally apply to the rest of the community. While, granted, generalizations are inherently risky and potentially unfair, they offer the expatriate teacher an important leg to stand on—providing the other two legs are in working order. In East Asia, a teacher is accorded automatic respect (which, however, is not always reflected in the pay envelope); in Africa, the students and the parents suspend judgment, and after a while will treat you according to your merits. One of the most impressive statements that was ever made to me as a teacher was in the Ivory Coast. Due to the importance of the subjects that one girl (well, woman—probably about twenty years old, but in the tenth grade) took from me, my evaluation (grades) for her turned out to be pivotal. I caught her cheating, which lowered her grade enough to fail the year—the second time running, which shut her out from further education in that country. Afterwards she told me, "Monsieur, I want to tell you that you caught me fair and square, and I deserved what you did, but I want you to know that I think you are a good teacher." This comment was not rooted in sarcasm or bitterness. It was firmly planted in Africa. Many of my students there were poor, needing financial help from the Catholic Church for their educations. They knew they were special: In the Ivory Coast, education remains a luxury that not all children may enjoy, and the children highly value the chance to be educated.

In South America, on the other hand, teachers are rather low on the social scale. In many countries, if the parents are rich (as is often the case at international schools), you may be seen as a servant. However, this should not bother you. For example, in Italy, where one will also come across this attitude, one of my pupils had been out of school with a broken leg due to a ski accident. She then did poorly in mathematics. Talking to her mother, I said that I saw only one solution: the girl must stay after school every day with me until she caught up. She thought I meant for payment, but I explained the ethics of the situation: no payment. An Italian teacher would generally not do that: if the student fails, then the student fails. The girl caught up. The Italian mother was not only profusely thankful, but at Christmas I found a case of wine, a Pannetonni (special cake), and a membership card to a health club on my doorstep. In Colombia, where fewer research papers per professor were published than all other countries in South America, I was able to get my students, in higher level physics International Baccalaureate, interested in writing a mini-thesis. One student, for example, liked to play his (music) synthesizer. Fine. So he hooked up his synthesizer to an oscilloscope, took pictures of the screen as different musical instruments were simulated, and worked on the computer to analyze the resulting curves ("Fourier analysis") to predict how to create new sounds and new instruments. Excellent mini-thesis. Students came out of my courses with a higher respect for education than their parents had. Personal encounters helped as well; one student told me he was impressed when he came to my house and found a poor woman I had just taken to the eye doctor. That impression was perhaps more lasting than the formula of electromagnetism that he had had to master for the physics course, but it was all part of his education.

With all this talk about suiting your curriculum to the students in your classroom, you may worry and cry, "But resources! I may not be able to get all those wonderful audiovisual materials, computer labs, science gadgetry, books, and all that!" Resourcefulness and creativity is your answer. When I arrived in the Ivory Coast, the director proudly pointed me to a physics lab that he said was full of equipment. I went in, and it was indeed full of equipment—none of which worked, and repairs were impossible. However, one of my best experiments required me to saw out different shapes of wood for the students to find the center of gravity. In biology class we made yogurt to explain fermentation; I showed my veins where they could see blue blood (on their arms this was not evident). And so forth. In Colombia, although we had more equipment, a very successful experiment was to predict where a stone would land when propelled by a slingshot. (Not easy, but fun! Aiming at the director's window was discouraged.) An experiment to simulate a radioactivity decay curve was to graph the decay of the head on a glass of beer (older classes only!).

In mathematics, with a sheet of paper you can come up with results that are wilder than most people can imagine. For example, do a bit of geometry, not in a space where you can go from one point to another freely, but along lines in a grid, like streets in a city (thus this is called "Taxi-cab geometry"). Now apply normal definitions of geometry, and you come up with strange results—results that are wild, but which are similar to, but simpler than, those of atomic physics! A class discussion of axioms (basic suppositions) can bring more changes to a child's world-view than a series of videos. For example, after a few such discussions in Italy, where I used no audio-visuals, a pupil came up and told me, "Mr. Reid, you have destroyed all my foundations of thought!" This was expressed not as a complaint, but as a compliment. True, the audio-visuals are nice, but there is no need to despair when they are not there: teaching can still be worthwhile for both the teacher and the students. That is, if the teacher cares. And if you did not care, why would you still be teaching?

"But I will be a foreigner," you may worry. So what? How you are treated will depend, of course, on the country you live in, but also in the way you adjust. A trivial example: in South Korea it is traditional and polite to give and accept things with two hands (or with a symbolic touching of one hand to the wrist). The Koreans know that foreigners do not know this, but they are delighted when you do adopt this and other forms of politeness. Since Koreans do not have the same forms of politeness as Europeans or Americans, many foreigners may think the Koreans rude. What a mistake! It is so easy to adjust. In Africa and South Asia I ate with my hands, in East Asia with chopsticks. One is always better accepted when you do not insist on your own ways. Indeed, one must remember not only that customs but also laws are very different. In the days when Zimbabwe was Rhodesia, and racial discrimination was intense, I was kicked out of the country because of my discussions with black Africans, which were heard by a plainclothes police agent. I am a little bit more careful now, especially concerning stories about police.

"But what about the language?" you may wonder. Admittedly, I cheated for my first overseas job, as it was in Australia, but I didn't know I could get jobs in non-English-speaking countries. Even in such countries, it is a temptation to be lazy by sticking to one's native tongue, since one can usually get by using a combination of English, a smattering of the local language, gestures, common sense, pointing, drawing, maps, language guides, dictionaries, friends, etc. I do not pick up languages easily, and being lazy, I stuck to these basics for Korean, Farsi, Turkish, and others— learning a few key words is never difficult. But these key words are important: people are always much kinder when you show an interest in learning even "Thank you" in their language (always the first thing to learn, even before "where is the toilet?"!). Hand movements will get you far, although be careful: most gestures are not international. For example, the "thumbs-up" gesture continues to mean "very good" in Europe or Korea, but in much of the Middle East it means "up yours." Anyway, I only studied beyond pleasantries for a few Indo-European languages. Where? Yes, Germany for German and Italy for Italian, but when, for example, I did not get a job in France, I went to the French-speaking Ivory Coast in Africa for my French. Being in the country allows you not only to hear and practice the language, but also to find ready access to courses and tutors.

Another concern that many soon-to-be foreign teachers have is health care. This issue need not scare you. Usually you are well covered by enough insurance to go to the best doctors. There are, of course, occasional annoyances; for example, to get my visa to Kuwait, I needed to be tested for AIDS three times within five months. But on the other hand, I received a mouthful of crowns in Colombia by a U.S.-trained dentist at a price comparable to the cost of two crowns in Europe or America. In South Korea I received a month-long acupuncture treatment (which worked) free, simply because the doctor liked foreigners. In Taiwan a dentist was amazed that I should ask him how much I owed for a checkup: I had nothing wrong, so nothing was charged. An operation in Turkey was performed by a highly esteemed doctor trained in Europe. The list goes on.

"But," you protest. "What about the food? I might get sick." Quite the contrary! Your taste buds should revel in new experiences. Sit in your home country, and you shall always eat green-picked fruit, cloned vegetables, McDonald's, and the like. True, you can often eat McDonald's abroad as well, but you would be missing out on culinary delights. My mouth waters at the memory of tropical fruits, sumptuous fresh fish, vegetables that were real vegetables, and magnificent combinations of spices. The water? Maybe you have to filter and boil it, but that quickly becomes routine.

Housing is probably going to be different from what you may be used to. In the Ivory Coast, the director of the school was worried that he could not give me a big apartment, because he had seen the "typical" American homes in the TV show "Dallas" (a show which showed an oil-rich American family). True, I did not have a carpet, or glass in the windows, or a door, but the weather made these things unnecessary. I had a mosquito net, a fan, a bed, a desk, a light, shelves, and plenty of room. I was content.

Living quarters in international schools, however, are often downright luxurious. In Turkey, I had a huge apartment with heat, when most Turks had to content themselves with heavy sweaters. Such utilities are usually very cheap or free. Even when the conditions are generally poor, one often enjoys luxuries not found elsewhere. For example, if one is a hedonist like me with respect to hot, hot baths, then Russia can be marvelous.

Another advantage to international teaching is in the travel possibilities. Of course just living abroad is a sort of travel, but add to that the possibilities during school vacations and one can find a variety of excursions into local cultures richly rewarding. Holidays are often different but they are always sufficient to prevent teachers from going crazy. In Turkey we had only two days off for Christmas, but then several weeks in February. That was better as February was not the high season for international flights, but the Christmas season was. Between school vacations and years between jobs, I have had the opportunity to experience over seventy countries in the last twenty-six years, spread out over all the habitable continents. This schedule is perhaps a bit extreme, but it does give an indication of the possibilities.

As for intellectual and cultural life, the international experience will almost certainly be an enriching one. Indeed, I have been able to see a much greater diversity of spectacles than anyone who has stuck to his or her home country. In Minsk, Belarus, I could afford to go to the ballet (a passion of mine) and opera as often as I wished. (At the time, the Minsk Ballet Troupe was the third best in the ex-Soviet Union.) The Russian traditional dances that I paid through the nose to see in Europe, I saw for free in Russia; the Colombian crafts were an everyday affair; the rambles through Barcelona were not a holiday goal but my everyday walk home from school; the Turkish markets were a weekly pleasure; Italy was at my doorstep; the Koreans enchanted me for a whole year; a German castle looked down upon my shopping; Australia was not a faraway land; Zimbabwe was more than a word in the newspaper; and I had a front-row seat to view the revolution in Iran. (This may not have been to everyone's taste, but as it was, I am glad I witnessed it.)

Now, time to deal with the question you have pretended not to be so interested in: money. Some international schools pay handsomely, tax-free (or almost), with lots of benefits. However, this is not what keeps me in international teaching. I have also taught at local salaries, one of which was best described by an Austrian friend in Japan: "If I made only as much per hour as you made per month, I couldn't survive!" I survived and hold no regrets about the salary. But if you want to save money, you can often do it more easily at an international school than in your home country.

Now, you're at the point where you are actually determined to teach in a new environment. Then you look at the visa requirements and become horrified. If you are lucky, the school will take care of everything, but you start to get an idea of the bureaucracy that you will have to live under. Even if the visa is handled entirely by the school, it is unlikely that you will escape the bureaucracy the entire length of your contract. My Russian visa is a good example. As this was not an international school, the visa was my affair. When no one in one office knew what to do about me, I would be referred somewhere else. When there was nowhere else to refer me to, some bureaucrat would stare at the paper for a while, and then go and type something up, as long as it had a stamp on it. This took weeks and a lot of help by a very lovely Russian. In Colombia it was not uncommon to get your ID after it had expired. (I carried around a receipt while waiting. After a year, the paper receipt gets unrecognizable, but the police usually do not let that bother them.) You want to learn how the other 95 percent live? Don't expect efficiency. On the other hand, my work visa for Germany took about five minutes.

Surprisingly, if you are flexible, the bureaucrats usually are too. One standard document for a visa is a police report. Fine. But from which police, if I am officially without residence? For my Spanish visa, the police were quite accommodating, but a few years later, in trying to get something equivalent in Belgium, no one—neither Belgian police, nor Interpol, nor the American consulate—would issue such a report. So, I got an official-looking affidavit in which I said that I was not a criminal. Even though any criminal can get this affidavit, I got the visa. Sometimes officials can be amazingly nice. In Russia, during the Kosovo bombing, I was visited by a policeman, then a few days later by the passport office, who wanted to make sure that neighbors did not harass me for being American. (They didn't. Most people distinguish between a government and its citizens.) These issues are national, as opposed to professional, and ultimately not a great concern.

More important than minor civil servants are your superiors. Hierarchy is a sticky question in any school system. In general, one has more to do with one's immediate superior (head of department) than with the director of the school. The director may know little or nothing of what is going on with your subject. One director I had in Italy asked me during the interview whether I, as a mathematics teacher, could handle the computer classes. The pure mathematics I had studied had absolutely nothing to do with computers, but of course I said I could. He told me casually that the school had "the usual Apples"; I nodded, and changed the subject. Back in Germany I grabbed a friend and asked frantically, "What's an Apple? I have three months to learn!" I learned, not only about computers, but also about directors. Despite this awkwardness, directors can be an immense help. On the other hand, in a local school in the Ivory Coast, when the director just shrugged when I reported a case of attempted bribery, I resolved not to extend my contract. Of course, in some countries one knows that the business manager—rarely a beloved part of the school, as he is the one who has to keep appetites in check—must give bribes to keep the school going, but this is a different matter.

If these unusual incidents haven't shaken your resolve, or conversely, they have motivated you to teach internationally you may still cry, "But I have a family." All the better for your family. Of course, there is the consideration about whether your spouse wants to move to that country. If there are children, and if you teach in an international school, then you can usually enroll your children in that school free, and it will be a positive experience for them. (Although I myself do not have children, I have observed many colleagues with children.)

Why, I think the next time I go to Turkey, I shall rent/hire a child: the Turks go ga-ga when they see a child. They love children. Also, no matter what the language, your children will pick up the local language a lot faster than you do, and this will be valuable to them later.

What about your colleagues? There are the foreign colleagues and the local colleagues. How you get along with them depends on how you get along with people in general. In many international schools, the expatriate teachers tend to clump together. This is often encouraged by the language barrier, housing arrangements, and even economic status (you will get benefits that your local colleagues do not). But these are illusions: none of these need to be an insuperable barrier to close and rewarding professional and personal relations with your colleagues. Indeed, without the effort on your part to establish these relations, what sense would teaching abroad have?

But the students are of course why we teach. Schools made up purely of foreign nationals (i.e., students not from the host country) are rare. So, to be effective, you have to understand something of the way your students think, and that is based not only on age but also culture. This does not mean that you cannot have influence on their ways of thinking. The curricula always allows the teacher a certain amount of freedom in teaching methodology, whether the curricula is a mixture of an international curriculum (the American program and the International Baccalaureate are common) and a local one, or purely the local curriculum. Indeed, many students have told me, even years after, of the influence I had on their ways of thinking, long after they had forgotten the formula for integrals or gravitational attraction. The students, of course, may have either a disdain for teachers, as in the Americas, or an exaggerated respect, as in the Far East, but most of the time they are in the middle, like the African students who wait to see how you are, and then accord you the respect (or lack thereof) that you merit.

There you have it: overseas teaching—welcome. Once in, you will find the inconveniences smaller than you imagined, and a small price to pay for the wonders which you will experience, both in and out of the classroom. Good luck!

Appendix A

Risky Business: Extreme Educational Environments

Dan Davis

Educators with fairly sane venues for their lives hear reports of teachers being evacuated from Pakistan or similarly dangerous sounding places and wonder, "What is it like to live in a country where daily security is not something which can apparently be taken for granted?" I was handed the mission of trying to answer this riddle. On pondering the issue, however, I realized I must first consider a couple of other questions—Why do people travel or live overseas? And, just how risky is it, anyway?—because the answers to these questions dictate the attitudes people have toward their particular lifestyles.

Most people like to travel, even ensconced Middle-Americans whose idea of adventure is witnessing license plates from states they can't even spell. Far fewer, however, opt to actually live in places they would consider foreign. The numbers drop dramatically when one excludes countries in western Europe, a place which differs from America only in the price of gas, funny little road signs, the greater average age of buildings, and the tendency of natives to speak in a dialect that is not quite understandable.

But why would anyone live in a country considered dangerous, one of those names on the State Department list of undesirable destinations? Many Americans have continued to do so, and are not terribly concerned about all the hoopla. Of course, tax-free status, free housing, and inexpensive domestic help might explain the fascination, but such benefits are available in calmer locales. So why indulge in all the risk? One answer, I realized, might rely on a teacher's definition of risk.

People have long kidded me about my fascination with risk, primarily because of my enjoyment of sports such as skydiving, BASE jumping (par-achuting off of fixed objects), paragliding, and rappelling, and thought I was perfect for living in extreme environments. Similarly, my wife, although she is not much of a thrill-seeker nowadays, has tried most of these sports, and could therefore be assumed to be a fit candidate for life on the global edge. But how does one explain the presence of so many rational people whose idea of a thrill is a well-hit shot down the fairway?

By analyzing the exact dangers in skydiving, for example, I had long ago realized that the sport was not as dangerous as many—out of sheer igno-rance—believe it to be. Likewise, every country has its own characteristic problems, facets that often vary by city. A prime example in this case would be my current place of residency, Pakistan.

Although I feel perfectly safe living in Lahore, the thought of residing in Karachi frightens me. I'm sure there are plenty of ex-pats in Karachi, how-ever, who feel perfectly safe living there. They know the exact risks, and therefore are not ignorant of the true facts of living in what others consider a dangerous environment. Perhaps, then, a big part of the mystery is how residents see their environments, the realities they see on a daily basis.

Most people form their opinions of a place, be it a city or a country, through what they hear in the news. Indeed, I have come to realize the media is too often the supreme judge when it should really only be regarded on par with an opinionated trial lawyer: they are out to sell themselves—their papers or airtime—and sensationalism sells. As a result, what you see is not what you get, and if an expatriate looks behind the headlines she will often find a more peaceful reality. Before we met, my wife learned this lesson well when she took a position in Israel just as the Intifada began. Her family and friends berated her for moving to what appeared to be a war zone, but what she found in Tel Aviv was a sense of security, which allowed her to feel perfectly safe strolling along the beach at 2 A.M. if she so desired. The lesson from this example is that teachers are as safe as you feel. Quite simply, safety is a matter of personal perception and comfort.

When the decision to work and live overseas is final, it is this attitude that dictates how successfully people live in extreme educational environ-ments. During the interview for our first position overseas together, the American School of Kinshasa's director, Stephen Kapner, did his best to frighten us with stories of the September 1991 looting in the Zairian cap-ital, events which resulted in the closing of school for the 1991–1992 school year and the evacuation of all teachers. Linda had recently learned her lesson in Israel, however, and I was reminded of the several times the Ecu-adorian government had been overthrown between 1971 and 1979 when I was growing up in the South American country where my parents directed an orphanage. What I recalled most vividly about the coup d'etats was not being frightened, but rather being ecstatic because each one usually meant a few days off from school. The director in Zaire must have been impressed by our nonchalant reactions to his "reality tests" because we got the jobs. During the remaining months before our move, we witnessed on television the riots in Los Angeles, and were amused that the State Department had not issued an advisory against travel to Southern California.

Less than a year later we were beginning to wonder if we had made a mistake when, one afternoon shortly after an aerobics class, machine-gun fire began to be heard around Kinshasa, much like a bag of popcorn after about a minute in a microwave. Within forty-eight hours the city was under siege, and many businesses were quite literally shattered. The school closed for at least a month, but our attitude helped sustain us: In many ways, the whole episode was one great adventure, and I still think that my journal from those days sizzles. At one moment we could watch our predicament on television as the conflict became CNN's leading story, and the next we could walk outside to the front lawn with beer in hand and watch the tracers dissect the African sky. Far from seeming risky, this experience was almost magical. Even dispatches overheard on various civilian radio frequencies were not considered so much bad news as they were electronic doses of adrenaline pulsed directly into our bodies by way of our ears. As I said earlier, risk is a matter of perception.

Some of our colleagues, unfortunately, were not able to maintain the same attitude. Their feelings were compounded by the fact that they would tend to isolate themselves where their worst fears could replicate faster than any petri-dish-bound bacteria—a situation we survivors realized was fatal. To stay emotionally healthy in times of crisis, it is essential to have human contact, discuss your fears, and stay as informed as possible while at the same time taking each rumor with an ocean of salt. After being evacuated for two or three weeks, most of us returned to finish the year, although there were some notable absences among the list of returning staff.

Our next overseas position was in Romania and, as expected, many of our family and friends thought we were insane for taking our newborn son, only six weeks old, to a place infamous for breeding such fiends as Vlad Tepes (the original Dracula) and the communist madman Ceaucescu. Despite articles in leading magazines depicting a horrendous level of environmental degradation, we found much the opposite. There were some bleak places and, on occasion, the aerial pollution rivaled that of Los Angeles on a bad day, but mostly we were delighted by the green countryside, the soaring Transylvanian Alps, and historic cities that had yet to be desecrated by the mobs of tourists which overrun every known vestige of history in Western Europe. The people were absolutely magnificent, and I forged such strong friendships there that I will be returning every summer to visit. The lack of danger was so overwhelming, in fact, that about the only way I kept my sanity was by paragliding several days every month, snowboarding in the winter, and occasionally skydiving from a decrepit ex-Soviet Antonov-2 biplane.

Last year we left the paradise of Romania and came here to Pakistan with demanding jobs to keep us busy. Since at the time most of our relatives knew nothing of this South Asian country—other than that our style might be somewhat cramped by the Muslim culture—we were mercifully spared the usual inquiries into our mental fitness. Then came the nuclear tests, and suddenly our home was on the global stage, with many people fearful of war with India or the dangers of radioactive fallout from the tests. For us, however, life continued its mundane pace, and by the end of the summer we felt no qualms whatsoever in returning. Our piece of mind was brutally shattered on the first day of school, however, when we were bluntly informed we would be evacuated the next day. Threats of imminent action against American interests in Pakistan had the State Department nervous and, of course, two days later the United States attacked Osama bin Laden's camps in Afghanistan and the pharmaceuticals plant in Sudan, so the American government was apparently trying to keep us safe from the collateral damage or brunt of locals' retaliatory fury. But when a month had passed and we were assured sentiments and safety had returned to their normal levels, we dutifully resumed our positions at school.

One considerable difference between our attitudes in Zaire versus our attitudes here was obvious, however: we now have the safety of our two young sons to keep in mind. Suddenly our mighty roar in the face of adversity has sunk to a calculated squeak, and we do nothing important before considering all the risks. Still, we never seriously entertained the idea of returning to the dubious safety of the United States. From all the media reports we have seen, our minds have been programmed to believe the danger from the violent crime in the states is comparable to any risks we might face here. After all, I have never heard of an American/International school where one of the students came to school just so he could murder his classmates with some NRA-approved toy.

In the end, the simple fact of the matter is that our daily routine continues its usual pace regardless of the presence or absence of any earth-shattering concerns. Although we might ponder our safety once or twice throughout the day—especially when driving about town—there are classes to prep and teach, meetings to attend, and extracurricular activities to lead. On weekends and after school we are careful to spend ample quality time with our kids. And every evening, dinner takes place at its usual time at home—the only place we could, or would, call home at this moment in our lives.

Faculty of Education Initiatives in International Teaching: Indiana University's Student Teaching Program and Queen's University's Teachers' Overseas Recruiting Fair

Going Global: U.S. Educators Living and Working Abroad
Laura L. Stachowski and Susan Johnstad

Being able to live and teach with members of a community that is in another country is just the beginning to developing a truly global view. This experience will have a positive and dramatic effect on my entire life, and since I am going to teach, it will also affect others. People here have taught me so much.

—Bruce, student teacher in Wales

This project gave me access to the true Indian culture. Indian culture is so radically different from the West that every moment gives you a totally new understanding of life. When one witnesses such a contrast, they come to better understand their own culture. Within India you will experience the highest of the highs and the lowest of the lows. But it all positively adds to your character.

—Chad, student teacher in India

I have learned to be more observant and appreciative of the little things. . . . My neighbors will call to alert us that a rainbow is in the sky, for example. People [back home] don't often appreciate or comment upon the little joys in life. Also, I have learned that I have potential as a teacher and have a positive effect on some hard-to-work-with students. One of my supervising teachers made a special point of telling me what

a great response I had elicited from a boy who could barely read and
usually felt stigmatized. The teacher said she is thrilled with the student's effort and more frequent smiles.

—Lauren, student teacher in Scotland

The reflections of these young, preservice educators—participants in an
international student teaching project—demonstrate that teaching and living in foreign schools and communities is a complex dynamic. The experiences of Lauren, Bruce, and Chad were as unique as their own
personalities and shaped by their particular goals and insights. As U.S.
educators increasingly venture beyond our national borders to teach youth,
they encounter, literally, a world of opportunity. Whether seeking to enhance their pedagogical skills, develop global perspectives, or better understand themselves, U.S. educators traveling abroad—preservice and
in-service alike—will find rewarding experiences which extend beyond the
scope of the less adventurous professional.

Since 1975, the Overseas Project, offered through the School of Education at Indiana University, has provided hundreds of student teachers with
international classroom and community experiences, launching them into
the teaching profession with a solid and realistic sense of life and schooling
outside of the United States. An optional supplement to conventional student teaching, this popular project places students in the schools of England, Wales, Scotland, the Republic of Ireland, Australia, New Zealand,
and most recently, India, Taiwan, and Kenya. During the student teaching
semester, participants first teach in-state for a minimum of ten to sixteen
weeks to receive certification; they then spend at least eight weeks in their
host nations, where they live with families in the community and teach in
national schools. The Overseas Project has enjoyed much success as an
avenue by which beginning teachers can move beyond the "familiar" to
explore other nations and other cultures within the context of a school-
based, community-focused experience. In fact, the Overseas Project's contributions to teacher education have recently been recognized by the
American Association for Colleges of Teacher Education as the recipient of
AACTE's 2001 Best Practice Award for Global and International Teacher
Education.

In this chapter, we will use the Overseas Project and our student teachers'
own words as a springboard to share some of the insights we have gained
over the years regarding the multidimensional characteristics of international teaching.

STATESIDE PREPARATION

The Overseas Project participants undergo extensive preparation, spending the academic year prior to student teaching exploring the schools and

cultures of the placement sites to which they have applied. Obviously, these requirements serve to familiarize student teachers with the educational practices, cultural/national values, beliefs, and lifestyles they will likely encounter abroad. Such intensive study also allays many of the student teachers' worries about the "unknown," such as school organization, national curriculums, external examinations, religious and spiritual beliefs, social and political structures, and general cultural profiles. Finally, the preparation requires a significant commitment and discourages applicants who might view international student teaching as merely a justification to "see the world."

The preparatory phase sets a serious tone for the Overseas Project, and the breadth and depth of this year-long study are crucial. Before they embark on their overseas travel, we ask our student teachers to reflect upon their involvement in the project, describing the evolution of their thinking about their host nations, as well as their fears and concerns regarding their upcoming international experiences. Aaron, destined for the Scottish Highlands to teach English, wrote that prior to his Overseas Project participation, he understood the study of other cultures as a "fun and interesting pastime." He added:

I see it now through a critical and scholarly lens as well. Through reading Scottish literature, studying the social constructs of their system of education, and analyzing the complexity of Scottish heritage, I am now able to more completely understand those same complexities in my own culture as well as myself.

Shannon, who was preparing for placement in an Irish primary school, also recognized the importance of preparation when she wrote:

There are many things that I have learned about Ireland's culture, history, and people that will enable me to be an educated visitor in that country. I used to think it would be so easy to live in another country for two and a half months, but now I realize how unrealistic that is without taking part in the proper groundwork first.

Of course, no preparation can eliminate all pre-trip anxieties. The student teachers still express concerns about being far from family and friends, effectively teaching the pupils in host nation classrooms, sharing compatible educational philosophies with cooperating teachers, and getting along with host families. For Kristy, preparing to fulfill a dream of teaching in Australia, an added worry was "that the reality will never live up to my expectations." Yet, a sense of the empowerment that comes with new knowledge is reflected in the student teachers' essays. While recognizing that there will likely be bouts of homesickness and moments of feeling overwhelmed, most of the student teachers feel ready for the challenges awaiting them, believing that patience and open-mindedness will be keys to their success.

ARRIVING AND SETTLING IN

Throughout the year of preparatory work, project participants anticipate their dates of departure, and when that date finally arrives, many report feelings of unbridled enthusiasm. Kristina, upon arrival in Australia, was invigorated by her new environment, writing:

It even smells different here! It smells fresh and beautiful, and I never want to go home. It is only the second day, and I am ready to travel all over the world to explore other lands and other schools!

However, for a number of student teachers, the first few days in their host nation communities are marked by a rash of sudden fears and anxieties as they cope with culture shock, adjustment difficulties, and the realization that they are a long way from home. Joanna described her feelings in this way: "Before I came to Australia, I felt prepared and confident. Once my plane landed in Melbourne, all of that confidence slipped away. I was terrified!" *Homesick*, *scared*, *overwhelmed*, *nervous*, and *anxious* were words student teachers seemed to use most frequently in describing their first forty-eight hours in their overseas schools, homes, and communities.

Jeremy, overwhelmed by the differences he encountered in the remote Himalayan hill station where he was placed in India, reported that initially he was very frightened:

I am alone in a place halfway around the world. I have to make the best of it for seventy days or so. I am very glad that everyone is so nice, for if not for that, I would be more of a blubbering mess than I am now.

Suzanne, on the other hand, felt as though she was starting over in terms of her actual teaching in England, having just completed a highly successful ten-week student teaching assignment in Indiana:

Now I feel like I'm back at the beginning again. Instead of a confident teacher, I feel like a shy tagalong. I will be observing this week, so I hope to have the system figured out for next week when I start my own units. . . . In a way, this is all very unreal. It's a strange and empowering feeling to know I can get myself to another country on my own. I think much of the reality of **being** in this other country has not yet set in.

The preparatory phase that student teachers undergo at home provides a framework for understanding many of the school and cultural features they encounter abroad. Thus, the stage is set for the student teachers to become contributing, active members of their host nation schools, families, and communities, and to reap the rewards of an experience for which they have planned and prepared for such a long time.

ON-SITE INVOLVEMENT

The immersion component of the Overseas Project, like the preparatory phase, is structured to guide student teachers toward reflective and responsive experiences. While at their sites, project participants are expected to engage fully in all teacher-related functions of the school; foster friendships with community people and seek involvement in their activities; and submit written reports identifying local attitudes, cultural values, world and host nation issues, and personal and professional insights. The reports encourage student teachers to consult a variety of resources, including media and community members, while their assigned tasks require them to venture beyond the school grounds, to visit important cultural and historical sites, and to plan and perform service learning projects. For example, they have helped out in nursing homes and in the delivery of meals to the homebound, served as leaders for scout troops, provided adult literacy instruction, and assisted on village planning committees and at national wildlife parks. Through this assignment, student teachers like Kellard, who labored on a farm in rural Ireland, often find they can move beyond their "outsider" status and perspective. Kellard wrote:

I was privileged to work within a community not as some daring do-gooder, but as a member of that community. This allowed me to experience rather than just watch how the people of Ireland live, work, and enjoy their lives.

FEEDBACK FROM HOST NATION EDUCATORS

As U.S. teachers prepare for international work, it is essential that they keep in mind the perspectives of those foreign educators who will host them. The experience, after all, is only viable if there is an expectation of mutual benefit. Components of the Overseas Project are routinely honed in response to the professional concerns expressed by those host nation educators who have accepted U.S. student teachers into their schools in recent semesters. A recent survey mailed to educators in England, Scotland, the Republic of Ireland, and Australia explored their reasons for accepting U.S. student teachers, the benefits they perceived for school pupils in working with the student teachers, and the assets and adjustment/adaptation difficulties of the student teachers.

ACCEPTING U.S. TEACHERS

The thirty-six host nation educators who responded to the survey reported having accepted the U.S. student teachers into their classrooms and schools for a number of reasons, including cultural enrichment and exposure to U.S. teaching ideas and approaches. For example, this comment from a head teacher in England was representative of the hopes educators expressed for hosting U.S. student teachers: "We felt it would broaden the children's perspective and be useful for the staff also to learn of different viewpoints and methods from a different culture."

Several of the educators who believed their schools would benefit by accepting U.S. student teachers observed that "static staff situations" needed the fresh ideas and enthusiasm that the visitors brought with them. An Australian Year 1 teacher pointed out that "many hands are needed in my area," while a teacher of theater at another Australian school, in noting that the timing of the student teacher's arrival coincided with a Year 11 school production, wrote: "The chance to have new ideas and young, fresh input into the play was very attractive!"

BENEFITS TO SCHOOL PUPILS

Host nation educators identified a number of noteworthy benefits for their primary and secondary school pupils who interacted with the student teachers. Nearly half believed that one of the most important outcomes for the children was the "realistic, accurate information about the United States" that the student teachers imparted. Learning about contemporary U.S. lifestyles, customs, and values from an actual citizen helped the pupils separate the "bigger than life" impression of the U.S. conveyed by the media from the reality. Plus, as an Australian educator observed, the children "learned that Americans do not all live like or look like *Melrose Place* actors." A related benefit noted by foreign educators was that their pupils developed a "broadened world perspective through cultural exchange."

ASSETS

When asked to identify the greatest professional, personal, and social assets U.S. student teachers bring to the overseas setting, two-thirds of the host nation educators described personality factors, repeatedly using words such as *enthusiastic, positive, undemanding, confident, cooperative,* and *adaptable* to characterize the student teachers with whom they had interacted. Somewhat fewer educators believed that the student teachers' subject matter expertise was especially strong, although they did recognize their knowledge of the United States, experience with special education, and skill in planning and executing lessons. The observations of an Australian educator perhaps best represents the consensus:

I've had three U.S. student teachers to date, and all were excellent. They were very adaptable, undemanding, and fitted in well socially. Personal and social skills outweighed their professional capabilities at this stage, but they were all good trainee teachers. Keen to work, keen to do well, and keen to learn.

DIFFICULTIES

Still, the identification of adjustment or adaptation difficulties experienced by U.S. student teachers is important in fine-tuning the Overseas Project. In this survey, one-fourth of the foreign educators believed that the most significant difficulty for student teachers was adapting to new and different practices and demands in the classroom; respondents identified the implementation of a national curriculum, use of whole language teaching methods, and management of children representing a mix of ethnic and socioeconomic backgrounds as somewhat problematic. Other educators felt that the isolation of some host communities and the relative lack of social contact with other young people were difficult for the U.S. student teachers they hosted. The various other concerns they reported included:

- "language and speaking," involving differences in word meanings and accent;
- "coping with host families," which applied to both personality conflicts and differing expectations for the experience;
- "relations with school pupils," which most often referred to the student teacher being too informal in interactions with youth.

However, by far most of the adjustment and adaptation difficulties reported were neither insurmountable nor reflective of the majority of U.S. student teachers in overseas schools and communities, and over one-fifth of the host nation educators reported that their student teachers exhibited "no difficulties" or that they were "too minor to identify."

LEARNING OUTCOMES OF OVERSEAS TEACHING

Overseas experiences in host schools, communities, and families are rich sources for learning. Project participants gain important insights into educational practices and human relationships at several levels and make significant self-discoveries while navigating through their daily activities without the close guidance and support of "back home" family and friends. Much has been written over the years about outcomes of the Overseas Project, with the underlying theme being that most of these outcomes could not have been achieved had the student teachers simply remained at home and completed their student teaching assignments stateside.

SCHOOL OUTCOMES

Clearly, much of what is learned by U.S. educators abroad can be classified as professional development. The student teachers work to reconcile their experiences in overseas schools with what they have studied and witnessed in the United States. Working side-by-side with educators in Australia gave Mary Jo new insights into schooling and her role as a future high school teacher:

I never realized how narrow-minded I had become about education. I always assumed that all schools had to run in a similar fashion. Now, I have many new ideas and different opinions on education. I said just the other day that I cannot imagine stopping my preservice training after student teaching in Indiana. I have learned so much more in these past two months than I ever could have in a lifetime.

Similarly, Emily reported that student teaching in England "enabled me to add to and redefine my teaching methods and philosophies," an outcome she felt was especially significant prior to acquiring her own language arts classroom as a certified teacher. The specific areas of professional learning identified by the student teachers as increasing through project participation are:

• knowledge of curriculum and assessment,
• application of general teaching methods,
• acquisition of new lesson and unit plan ideas,
• experience with thematic and integrated teaching approaches,
• creative use of often limited instructional materials and resources,
• enhancement of classroom management and discipline strategies, and
• better understanding of relationships with teachers, pupils, administrators, and parents.

Sometimes years after students have participated in the Overseas Project, we discover that many are continuing to apply these and other professional learning outcomes to their elementary and secondary classrooms across the United States. For example, Jodi, who now teaches secondary English in rural Georgia, recently communicated:

I use things that I learned in England in my classroom all of the time. I just finished Great Expectations in my 9th grade lit/comp. class. These Georgia farming community students have no idea what Pip's village might have looked like. I got out all of the photos, posters, and keepsakes and did a whole England Day. I have done that with EVERY group of students I have had since I got back! I vowed that I would always share my experience. I also really use the type of portfolio assessment they use in England. It seems much more fair to me. So, the entire way I give assignments and mark them was learned there. I could go on and on.

COMMUNITY OUTCOMES

As with host nation schools, the communities in which project participants are placed serve as rich sources for learning. Through their specific roles in the community—as a member of the local host family, or as a contributor in the service learning projects described earlier—project participants demonstrate a commitment to understanding the lifestyles of people in their host nations. In reflecting on their service learning activities, for instance, participants reported important gains, such as a greater understanding and appreciation of other people's lives, a greater awareness of their own strengths and weaknesses, as well as a sense of belonging within their host communities—all things that cannot be learned in a classroom. Wendy, who student taught in India, assisted in administering polio vaccination drops to hundreds of children under the age of five outside of a Hindu temple:

When you are walking in the streets of India, you can easily cross the street, ignore, or choose not to interact with the beggars, the sick, and the homeless, but on this day I was in constant interaction with them. . . . This activity reaffirmed my opinion that the people of [this community] are some of the friendliest people I have ever met.

The acceptance Wendy felt by both her fellow volunteers and the mothers who brought their children for the vaccinations, and her ability to communicate with the mothers and children through smiles, gestures, touch, and other expressions and body language, left lasting impressions on Wendy and made her service project especially meaningful.

PERSONAL OUTCOMES

Finally, living and teaching overseas enables the student teachers to make important self-discoveries and to grow in significant personal ways. Most report that their self-confidence and independence increase exponentially and that they possess inner resources they never knew existed. Some also come face-to-face with less desirable personal traits, such as an overreliance on family and friends, a tendency to talk rather than listen, and difficulty adapting to the life outside of their "comfort zones."

Krista, for example, found her personal insights to constitute the most important set of learning outcomes she achieved during her overseas student teaching:

Teaching in England was an opportunity to explore myself through quiet reflection. My host family was wonderful and my network of friends was always encouraging, but in the end, I had to rely on myself. I had to teach the foreign material. I had to board the train all by myself, and I had to manage my budget. I gained light years in self-confidence and independence. I had to fend for myself while in England, and now I know that I can handle any situation presented to me in the future. Gaining this kind of trust and self-esteem can't be bought or sold—only earned. Teaching in England gave me the opportunity to earn it.

Christy poignantly described the personal meaning she attributed to her teaching and living experiences in Australia:

As strange as it sounds, I truly understand what someone means when they say that you have to lose yourself to find yourself. I have never felt as lost and alone as I did my first couple of weeks here. All I was thinking was, what was I doing here. All my life I have wanted to travel and learn about other cultures. Then I got here and I couldn't imagine why I ever thought it would be so fantastic. I felt ripped off, really.

Now, I am beginning to understand why those first couple of weeks were so hard. I brought my old, tattered attitude with me to this new, beautiful land. It nearly destroyed me. I cried, I got sick, and I was ready to leave, but now I can see so much more clearly why I am meant to be here. This is all happening for a reason, and I know it holds great significance in my life, now and in the years ahead.

I can feel peace like I have never experienced before. I truly know what it means to be relaxed and to simply enjoy being with people. I have found a part of me, here in Australia, that I have never known before. Isn't it funny that it has taken me this long to find the answer? I never would have guessed that this trip held the key. Strange, an American finding herself in Australia.

CONCLUSION

At the conclusion of her student teaching assignment in India, where initially the cultural differences are so striking, Wendy reflected on the many things she had learned:

I have learned new methods of teaching and have learned so many other things since I've been here, such as yoga, sitar, Hindi, needlework, etc. It has also given me a chance to realize that there are so many similarities between us and Indians. Every day someone says to me, "You don't seem like a foreigner, you seem like one of us." Being here has shown me that people are basically the same wherever you go.

In discovering that human beings the world over share many of the same dreams, fears, and aspirations for themselves and their families, the idea of membership in a global community becomes easier to understand. Indeed, Cathy described her student teaching experience in Australia as "looking beyond my narrow tunnel of life to a life that is more globally aware."

Clearly, international teaching experiences make a significant impact on those with whom the teachers interact on a daily basis—the elementary and secondary school pupils, teaching colleagues, and administrators who open their school doors and lives to the visitor from abroad. Even more certainly, however, the experiences greatly impact the professional and personal lives of those U.S. educators who actively seek new challenges abroad with an open mind and reflective spirit. Wendy, Cathy, and their counter-parts in the Overseas Project are on their way to cultivating that global perspective which is vital for teachers in today's increasingly interrelated world. Reflecting on his work in Scotland, Andrew wrote: "In an age when globalization demands increased tolerance, overseas teaching ensures that the teachers who will shape our kids' futures have first-hand experience with cross-cultural relationships." Working in another country—whether for a handful of weeks, as the student teachers described here have done, or for a year or longer of contractual teaching—enables educators to de-velop the skills, insights, and knowledge needed to be effective, "world-minded" teachers in U.S. classrooms and beyond.

Recruiting for a Global Society: Teaching Internationally Through Queen's University, Faculty of Education
Alan Travers

Working with students and staff from forty-six different nationalities certainly has its share of challenges, but my time here has been an extremely interesting and rewarding experience. Working in an inter-national educational setting has been one which I feel will enrich my future teaching experiences.

—L. B., Kampala, Uganda

It is really quite amazing to see how many different languages are spo-ken on the playground and how children playing soccer on the field try to negotiate rules though they don't speak the same language.

—G. F., Budapest, Hungary

I never anticipated the "where the hell am I?" effect . . . but having lived in Turkey for a number of months, everything began to seem "normal." Horse carts, the call to prayer, the dust, the five men riding on a single moped, the incredible service in restaurants, the Roman relics being used as flowerpot stands in the garden . . . these are part of everyday life.

—F. V., Tarsus, Turkey

These three testimonials illustrate not only the range of exciting and en-riching opportunities involved with overseas teaching, but also the success of a Teachers' Overseas Recruiting Fair, which is the centrepiece of an effort by Queen's University's Faculty of Education and its placement office to enhance the international experiences of education students and faculty. International recruiting fairs are held in many parts of the world, but for eight years the Queen's University fair in Kingston was the only one in Canada. Now one of three in the country and the only one that is a

university-sponsored event, the Queen's Recruiting Fair attracts schools
from around the world to Queen's each year to recruit both inexperienced
and experienced teachers for teaching overseas. Thus far, recruiters from
about 125 schools representing almost sixty countries in Latin America,
the Middle East, and Asia, and to a lesser extent, Europe and Africa, have
attended. Through the Recruiting Fair and other ongoing placement office
activities, Queen's B.Ed. graduates have secured teaching positions in over
ninety countries in recent years. This initiative has also led to the creation
of other programs, namely an International and Development Education
program at the undergraduate and graduate levels.

DESCRIPTION OF THE INITIATIVE

In 1986, administrators from two international schools in Columbia approached the Placement Office of the Faculty of Education at Queen's.
Based on the quality of two Queen's graduates hired in 1984, they expressed an interest in recruiting at Queen's as an expansion of their usual
recruitment itinerary in the United States. Our faculty placement coordinator brought interested education students and the recruiters together; the
students found new challenges, both personal and professional, and the
recruiters filled their staffing needs. The overseas schools were soon impressed by the quality of the new graduates they were finding at Queen's
and word began to spread. One such exemplary teacher, L. B., who taught
in Nairobi, Kenya, was even asked to offer professional development to
her colleagues: "I love teaching and have felt a lot of support for my approaches and ideas—to the point where I'll be leading a workshop at the
East Africa International Schools Conference in October. So there is space
for professional and personal experience," she reports. Between six to eight
graduates who return from successful international positions to teach in
Canada also return to Queen's on the Fair weekend as part of a twenty-
five-member planning committee to assist and advise the new applicants.

In February 2002, the 14th annual Teachers' Overseas Recruiting Fair
was held at Queen's with eighty representatives from fifty-two schools
drawn from nearly thirty-three countries. The nature of these schools varies, but most provide an English language curriculum across the grades.
They may have an international mix of students or a student body entirely
from the host country. The teaching staffs of the schools are often a blend
of host country and import teachers. Some schools are large; others are
small. Most undergo rigorous screening in order to secure accreditation in
the United States, Great Britain, Canada, or with the International Baccalaureate Organization.

FEEDBACK FROM APPLICANTS AND SCHOOL ADMINISTRATORS

Reactions to the recent Recruiting Fair were very positive and covered a wide spectrum of topics. Cynthia Murnaghan reported that "the entire weekend was a big learning experience for [her] and one that has whetted [her] appetite even more to go overseas. It was wonderful to meet so many enthusiastic educators from all parts of the globe." Lisa and Philip Bistret-zan echoed these sentiments: "We learned so much about other countries and cultures, and we met many people who shared our sense of adventure and openness to new experiences." In addition to the teachers, whether they are new graduates or seasoned educators who facilitate and benefit from this exciting atmosphere, the school representatives are equally positive. "I was impressed with the organization, the staffing, the candidates, the setting. But most of all, I was thoroughly impressed by the tone and spirit that the Queen's team brings to it all," said John Chandler, director of The Koc School in Istanbul, Turkey. The president of Ibn Khuldoon National School, Bahrain, Samir Chammaa, was also present, and he noted that "through its Recruiting Fair, Queen's University is providing an immense service to international schools and to young Canadian teachers."

Many of the teachers hired, by design, are those with limited teaching experience, the recent graduates of our teacher education program. Based on initial data from a survey underway, most of these young teachers work overseas for two to five years, and then return with their multicultural, multiethnic experiences to enrich the lives of Canadian children. The Fair itself reflects Queen's stated objectives to make itself into an institution that reflects the world around us.

The initiative has met its original objectives but goals continue to change as new elements are added to the original program. The original objective of providing graduates with teaching places is documented annually by the placement office. Since the mid-1980s approximately 1,200 Bachelor of Education graduates have secured their first teaching positions in overseas schools. A comparable number of experienced teachers from across Canada have also been placed over the same time period, attesting to the strength of the Queen's program.

IMPACT AND RELATED INNOVATIONS

Several initiatives have come out of this continuing activity. An innovative teacher preparation "program focus" for International and Development Education, including an optional overseas practicum, is now part of the undergraduate teacher education at Queen's. In addition, a travel fellowship program for both students and faculty complements and expands the effort. In all these programs, the overall goal is to provide Canadian teachers with an international perspective to broaden and deepen our understanding of who and where we are. M. R., who teaches in Bahrain, attests to the broader outlook he has gained: "Bahrain feels like another planet sometimes, especially during Ramadan, the month of purifying the soul, thus bringing the true Moslem closer to God. The locals take this religious time very seriously, even those who are not strict Moslems . . . [my] thoughts of Canada are distant," he adds, emphasizing the cultural education he is receiving. And although he feels far from home, his feelings are definitely relevant to Canadian society and its increasingly multicultural character. Another teacher, whose international experience will develop her sense of who and where she is, whether in Canada or Seoul, Korea, says: "We live in a sea of Asian faces. I wanted to know what it was like to be a racial minority. Now I know." Individuals and the faculty at Queen's, then, are truly achieving insight in internationalization in so many ways.

Their course work and teaching practice in the International and Development Education program reflect their desires to understand and often participate in educational experiences outside the boundaries of Canada. This drive is exemplified by H.R., a teacher in Shanghai who says: "We are still going twice a week for our Chinese lessons at Fudan University and learning a lot. We have had many incredible experiences with taxi drivers who love to talk, practice their English, and help us with our Chinese. We get to know everyday Chinese and their lives." Teachers are encouraged to actually participate in the culture, such as taking language classes. In addition to contributing to the international education community, it is a program objective for teachers to return and integrate their insights into Canadian classrooms. D. A.'s exploration of Syrian culture, for example, would be excellent material for cross-curriculum study, including a look at North American perspectives. "Last weekend I saw a ballet in a Roman amphitheatre which was at least 1,500 years old. The next day I was riding in a U.N. armoured personnel carrier in the Golan Heights," he says enthusiastically. The potential for enrichment across the curriculum, and, indeed, across the globe, abounds when personal experience is involved. For those students who enroll in this International and Development Education program, who are seeking both the practice and the theory behind the kind of experience teachers such as D. A. are having, there are two focus sections of twenty-five participants, comprising nearly 10 percent of each year's graduating class. The program focus is normally taught by one faculty member with a continuing involvement in the Recruiting Fair, and by two graduate students with international teaching experience. The instructional team is supported by the Faculty's placement coordinator who has visited over fifty overseas schools.

An Alternative Practicum during the second semester is designed to encourage current students to experience teaching in another context. Approximately 100 students in 2002 took advantage of this opportunity to teach in overseas schools. The overseas practicum is an option for all students, but some who have sought out Queen's for its international expertise choose to broaden their academic and cultural awareness through participation in both the International program focus and the overseas practicum.

Complementing and extending this program is an international travel fellowship program for students (who qualify for financial assistance) and faculty to enrich their experiences. The fellowship facilitates the creation of new types of practica. Some students volunteer to help at aid agencies; others work at schools where help and expertise are desperately needed; still others do more traditional practica at overseas schools with educational systems different from our own. The Faculty of Education supports students and teachers in overseas schools through Professional Development International, a program by which Queen's faculty members engage in on-site development. Inspired by these visits, in addition to their own insights and experiences, some graduates choose to return to the Faculty for graduate work at both the master and doctoral levels. They come to research and reflect and learn about their experiences and to prepare for the next teaching challenges. J. L., for example, a graduate who has been teaching for three years in Graz, Austria, "believes [he] has a lot of valuable knowledge and ideas to share with soon-to-be teachers." He adds: "I want to teach, but at a different level. I need to study education further, including culture and education, which needs more development as a course of study."

CONCLUSION

With Queen's graduates teaching in English-speaking schools in Brazil, Egypt, Portugal, Germany, Trinidad, and Spain, to name just a few of the more than fifty schools now participating in Canada's oldest international Recruiting Fair, Queen's University has defined itself as a national university with an international reach and perspective. More importantly, however, beyond the limits of school or national reputations, Queen's faculty and alumni are contributing to an important education community that is diversifying, growing, and improving with every new teacher that decides to prepare and apply for employment overseas. The criteria for applicants to consider, whether entering the undergraduate International and Development Education program focus or the Recruiting Fair is at once complex and very simple. C. M., whose experience lies in Laos, Vietnam, states the criteria succinctly and personally: "In my kindergarten class this year I had eighteen students from twelve different countries. Laos is truly a unique country and requires special and unique, or perhaps better yet—just open-minded individuals to teach there." As a result of international placements for student teaching and full-time teaching, Canadian teachers have the opportunity to develop new professional skills, new language skills, greater cultural awareness, and increased tolerance. These assets, as well as the opportunity to share them when mentoring others, builds the capacity of our teachers and our citizens to operate effectively and compassionately in a global arena.

Appendix C

Contributors' Review

Contributors were asked to comment on the following topics to provide additional insight on the overseas teaching environment.

1. The names of the institutions where they taught
2. How they found their positions
3. How they were compensated
4. How they prepared personally
5. What is a favorite memory about the experience

JERI HURD

1. Bilkent International School, Turkey.
2. I found the position through International Schools Services, but Bilkent International School, now hires almost exclusively through Search and Carney-Sandoe. Search is generally considered to be of better quality than ISS/ECIS because they screen both applicants and schools and limit the size of their job fairs.
3. Compensation: Without being specific about dollar amounts, Bilkent International School pays on the higher end for Turkish schools, and includes apartments, health insurance, and biannual flights home. It also offers an excellent orientation program, one of the best on the international circuit, from what I've heard. Salaries are tied to the U.S. dollar, so are relatively unaffected by the rampant inflation in Turkey. In general, a childless couple could probably save one salary and live on the other.

4. Other than required vaccinations and reading up on the country, my personal preparations were relatively limited.

5. Favorite memory: I was chaperoning a seventh grade field trip to Cappadoccia, and was having the kids write a story about life as a Hittite. One of the students couldn't think of a name and decided to name his character "Bob." His room-mates and I howled with laughter when he told us this. Poor Gokhan! We still talk about Bob the Hittite! (Probably one of those "you had to be there" sto-ries)—or—My third day teaching, the British Deputy Director's eighth grade daughter commented in class: "I need a rubber!" I picked my jaw up from the floor and started scolding her, only to be told that in *real* English, a rubber is an eraser!

KEN LOCKETTE

1. The Almaty International School, Kazakstan.

2. I found the position through a job fair sponsored by International Schools Serv-ices.

3. Compensation: Base salary around $25,500, $4,000 COLA, $2,000 end-of-year bonus, initial $900 shipping allowance ($500 each year after two years), TieCare Insurance (major medical, $2,000 deductible), apartment, and flights to and from home each summer are provided.

4. My personal preparations were few: My wife and I were part of the first Peace Corps group in Kazakhstan (1993–1995), so we knew what to expect when we returned in 1997. If anything, we brought too much, for product availability was much better after two years.

5. Most of my favorite memories of Kazakhstan come from my Peace Corps stint in Karaganda, Kazakhstan, a depressed mining town in the center of the country. For a favorite memory with my current position, it is difficult to pin down one instance. The best part of my job is the relationship that I have with my students here, relationships that would not occur in a public school setting back in the states. In Almaty everything is much more informal. The secondary students spend the night at school for our get-to-know-each-other Lock-in and hike, and we take annual excursions to other countries.

MIKE KIELKOPF

1. American Community School of Abu Dhabi, United Arab Emirates.

2. I was hired at the recruiting fair of the University of Northern Iowa, Cedar Falls/Waterloo.

3. Compensation: Salary is about $35,000 with no local UAE taxes or no USA tax liability; a furnished three-bath, three-bedroom older villa two blocks from school is paid for by the school; the school also pays local phone bill, all utilities, and all villa maintenance. The school provides health and minimal dental cov-erage through TIE Care. Children are also covered at no expense to the teacher. The school also pays for a round-trip flight to the U.S. for all overseas teachers and all members of their immediate family.

4. Our amount of preparation was considerable. My wife, Mary, an elementary specialist, spent almost one year researching international schools and the living conditions in a variety of countries, gathering all the paperwork, obtaining passports, visas, work permits, and so on. We went to the recruiting fair with a preliminary list of Top Ten schools. The American Community School of Abu Dhabi was *not* on that list. In fact, it was on a short list of Middle Eastern schools that we had ruled out prior to the fair. Now in our sixth year here, we don't think we could have made a better choice.

5. By the very nature of the international school situation, favorite memories abound. But there is no doubt that it's the people that make the difference. My favorite memory, then, will be of all the great people I've met: students, faculty, and staff, people from more than fifty nations, many of whom we hope will be friends for the rest of our lives.

VERNON OLSON

1. Due to the nature of the article, I would prefer not to specifically identify the school. I have taught at a number of academic institutions in the Middle East, including the American International School in Egypt.

2. I found the position through a friend who had studied and worked in the United States and then moved back to Lebanon. He made all of the arrangements before I traveled.

3. The compensation package sounds modest, but this was at an earlier time, when costs, especially in Lebanon, were cheap. I believe that I received $100 a month plus a room, meals, and laundry. There was no health insurance. This sounds like a compensation package geared more for a Peace Corps candidate than a teacher, but my needs were met.

4. Preparation of the academic type was minimal. One reason why I worked there was because I had not had any formal teacher preparation in college, only a liberal arts program and some graduate work in social work. Later, I went back to college to get a degree and certification in elementary education.

5. My favorite memory involves the utter energy of the Lebanese. Having come from a somewhat restrained culture in Minneapolis, I was not used to the explosion of activity and interaction of the people. The quiet, reserved Scandinavian temperament of a Minnesotan found the craziness, the color, the humor, and the lack of emotional reserve utterly exhilarating.

TREVOR DODMAN

1. Name of school: ESL Japan (since the school is now defunct, I won't bother to include the contact info!!). The school was located in the city of Hanyti, Japan.

2. How did I find out about ESL Japan? A university acquaintance who had previously taught at ESL Japan helped us to make the initial contacts and arrangements with the owners of the school.

3. My compensation included the following items: Monthly salary was 250,000 yen (I'm certain that the yen figure is correct, but I'm not sure what the exchange

rate was at the time. It seems to me that in 1997, 100 yen was roughly $1.00 Canadian, but I can't be sure!), health insurance, subsidized rent for a nicely furnished and spacious apartment, and plane tickets to and from Japan.

4. My preparation was limited: Aside from securing visa paperwork at the Japanese consulate in Toronto, I simply planned what clothes to bring.

5. A favourite memory is difficult to pinpoint, as there are so many. The very first time my boss invited us to his house for a traditional Japanese dinner with his family will always be special to me. It was the day after we arrived, and Amy and I were both severely jet-lagged. We spoke no Japanese and had never eaten any Japanese foods before. As we rode our bicycles to his house that evening, we could only marvel at the complex mix of profound excitement and sheer terror that we were feeling. Needless to say, the dinner was a delicious adventure, filled with laughter and chopsticks tutorials. Inviting and warm, our Japanese hosts welcomed us into their home with enthusiasm, grace, and a genuine interest in building new international friendships—an altogether invigorating introduction to the Japanese way of life!

MICHELE E. GORDON

1. Zhaotong Teachers' College, Zhaotong City, Yunnan Province, China.

2. The Canadian Voluntary Service Overseas (VSO) placed me. I found VSO through personal contacts as well as through addresses in the two books mentioned in the article.

3. The compensation included the following items: I was provided with a fully furnished apartment, and paid no rent or utilities. The apartment had a television, telephone (after six months), washing machine, refrigerator, and hot water heater, most of which was required in the VSO contract. I received 1,200 yuan (US$145) a month the first year, and 1,500 yuan (US$180) a month the second year, as well as periodic but irregular bonuses for things such as Women's Day and the Start of Spring. I also received a Mid-Service Grant of US$500, after completing my first year and agreeing to continue, as well as an End of Service Grant of about $2,200 (it was converted from British pounds). VSO also wired in Canadian $600 per quarter (about $130 to $140 per month) to my American bank account to be used for any ongoing expenses, such as mortgage or loan payments. This has, however, been reduced, with volunteers now needing to demonstrate that they need the money before they will get such a large amount. Normal wire amount is something like Canadian $250 per quarter, with the possibility of increasing it according to the volunteer's situation. I also had full health insurance and evacuation insurance while serving my two years, and it continued for three months after returning to the U.S.

4. For preparation I read as much as I could and watched as many films as I could about China. I talked to many people who had been there to find out what life was like for foreigners and English teachers. VSO also arranged a four-day weekend to prepare volunteers for departure, as well as a week-long China-focused training just before departing. I had been overseas many times before,

but China was vastly different from any country I had been to, and even though I felt I had done a lot of preparation, upon arrival, I felt I had much to learn.

5. I have so many positive images and memories about my two years in China that it is hard to pick just one. Without any hesitation, I can say that the people were the highlight of my time there. They were friendly, helpful, inquisitive, generous, and displayed a beautiful innocence of life that one rarely sees among young adults in the West. One very clear memory is of a student, Victoria, with whom I was very close. She often came to visit me, and on one particular occasion, she knocked on the door around dinnertime. When I answered, she proceeded to go into my kitchen, take out all of my food, and prepare a wonderful feast for us. Over dinner, we discussed my "double-folded upper eyelids," which are different from hers and other Chinese. She also told me that when I first arrived, she had been afraid of me, but once she knew me better, she viewed me in the same light as other Chinese!

JOHN A. HANSEN

1. Escuela de las Americas, El Tigre, Venezuela.

2. I found this position by registering with the International Educators Cooperative, an advertisement that I found in the back of *The International Educator*, a quarterly newspaper.

3. For compensation in my first year I was paid $1,100 a month, an additional $1,100 Christmas bonus and a $2,200 bonus at the end of the year. A travel allowance of $1,500 was given as well. The second year, compensation included a $1,200 travel allowance and a salary of $1,500 a month with a 10 percent bonus at Christmas and a 12 percent bonus on completion of the contracted tenth month.

4. For preparation I read about current travel conditions, safety, and health concerns at the United States State Department website, http://www.state.gov/www/services.html. I received vaccinations for yellow fever, typhoid, and hepatitis B and C. Malaria was not considered a problem, however, I did bring a two-month supply of malaria pills just in case I wanted to travel to other countries.

5. My favorite memories involve the natural world. As a natural scientist, being exposed to a new region on planet Earth was wonderful. Our school was located in the Savannah of the central region of Venezuela called Los Llanos, the great plains. The plains are a beautiful region of Venezuela. Every moment of every day the wind is alive as there are no hills, mountains, or stands of tall trees to quell this breath of living Earth. I had only one responsibility that came with my role as the school's science teacher—teach the students science. Dwarfed by the tall grass, our two student biology classes would go for walks in our "Living Laboratory," as we set up experiments, collected data, or identified some of the native terrestrial orchids in the region. Students in the school came from around the globe and they brought with them their stories and observations from their native lands. We began our exploration of science with the few books in the library and our class text, laying a basic foundation for scientific inquiry. During

a visit to Caracas I happened to meet one of the curators of the National Science Museum. As a fellow scientist, we quickly became friends, and when I told him of my difficulties finding regional maps of Venezuela's climate, fault lines, minerals, etc., he invited me into their private library and gave me carte blanche of the seemingly limitless resources.

The limit of resources in the classroom, however, was an opportunity in disguise. Students brought in books from home in a variety of languages. Locals provided identification keys and traditional knowledge about plant and animal use in their culture. We would collect rock and mineral samples whenever an excursion sent students into various regions of the countries. And we would bring back our stories and sketches of geographic features, biodiversity, and weather patterns to the class. This was science. Our small groups would explore, collect, and identify folklore from facts, draw conclusions, and assimilate new elements into our existing model of Earth and its systems. Questions bloomed regularly from this rich foliage of discussions and scientific inquiry. Students not only learned science but they also learned how to approach the world as their laboratory.

EVAN M. SMITH

1. Escuela de las Americas/Colegio Internacional de Anzoategui.

2. I found the position through the Queen's University Placement Coordinator. A fax was sent to him by the E.L.A. principal.

3. The compensation included a $1,200 travel allowance and a salary of $15,000 with a 10 percent bonus at Christmas and a 12 percent bonus on completion of the contracted tenth and final month. The form of payment was negotiated. Cheques in U.S. funds were sent home while a certain percentage was issued in a cheque of Venezuelan bolivares. That cheque could then be cashed at a nearby bank—usually involving a one- to two-hour wait.

4. For preparation I visited a doctor two months before departure to learn about and receive the required vaccinations. Yellow fever, typhoid, and hepatitus B were all necessary. Malaria was not required, even in the jungles near the Brazilian border.

5. One of my favourite memories involves Nicholas, an ADD student in grade five. Intellectually, he could have and should have been in grade six or seven. He frequently lifted his head from the story he and the five other grade fives were reading to answer questions I was asking the grade six students on the other side of the room. "Nicholas, thank you, but do your own work please," I said sternly. You couldn't ignore Nicholas. His voice was distinctive—reminiscent of Owen Meaney's, if you've read the John Irving bestseller: loud, strident, with a nasal quality and the impression that he had too much saliva in his mouth. He was one of the few Venezuelans among many Argentines at the school, but his English was one of the best.

The ADD caused not only excessive swinging of his legs, which usually involved kicking the desk in front of him, but also an exuberant rearing up on his haunches. He'd kneel on his seat, blocking the view of those behind him, and lean over the desk. That way, his answers were as loud as they could be and were always directed at your face. He usually needed a "time-out" in the hall at least twice a day.

Although I feel a simple description of Nicholas suffices as one of my favourite memories, I will provide one event that I won't forget. His notes were a mess, loose and scrunched at the bottom of his bag. A fancy new school suitcase on wheels with a handle at least kept the whole mess in one place. His creative insight, however, as with his comprehension, was wonderful.

One day, after the bell had gone, I drifted over to the science teacher's (John Hansen's) classroom. The back table was being used to display cells made out of everything from cake and candies to cloth and buttons. And then my eyes fell on a large aluminum plate, messy with scrunched-up bits of paper stuck to it. Noticing my smile, John said, "That's Nicholas's model. The thing is," he said after we laughed, "is that he has all the required parts here. It's perfect." I was proud of Nicholas, and I wondered if any of that paper had on it a grammar lesson or comprehension questions.

SHIRLEY HOOPER

1. First, I was a Peace Corps volunteer in Northern Peru and a trainer for two groups of volunteers: one which was placed in Peru and the other which was placed in Paraguay. I have taught for the following institutions: Anion Corporation (mining camp, Slidell, Chile), British School of Rio de Janeiro, British Cultural Institute, Rio De Janeiro, Colegio San Carlos (Benedictine school run by North American monks in Bogota, Colombia), Colegio Nueva Granada (American school in Bogota), Escuela Americana (San Salvador, El Salvador), and Colegio Americana de Torreon (Torreon, Mexico).

2. The first three jobs above I obtained while backpacking my way around South America after my Peace Corps experience. Both jobs in Colombia I obtained because my husband received job offers there. The big drawback to this method of employment is that I received only local salary with no benefits as I was considered a walk-in off the street. The job in El Salvador was the first and only one I got through an employment agency: ISS. After my husband died in El Salvador, I found this job in Torreon through friends so that I could be closer to the states to visit my sons in college.

3. Compensation varied from school to school and year to year. My job in El Salvador and here in Torreon pay more than double a local salary and half the salary is in a dollar check once a month for ten months. I received about $17,000 in El Salvador, but I understand they pay better now. I was there from 1990–1994. Here in Torreon I teach two classes (tenth grade English) and am the Curriculum Coordinator K-12 so I get about $22,000. For the previous two years I was the coordinator but didn't have to teach and had the same salary. The school believes it has fallen on hard times and has made various changes, none of which have helped improve the morale of the teaching staff. I have been here since the 1994–1995 school year. I get medical insurance (a Mexican company) and a round-trip ticket home yearly (after having completed the original two-year contract). I also received a master's degree in Educational Leadership from the University of Alabama. I received it while working for Colegio Nueva

Granada. This was a big plus as it was quite cheap, with some of the courses being paid for by a State Department grant. For a couple of years I coordinated the program for Colombia and received my courses free from the university. Another important benefit was the education of both my children and the opportunity for them to become proficient in Spanish as they were in regular Spanish classes with native speakers from the time they were in grade school.

5. Some favorite memories (even the bad ones become good with time): living within sight of Aconcagua Mountain in Chile, being scared out of the sea in Northern Peru by sharks (I was told they were only sand sharks, but I wasn't about to verify it), seeing the sunrise at Macchu Pichu, traveling from Manaos on the Amazon to Rio Prieto to Central Brasil, visiting a cloud forest in El Salvador, riding trains nearly everywhere, getting married in a civil ceremony on a Saturday morning along with sixty other couples in Rio, watching a tree sloth, hitchhiking in the Patagonia, standing on steaming volcanoes, having friends and acquaintances strung all over the continent, realizing how fortunate I am. Torreon is located in the north of Mexico in the desert. It is not an attractive city partly because it is only about 100 years old. When it cools down I've taken up fossil hunting and enjoy being out-of-doors with my dog. I also like visiting with my Mexican neighbors and traveling in this gorgeous, interesting country. Things are pretty slow here by states' standards, and I guess they're pretty disorganized but that keeps me alert. Something unexpected is always happening. I've seriously considered moving on next year, but I would still like to be able to visit my sons in Tucson so I'm kind of limited. Perhaps I'll head back to the states to work on a principal's certification.

ELIZABETH WIGFUL

1. I taught at Outapi Senior Secondary School in Ombalantu, Namibia.

2. I was matched to the position by Voluntary Service Overseas Canada (for whom I now work as a program officer). I applied to VSO, was selected after an assessment day, and was matched to the job before attending training for about ten days. I was able to say no to the job if I didn't feel it suited me, but I felt it was perfect and did so throughout my placement.

3. For compensation I was paid a local salary by my Namibian employer (the Ministry of Education), and I received a small amount of money at home at the same time. On leaving my job, I received a resettlement grant of a few thousand dollars (Canadian). My accommodation was provided by the school, as was electricity and water. I shared a house with two other teachers. We each had our own room and shared a kitchen, bathroom (with running water), and a living room. We had a large yard that we used for gardening and hanging out in. We lived across the road from the school, which is a boarding school. Health insurance was paid by VSO but didn't cover eyeglasses or dental checkups, just emergency dental treatment. All medical treatment, including prescriptions, was covered by VSO.

4. I prepared by asking lots of questions of people who had worked as volunteers overseas before, especially in the Southern African region. I read books about

Namibia. I attended VSO training. I saved some money so that I could travel far during my holidays! I read VSO literature about similar placements in Namibia. (I was the first VSO volunteer to go to my school.) I made sure that I got my vaccinations.

5. Favourite memory? How can I pick one? I guess one of my favourite memories was the day sixty-five students crowded into my classroom for one of my additional classes at 7 A.M., just so they could practice their listening skills in English. They were so keen and motivated. It was very inspiring. Another memory (or serial memory, I guess) is of my students singing in English on a Friday afternoon. They loved to sing and with such joy! I taught them lots of songs in English and found them to be a great teaching tool.

KAREN NEWMAN

1. I was offered placement by the Austrian Ministry of Education as an English teaching assistant at GRG 23, Bundesgymnasium/Bundesealgymnasium Alt Erlaa, in Vienna's 23rd district.

2. The Fulbright Commission assists in the application process and placement of American teaching assistants throughout Austria and other countries. Complete information may be obtained from the Fulbright Website at: http://www.iie.org/fulbright/

3. My salary for the 1997–1998 school year was ATS 15,073 per month (approximately US $1,200), minus an 18 percent deduction for mandatory social security, which included full health insurance coverage. This was enough for one person to live comfortably, if not spartanly, in Vienna, Austria's pricey capital. The first salary payment did not occur until six weeks after arrival, so it was necessary to bring adequate funds to cover this initial adjustment period. Finding accommodations is the responsibility of each teaching assistant, as the Austrian Ministry of Education does not assist in housing placement. However, the Fulbright Commission in Vienna does, occasionally, have leads on vacant rooms and apartments for American exchange students and teachers. I was quite fortunate to rent a small, furnished apartment from a teacher at my school.

4. The teaching assistant program requires proof of having completed a B.A. degree before participation. It is also necessary to complete a health exam and obtain a visa for Austria prior to departure from the US. Since I was enrolled in a doctoral program, I needed to obtain permission from my advisors to take a one-year leave of absence to supplement my professional preparation as a language teacher. My parents agreed to care for my cat and look after my car in my absence. Prior to departure, I put my personal belongings in a storage shed, which I rented for US $65 a month, and paid in full for 10 months. While my belongings did not sustain any damage, upon my return, all clothing required a thorough washing and all books needed an airing out.

5. A colorful mosaic of memories characterizes my year of teaching in Vienna. The continual support of teaching colleagues and school staff, along with students' level of maturity and enthusiasm for learning and speaking English, deserve particular recognition here.

ROSS LAING

1. Morley Senior High School, Dianella, Perth, Western Australia.

2. International Teaching Exchange Program, Ministry of Education, Ontario. The Ministry of Education no longer provides this service.

3. For compensation I maintained my salary, benefits, etc., and was paid from my local school board in Canada. Regarding accommodations, each partner in the teaching exchange also exchanged homes and two cars from each household. Mutual agreements were reached regarding care of the homes, and servicing schedules and kilometer usage for each of the cars. Cars are extremely expensive in Australia, and while the exchange of cars is not usually recommended, our experience was positive. These agreements were put in writing and signed by both parties. While our agreements may not have held up in court, I thoroughly recommend some type of formal agreement. There are too many stories of exchanges gone seriously wrong.

4. My preparations were considerable. Preparations had to be made for medical examinations and for numerous legal requirements, such as wills, power of attorney, banking instructions, and insurance waivers. In addition, there were visa requirements to be met and strict deadlines for the paperwork. There was also a minefield of Revenue Canada regulations to deal with upon returning to Canada. The people at the International Revenue Canada office in Ottawa were very helpful. It should be noted that many of the preparations for the exchange are costly.

5. My favourite memories revolve around the wonderful, lifelong friends I met; many are true characters. The lack of pretension on the part of most of the people I met. My students. New expressions. The beautiful city of Perth and the sublime beauty of the Australian landscape. The glistening view of the sun on the Indian Ocean as you reach the crest of the hill on North Beach Road.
In particular, I vividly remember my numerous encounters with the bug, reptile, and animal life of Western Australia—red back spiders, rhinoceros beetles, giant cockroaches, the possum that scratched nightly in the attic, geckos on the kitchen floor, the blue-tongued skink in our backyard, and the huntsman spider as big as my hand that crawled out of the defrost vent and crawled up the inside of the window of my car the second day in Oz. I drove onto the median and jumped out of the car!

DEBORAH M. BOUCHER

1. I am currently teaching at the American Cooperative School in La Paz, Bolivia. I also taught at Asociación Escuelas Lincoln in Buenos Aires, Argentina, and Colegio Nueva Granada in Bogotá, Colombia.

2. I found my positions the last two times by writing a letter directly to the schools in Bolivia and Argentina. When I received a favorable response from each, I planned to meet (along with my husband) the administrators at the I.S.S. recruiting fairs. For Colombia, we went directly to a recruiting fair that was held at the University of California, Los Angeles.

3. As compensation, all the positions included housing, which was subsidized 100 percent for rent and a varying rate for utilities. Salaries ranged from $12,000 per year in Colombia (1981) to $33,000 per year in Argentina (1990) to currently $28,000 per year in Bolivia. Remember that these figures do not include housing allowance, retirement fund contributions, COLAs, or health insurance. While it appears that I took a cut in salary to work in my current position, the cost of living in Buenos Aires, Argentina is much higher than living in La Paz, Bolivia. These positions all included shipping allowances and round-trip airfare home after the initial two-year contract, and then airfare home every year after that.

4. My personal preparations were many and varied. Tuition for our children was covered by the contract. In Argentina, this was worth over $20,000 per year. This may explain why some schools don't want more than two dependents in a family. Before my husband and I went to Colombia, we studied Spanish for three weeks in an intensive program. This really paid off since outside of school, no one spoke much English. The Colombian school and the Bolivian school provided free Spanish lessons to the staff. We always read about each country we went to before getting there, which really helped. We bought good travel guides since that was one of our goals while in each country. We got international driver's licenses, passports, visas, shots, etc. The schools will give you advice on that.

5. My favourite memories are encapsulated by one word: Colombia. I loved seeing much of the beautiful countryside from the back of a Toyota Landcruiser. I learned quickly that the question was never "How far?" but "How long?" The best snorkeling of my life in Parque Tayrona, on the Caribbean Coast. Argentina: Living in a Tudor-style house with a flagstone patio and a pool big enough for lap swimming. Playing tennis on clay courts. Eating Italian-style ice cream in summer at 2 A.M. and having the streets packed as if it were 2 P.M. Bolivia: Having an indigenous culture that surrounds you and is open to the sensitive Westerner. Day hikes in the incredibly high Andes Mountains. I've been over 17,000 feet, but several colleagues have scaled peaks over 20,000.

VICTORIA EGAN

I Nigeria

1. Government Junior Secondary School, Kutigi, Niger State, Nigeria.

2. I applied to CUSO (a Canadian Volunteer Development Organization).

3. The Monthly salary was minimal, but there was a resettlement allowance on return to Canada ($1,500 in 1985). Living accommodation was paid for and provided the very basics—no electricity or running water and very little furniture. There was health coverage but minimal health facilities to choose from.

4. Personal preparations were pretty much the same for each of the jobs. These involved reading as much as I could about the country and people; sometimes trying to learn a little of the language beforehand, and buying things to take.

5. My favourite memory of Nigeria is lying in my bed under my mosquito net during a heavy rainstorm imagining that I was in the movie *African Queen* (even though I've yet to see the movie!).

II Mexico

1. Escuela Americana, Pachuca, Hidalgo, Mexico.

2. To find this position I sent out lots of letters to schools. I got the addresses from a book in the library. I don't remember what it was but something like E.C.I.S. Directory of Schools.

3. The monthly salary was minimal—enough to get by and do some local traveling, and there was a resettlement allowance but it was in pesos and had devalued immensely between the time I signed the contract and finished it. Shared living accommodations were provided but we paid rent. I think medical coverage was provided but I don't recall.

5. Here, my favourite memory is eating fresh red snapper cooked up on a barbecue at a beach at three in the morning after an evening of revelry.

III Turkey

1. Ihsan Cizacka Lisesi, Sirameseler, Bursa, Turkey.

2. See II, 2.

3. The monthly salary was minimal—enough to live on and do some local traveling. Accommodations were provided. I had my own small but pleasant apartment in the school and I shared a kitchen with a couple. Maid service was provided, and I think that health coverage was too.

5. Here, my favourite memory is going to the Turkish baths in the cold winter and leaving totally relaxed and feeling wonderful!

IV England

1. Linguarama, London, England.

2. To find the job I visited language schools in London.

3. The salary was minimal. No accommodation and I'm not sure about health coverage.

5. Spending a week working at a resort in Winchester comprises my favourite memories during this stay in England.

V England

1. Laycock School, Islington, London, England.

2. To secure the position I wrote applications and sent them out to several local school boards.

3. Here the salary was very minimal but I was told that once my Canadian qualifications were recognized, I'd receive back pay. I never did. I can't remember if medical coverage was provided but there was no accommodation.

5. My favourite memory is taking the whole school on an outing to the beach.

VI Greece

1. Katsari Frontisteria, Arta, Greece.

2. This position I found in a London newspaper advertisement.

3. The monthly salary was minimal, housing conditions poor and not what was promised: not sure about health care.

5. Quite simply, my favourite memory is the whole thing. Living in Greece.

VII Singapore

1. Canadian International School, Singapore.

2. I found the position at the Job fair—Queen's University, Kingston, Ontario, Canada.

3. The salary was good and at that time 40 percent of what you made was held back until you finished your contract. There was no housing allowance though and rent at that time was very high. You also had to find your own accommodation. We had both medical and dental coverage.

5. Super traveling opportunities were the highlights here.

VIII China

1. Beijing BISS International School, Beijing, China.

2. I applied to the sister school in Singapore and was offered the job in Beijing.

3. The salary (in U.S. currency) is good. Accommodation is provided free and is very comfortable. Medical coverage is provided.

5. Again, my favourite memories are the super traveling opportunities.

DAVID REID

1. My international experience does not restrict itself to a single institution; I have taught at: Universal American School (Kuwait); Samara Lycée PHP (Samara, Russia); Koç Özel Lisesi (Istanbul, Turkey); Minsk State Pedagogical University of Foreign Languages (Minsk, Belarus); Colegio Colombo Británico (Cali, Colombia); Benjamin Franklin Int'l School (Barcelona, Spain); A.C.A.T. School (Turin, Italy); Yon-sei University (Seoul, South Korea); Collège Catholique S.C. (Gagnoa, Ivory Coast); Royal Navy Language Training Center (Rasht, Iran); Big Bend Community College (Mannheim, Germany); Churchill High School (then Salisbury, Rhodesia, now Harare, Zimbabwe); and Finley High School (Finley, Australia).

2. I found the positions in Russia, Korea, the Ivory Coast, Iran, Germany, and Zimbabwe by going to the respective countries, looking around, and applying. The positions in Turkey, Colombia, Spain, and Italy "international schools" I found through the efforts of the European Council of International Schools (ECIS) in England. The positions in Minsk and Kuwait were obtained by writing directly to the institutions involved from another country, and finally the position in Australia was through a recruiter for the Australian Department of Education.

3. The salaries/benefits in the schools, roughly converted into U.S. dollars, ranged from a high of U.S.$26,000 a year with free housing in expensive Kuwait to U.S.$15 a month with a free room in student housing in hyperinflating Belarus. Accommodation was provided by the schools in Kuwait, Turkey, Belarus, and the Ivory Coast, a housing allowance was given by the schools in Colombia and Italy, otherwise I was on my own resources (including my $50 per month salary in Russia) to seek my own apartment. For easy access and payment to good medical care, Colombia was excellent, followed by Germany and Turkey. In Kuwait, Turkey, Colombia, and Italy, the health coverage was covered by the school. The others were simply covered under the national health schemes of the respective countries. Bonuses were never paid, except insofar as part of the salary was renamed a bonus (in Turkey) to obtain a better tax deal. Other benefits by the four international schools mentioned above were flights to and from the schools (although I took a train to Italy) at the beginning and end of the two-year contracts (and, in Kuwait, another flight for the intervening summer), and some shipping allowance.

4. My personal preparations mainly included getting some of my books from place to place, and occasionally a few other belongings. With only a couple of exceptions I have relied on the international post office. Thankfully I have very kind friends in Europe that help me to store my possessions when I travel for a year or so between jobs.

5. I have many memories about the positions. The positions enable me to experience a country, inviting many memories of the culture and certain people, but on a strictly professional level, my best memories of the positions were the occasions I was able to change the basic way of thinking of certain pupils.

DAN DAVIS

1. I have taught at The American School of Kishasa, Zaire (now Democratic Republic of Congo) (2 years), the American School of Bucharest, Romania (3 years), and am starting my third year at the Lahore American School, Pakistan (where the article was written).

2. My wife and I found our positions here (and elsewhere) by interviewing at the SEARCH and ISS recruitment fairs, although we always send out cover letters and resumes to prospective schools before we attend any job fairs.

3. My salary has been fairly average ($25,000 to $35,000), but not paying taxes is a big bonus. I have also always had housing provided, medical insurance coverage paid, and fairly inexpensive full-time use of a school vehicle.

4. I lived in Ecuador, South America from the time I was seven until I was fifteen, so I've always been ready to live overseas. To secure jobs overseas my wife and I always send out cover letters and resumes to prospective schools, we study up on the benefits of the various schools we are considering, and we check living conditions by referring to guidebooks, magazines, newspapers, and people we know who are familiar with the area/country, and the State Department hotline. As far as the actual procedure of moving, packing up, shipping out, completing customs forms, making lists, buying whatever we cannot find in the new location, and getting up to date on vaccinations—it is not a part of the overseas life I look forward to.

5. This is where both of my sons came of school age, and their involvement in school has been touching for me—as a teacher—to see. Professionally, I am extremely grateful to have such overwhelming support from the administration as well as their complete trust in my abilities. As far as a single fondest memory here so far, I would have to say it has been seeing the scores my Advanced Placement calculus class obtained on the Advanced Placement exam—scores have literally doubled from those of the class the year before I got here.

Appendix D

The Guide to Finding a Job Abroad

Forrest A. Broman

A significant number of teachers at some point in their careers consider the appeal of an international assignment. The desire to work in an international school can occur at any time during an educator's career. Interest in teaching abroad may reflect a desire to experience the exotic, a way to improve a stagnating career, or aspirations to live and work in a new and challenging environment.

Whatever the reasons, the process of learning about opportunities abroad can be mystifying at best. Armed with a thorough understanding of how the system works, however, and with the proper qualifications and skills, a teacher stands a much better chance of heading off for her first job in an international school.

Scattered throughout the world are hundreds of international schools interested in employing American, Canadian, and British-trained teachers and administrators. This network employs approximately 35,000 professionals and serves close to 350,000 students. About 220 of these schools are run under the auspices of the U.S. Department of Defense. Around 200 are associated with the U.S. Department of State and the remainder are autonomous institutions, sponsored by a variety of different groups.

Curriculum varies from school to school and reflects the needs of the student body. Some schools offer a typical American or British program. If the school has a high number of host-country students enrolled, courses are often offered in both English and the host country language. Others offer both American and British tracks.

A growing number of schools are making the International Baccalaureate

(IB) available for talented, university-bound students and some institutions have developed their own unique educational program, culled from a variety of sources.

Here is a breakdown of the various types of international schools.

INDEPENDENT INTERNATIONAL SCHOOLS

There are approximately four hundred American, British, and other international schools in this worldwide network. Some may be operated by a single corporation: others are sponsored by the United Nations and their affiliated agencies. Some are religious or proprietary schools with boarding facilities. The majority of these schools are private, nonprofit institutions with considerable parental involvement in their governance. All offer instruction in the English language and there are usually American-trained teachers represented on the faculty.

With the exception of corporation-affiliated schools located in hardship settings, where salaries and benefits are often extremely generous, most schools tend to pay staff sufficient to provide both an opportunity for saving and a reasonable standard of living in the host country. Books, computers, science equipment, and other resources vary widely among these schools.

DEPARTMENT OF DEFENSE DEPENDENTS SCHOOLS (DODDS)

The U.S. Department of Defense operates around two hundred elementary and secondary schools located primarily in NATO countries, usually on American military bases in Europe, Great Britain, the Mediterranean area, Japan, Korea, the Philippines, Cuba, Panama, Canada, and other Atlantic region locations. Teachers and administrators for DoDDS schools are hired in the United States and candidates must have American training and certification.

Once hired to work in a DoDDS school, teachers will be U.S. government employees and their students will most likely be children of military and civilian personnel working on the base. Salaries are very competitive with those in the United States and the benefits are excellent. As federal employees, DoDDS teachers pay all federal and social security taxes required of citizens living within the United States.

U.S. DEPARTMENT OF STATE AFFILIATED SCHOOLS

There are nearly two hundred American overseas schools recognized by the U.S. State Department's Office of Overseas Schools. Located in many of the world's capital cities, most were established to serve the families of American citizens working abroad.

Over the years, rapidly changing political and economic factors in many countries have had a strong impact on these schools. Many are now educating children from many different countries. Several studies indicate that in the last ten years the typical American overseas school has experienced a drop in its American population from two-thirds of the student body down to one-half or one-third of the total student enrollment.

Hiring requirements, salaries, and benefits among these schools vary considerably. Indeed, the schools themselves are extremely varied. Some have a student population of 3,000; others run an academic program with fewer than ten students. Some are located in countries with very difficult living conditions, others can be found in locales described as "paradise." Some schools provide their staff free housing, a car for personal use, tax-free salaries, and a bonus upon completion of the contract. Others may offer only a subsistence salary and basic travel costs.

Keep in mind that Americans are generally entitled to a $70,000 exclusion of taxable income if they are employed abroad for at least eleven months of the year. However, many European countries levy local income taxes on foreign teachers immediately or after one, two, or three years of residence. Even if their incomes are excluded from tax, Americans must still file U.S. tax returns. Whether British or American, all teachers should check the tax situations concerning the countries they will be teaching in and should not make any assumptions.

If a teacher is just beginning to learn more about working in an international school and he wants to know where the specific jobs are, what they pay, and how to apply, there are a variety of resources available. How he proceeds should depend on his goals. If the teacher wants to work in a specific country, or within a small region, her best bet is to get a list of American and international schools in those countries and write directly to them. She should be forewarned that restricting the places she is willing to work will limit her chances of finding a job. Candidates who maintain an open mind on location have a far better chance of being hired.

Both the European Council of International Schools (ECIS) located in the UK and International School Services (ISS) in Princeton, New Jersey, publish comprehensive directories of international schools. These books will provide teachers with the names of schools, mailing addresses, telephone and fax numbers, headmasters' names, and a description of schools and their student bodies. In addition, both DoDDS and the U.S. State Department's Office of Overseas Schools publish booklets that list and describe the schools under their domain.

For teachers interested in British-oriented international schools, *The*

Times Educational Supplement (TES), published weekly in London, carries a few ads placed by English-speaking schools abroad. TES is available in the United States by subscription.

Most overseas schools assume individual responsibility for their own hiring and a personal interview is almost always required. It is difficult to know very much about either the quality of a school or the advantages and disadvantages of a specific job. For this reason, it is strongly recommended that all opportunities be explored with open-mindedness.

THE AGENCY APPROACH—RECRUITMENT FAIRS

There are several organizations that screen and recommend candidates for positions in international schools. You may register with one or more of these organizations. They will process your application materials and present your credentials to schools engaging their services.

Generally an interested candidate registers with the agency and completes a series of forms, which, together with confidential recommendations from former supervisors, makes up the candidate's file. These files may be forwarded to schools that require candidates for specific positions.

Throughout the year, these organizations host "recruitment fairs" in various parts of the world which bring together the schools and the candidates for several days of interviewing. Once registered, the candidate also has the option to attend one or more of the recruitment fairs being held by the agency. These may be attended by as few as twenty international schools or as many as 120. The ratio of candidates to schools can be anywhere from 1:3 to 1:6, although in recent years the number of candidates has dwindled while the number of schools in attendance has increased—all good news for the international candidate.

These job fairs are usually intense, three-day events where the agency will match the needs of the schools to candidates' qualifications. If a specific school is interested in the teacher's candidacy, he will be called for an interview. One clear advantage in attending a recruitment fair is that most candidates manage to be interviewed by representatives of at least three or four overseas schools. Moreover, many schools fill a significant portion of their openings with candidates they have interviewed at a recruitment fair.

Search Associates, a U.S.-based recruitment agency which hosts fairs all over the world, has established a strong record for placing both teachers and administrators in international schools. The European Council of International Schools (ECIS, based in Hampshire, England) is another major placement agency that hosts recruitment fairs in London attracting both British and American teachers working in international, American, and British schools.

International Schools Services (ISS) is a U.S.-based placement agency for international schools. ISS hosts several fairs each year where headmasters and candidates can meet in different regions of the United States.

UNIVERSITY-SPONSORED SERVICES

The largest university-sponsored recruitment fair for international schools is held at the University of Northern Iowa in Cedar Falls in February. In the past, over one hundred school representatives and between five hundred and seven hundred teachers have participated. Ohio State University and Queen's University (Canada) both run job fairs that are attracting a significant number of participants.

Generally the costs of registering with the recruitment agency or of attending a fair are fairly reasonable. But, depending on the location of the fair relative to the candidate's home, one might expend a significant sum in travel and up to four days of hotel expenses. At university-sponsored events, the costs are usually lower. Further information on these options can be obtained by writing to the organization directly.

Typically, overseas schools require at least two years of full-time teaching experience, although some schools may waive this criterion. Many international schools request that applicants have teaching certification in their country or state of origin, although many waive this requirement too. Most schools also request that teachers make two-year commitments. Other requirements, such as training in the IB (International Baccalaureate program) or specific language skills, vary from school to school.

Overall, international schools are seeking successful, flexible, and optimistic people with real potential for weathering the often-difficult circumstances of living and teaching abroad. Administrators frequently report that the most desirable candidate for an overseas position is the person who will be able to maintain composure despite difficulties, demonstrates a deep commitment to students, and has a strong sense of humor.

Since few schools hire teachers without an interview, teachers should make every effort to attend one or more of the recruitment fairs where their chances of securing interviews are high. Those teachers who have already responded to various schools directly after reading their advertisements in *The International Educator* newspaper should be successful in prearranging one or more interviews.

Although a significant number of teachers are hired at these events, teachers should brace themselves for disappointment. In certain cases there is just not time for a school to interview all interested candidates for reasons that have nothing to do with them personally.

Remember, if a teacher's first contact with a school was in response to an advertisement in *TIE*, *The New York Times*, *The International Herald*

Tribune, or others, she should not have to pay a placement fee unless the agency in question arranges the interview.

For the best results, we suggest the following sequence of activities:

1. Start the process early. Read *The International Educator* and begin contacting schools in November for employment the following September.

2. If you are interested in working in one or two countries only, write directly to schools located in these regions. Forward your resume, cover letter, transcripts, and at least two letters of recommendation.

3. Try to determine as soon as possible the specific jobs you are qualified for by reviewing the ads in *The International Educator* or other publications mentioned previously. If you find a possibility, send a cover letter, resume, two letters of recommendation, and your university transcripts. Also indicate when and where you will be available for an interview. Most administrators take the view that letters of recommendation from school supervisors are dramatically overinflated. Most have become quite adept at reading between the lines and ferreting out subtle reservations. Successful applicants usually produce very strong letters of recommendation, indicating, for example, whether the recommender would place the candidate in the top 10 percent, 25 percent, or 50 percent of teachers with whom he or she has worked. For these recommendations to be accorded validity, they should be sent out on a confidential basis.

4. After writing to secure information on services and fees, register with one or more of the private agencies of universities that specialize in placement of teachers in international schools. Then select the organization that seems most suited to your needs, taking into consideration which fair will be easiest for you to attend. Register for at least one recruitment fair and request information a month or two prior to the fair regarding how many schools are seeking candidates with the qualifications and experience you offer.

5. If a school wants to interview you at a recruitment fair, by all means register for this fair. Once registered, you can arrange to have other interviews as well.

6. Once the fair has ended, if you do not receive an offer shortly afterwards, don't give up. Inquire about new jobs that appear in *The International Educator* and other newspapers. Call or fax a school where you have a strong interest. Keep checking, as there are a significant number of jobs that open up between June and September. If you are traveling, pay a visit to any school where you might be interested in working. Remember that many international educators report finding their first job only during their second year of effort.

7. Your resume should be clear, informative, and professional in appearance. The cover letter should give the reader some insight into the strengths you have as a teacher, your reasons for wishing to go overseas, and the areas and levels at which you would prefer teaching or conducting extracurricular activities. One's willingness to get involved in student activities and coaching is often a very significant factor in the selection of staff by overseas schools.

The personal interview is extremely important in the hiring process. What transpires during this brief meeting will determine, more than any other factor, whether you receive an offer. The interview might be as brief as forty-five minutes, although very often, another half-hour or extended session is arranged. Most likely you will be talking to the superintendent or head of the school. You will find that some of these administrators are skilled interviewers, while others appear less sure of how to maximize their brief meetings with a stream of candidates.

Do your utmost to engage in a lively dialogue with the prospective employer. Try not to adopt a passive attitude in the interview. Ask interesting, thoughtful questions about the school, the country, and possible hardships. Reveal your curiosity and concern about the school where you may be working.

Remember that many international schools are unaware of legal restrictions concerning certain types of questions imposed by various U.S. state or federal laws. You may be asked to answer questions concerning your age, health, religious views, marital status, or sexual preference. Although these questions may appear to be a violation of your privacy, this information is being gathered for the protection of both you and the school.

Again, we urge you to carefully consider what kind of school you will be working for and how willing you are to adapt to local laws and customs, which in some areas of the world are extremely restrictive.

Appendix E

The International Educator: Periodical and Website

The International Educator (TIE) is a newspaper with an interactive Website (www.tieonline.com) serving four hundred to five hundred American overseas and international schools. This periodical comes out five times a year and is a great resource for teachers and administrators who may be considering overseas employment possibilities. The subscription price is $35 in the United States and Canada, $45 in all other countries. This includes all TIE Website services such as online access to Job Ads, the Resume Bank, News/Articles (current and past), International Community Message Board, and a Recruitment Fairs & Dates Calendar. TIE's Resume Bank has thousands of resumes placed by subscribers and can be viewed by heads of schools worldwide.

This seminal resource also fosters professional development for educators. There are frequent opportunities to publish articles about your international school and to list announcements and awards that colleagues have received in teaching and administration.

Another, more personal reason to become familiar with this organization is that many schools offer health insurance through TIECare. There is also a membership program that offers travel insurance, life, disability, and health insurance, hotel discounts, and international travel programs.

CONTACT PERSONS

TIE's staff helps teachers with subscriptions, memberships, technical support, general information, or schools advertisements. The TIE office is open

Monday through Friday from 8:00 A.M. to 4:30 P.M., Eastern Standard Time.

TIE—The International Educator
P.O. Box 513
Cummaquid, MA 02637 USA
Tel: (508) 362–1414; Fax: (508) 362–1411
www.tieonline.com
tie@capecod.net

Subscriptions, Memberships, & Tech Support

Janna Pereira
jpereira@tieonline.com

Kim Senior
ksenior@tieonline.com

Billing

Joe Parilla, Office Manager
jparilla@tieonline.com

Schools Recruitment Ads

Julie Thrasher, Director
jthrasher@tieonline.com

Articles/Editorials

Sherry Calef, Editor
tiedit@aol.com

Corporate & Website Advertising

Kate McGrail
kmcgrail@rcn.com

Marketing/Internet Links

Nikki Gundry, Marketing Coordinator
ngundry@tieonline.com

In the U.K.

Alexandra Broman, TIE(UK)
102A Popes Lane
London W5 4NS, UK
Tel/Fax: (44) 020 8840–2587
ABroman@tieteachabroad.demon.co.uk

Appendix F

Recruitment Fairs and Search Agencies

Association of American Schools in South America
1475 N.W. 77th Court, Suite 210
Miami Lakes, FL 33016
Tel: (305) 821–0345
Fax: (305) 821–4244

European Council of International Schools
21 Lavant Street, Petersfield
Hampshire, England GU32 3EL
Tel: (44) 1130–268244
Fax: (44) 1730–261914
http://www.ecis.org

European Council of International Schools (Australia)
P.O. Box 357, Kilmore 3154
Victoria, Australia
Tel: (61) 3–57–811–351
Fax: (61) 3–57–811–151

Southern Teachers Agency
2803 McRae Rd. B-4
Richmond, VA 23235
Tel: (804) 330–7880
Fax: (804) 330–5858
www.southernteachers.com

International Educators Cooperative
212 Alcoll Road

East Falmouth, MA 02536
Tel: (508) 540–8113

International Schools Services
P.O. Box 5910
Princeton, NJ 08543
Tel: (609) 452–0990
Fax: (609) 452–2690
edustaffing@iss.edu
www.iss.edu

The Ohio State University
110 Arps Hall, 1945 N. High St.
Columbus, Ohio 43210–1172
Tel: (888) 678–3382
Fax: (614) 292–8052

University of Northern Iowa
SSC #19
Cedar Falls, IA 50614–0390
Tel: (319) 213–2083
Fax: (319) 213–6998
overseas.placement@uni.edu
http://www.uni.edu/placement/overseas/

Queen's University
Placement Office, Faculty of Education
Kingston, Ontario, Canada K7L 3146
Tel: (613)145–6222
Fax: (613) 545–6691
http://educ.queensu.ca/~placment/

Teachers of English to Speakers of Other Languages (TESOL)
1600 Cameron Street, Suite 300
Alexandria, VA 22314–2751
Tel: (703) 836–0774
Fax: (703) 836–1864
http://www.tesol.org/

Search Associates
P.O. Box 636
Dallas, PA 18612
Tel: (717) 696–5400
Fax: (717) 696–9500
http://www.search-associates.com/

Search Associates Canada
RR#5 Belleville
Ontario, Canada K8N 4Z5

Tel: (613) 967–4902
Fax: (613) 967–8981

Teacher Recruitment International (Australia)
P.O. Box 177
Tumby Bay, Australia 5605
Tel: (618) 86–88–4260
Fax: (618) 86–88–4222
triaust@ozemail.com.au
http://www.triaust.com

Carney, Sandoe & Assoc.
Recruitment & School Services
136 Boyslton Street
Boston, MA 02116
Tel: (800) 225–7986
Fax: (617) 542–9400
http://www.csa-teach.com

Alaska Teacher Placement
P.O. Box 6880
Fairbanks, AK 99775
Tel: (907) 474–6644
Fax: (907) 474–6176
fytap@uaf.edu
http://www.atp.uaf.edu/

Department of Defense Education Activity
Personnel Center
4040 North Fairfax Drive
Arlington, VA 22203–1634
http://www.odedodea.edu/pers/

Educators Overseas Connection
27932 Camino del Rio
San Juan Capistrano, CA 92675
Tel: (949) 487–6745
Fax: (949) 487–6745
eoc4fredp@aol.com

ED-U-Link Services
P.O. Box 2076
Prescott, AZ 86302
Tel: (520) 778–5581
Fax: (520) 776–0611
jobfair@edulink.com
http://www.edulink.com/

New Zealand Qualifications Authority
P.O. Box 160

Wellington, New Zealand
Tel: (64) 4–802–3000
Fax: (64) 4–802–3401
http://www.nzqa.govt.nz

Quality Schools International
Sanaa International School
P.O. Box 2002
Sanaa, Yemen
Tel: (967)1–370191
Fax: (967)1–370193
jimgilson@qsi.org
http://www.qsi.org/

TimePlan Teacher Recruitment Specialists (England)
760 Eastern Avenue
Newbury Park
Ilford, Essex IG2 7HU
Tel: (020)8518–3311
Fax: (020)8518–3318
essex@timeplan.net
http://www.timeplan.com

International Teacher Training Organization
Madero No.469
Guadalajara, Jalisco 44100
Mexico
Tel: (52) 33–3658–3224
Fax: (52) 33–3614–2462
info@teflcertificatecourses.com
http://.teflcertificatecourses.com

ADDITIONAL WEB RESOURCES

International Employment Gazette
http://www.intemployment.com/

Overseas Teachers Digest
http://www.overseasdigest.com/

International Schools K-12
http://www.intlschools-k12.com/

Friends of World Teaching
http://www.fowt.com/

Teaching in the UK
http://www.education-jobs.co.uk

ESL Worldwide
www.eslworldwide.com

State Department of Overseas Schools
http://www.state.gov/www/about_state/schools/

University of California, Irvine, International Opportunities Program
http://www.cie.uci.edu/iop/teaching.html

Teaching and Projects Abroad
http://www.teaching-abroad.org/

TeachAbroad.Com
http://www.teachabroad.com/

University of Ohio English as a Foreign Language
http://www.ohio.edu/esl/teacher/job/efl.html

Appendix G

T is for Typhoon: A Beginner's Guide to the JET Programme

Laura Mann

So, this is what a typhoon feels like. Sitting in my new home, as the rain falls in sheets outside and the wind rattles my windows, I finally feel like I'm in Japan. Not long ago, just the thought of actually living in a foreign country intimidated me, typhoons aside. I love to be challenged, however, and the idea of moving to Japan kept turning around in the back of my mind. I first heard about the Japan Exchange and Teaching (JET) Programme from a regular customer at the Internet café in Canada where I was working nights. She told me over a double shot latté that her sister was in Japan with JET and was having a wonderful experience. Shortly after, I was researching the JET Programme in my spare time. There were numerous websites and brochures to be found, and in October informative question and answer sessions were held all over North America. When the time came, I applied. The entire application and interview process, which took a little over eight months, increased my trust in JET and my confidence in living abroad. Now, here I am, a newcomer to not only ESL teaching, but also Japan and my first typhoon.

The JET Programme is known as one of the largest international exchange programs in the world. Currently there are over six thousand participants working in Japan from thirty-nine different countries, but the majority of participants are from the United States, Canada, the UK, and Australia. The Programme is run through the Japanese government and has been in place since 1987. It involves collaboration between several branches of the Japanese government, including the Ministry of Foreign Affairs, the Ministry of Home Affairs, the Ministry of Education, and the Council of

Local Authorities for International Relations (CLAIR). Sorting out the re-lationships between all the government organizations can be confusing, but an ample supply of reference material is available.

The purpose of the JET Programme is outlined by CLAIR as follows: "[to] increase mutual understanding between the people of Japan and the people of other nations, and [to] promote the internationalization of Ja-pan's local communities by helping to improve foreign language education and developing international exchange at the community level" (CLAIR, 2001). To this end, the JET Programme has three possible positions for participants to fill.

The vast majority of foreigners working on the Programme are Assistant Language Teachers (ALTs). The role of the ALT is to work in the public school system as an assistant to Japanese teachers of English (JTEs), but of equal importance is the role of cultural exchange. A large portion of my job here is just to be myself, and share with my Japanese students my Canadianness. The ALT position itself is primarily an assistant position, much of the training is on-the-job, and many ALTs are underutilized by teachers. For ESL teachers with extensive experience and expertise, this may prove frustrating and limiting. As a jumping-off point into the international teaching community, however, JET allows for a relatively micromanaged transition. Positions are available in one-year contracts and a JET partici-pant can stay for a maximum of three years if both sides (JET and em-ployer) are amenable. The other positions available are Coordinator of International Relations (CIR) and Sports Education Advisor (SEA). The ALT position is available to those with limited or nonexistent Japanese language ability, which is why it was the position of choice for me.

Also, for those who wish to teach abroad but are intimidated by a storm of visas, alien registration, finding a place to live, and all the other simple details that seem torrential when combined with a language barrier, the JET Programme provides an astonishing amount of help and support to ease the transition. Ultimately, when you are accepted as a JET participant, you put yourself completely in the hands of the Japanese government and have very little say as to where you are placed or in which type of school you will work. The mantra that resounds throughout all the information on the JET Programme is that "every situation is different." A participant's situation depends largely on his or her local contracting organization (Board of Education) when it comes to the everyday workday details. The Programme is, however, a high priority for the Japanese government and uniform standards are ensured with respect to things such as working hours, insurance, salary, and vacation time.

It all began for me with Tokyo Orientation—a four-day jet-lagged haze of lectures, welcome addresses, and five-star hotel lobbies. The experience is a small typhoon itself, as hundreds of hurried introductions are made in lilting accents and the days are a strange mix of adrenaline and fatigue. Over a thousand new JETs are in attendance this session, sporting name tags that tell their names and nationalities. On the streets, no one raises an eyebrow at the groups of boisterous *"gaijin,"* a far cry from the stories I have heard about the Japanese fascination with foreigners. I even feel insulated, as all the comforts of home I have come to take for granted are here, and I am slightly disappointed at the thought that perhaps Japan isn't so different. Then I remember the lectures back in North America about the challenges. Titles such as "Cooking in Japan," "Using the Japanese Phone System," "Japanese Etiquette," "Gender Issues in Japan," and "Managing Your Money" all swim in my head while my arms begin to stiffen from the mammoth load of handouts and handbooks I'm carrying. I feel as though I'm learning the doggie paddle when I was expecting to be thrown into the deep end, and I secretly hope I forget some small detail at least.

There are sign-up tables for JET special interest groups, long-distance plans, and the foreign buyer's club; application forms run rampant for free Japanese courses, for travel packages, and for teaching resources. I'm utterly prepared and a little dazed by the organization and quantity of information. On the final night of the orientation we have the choice as to whether to attend our country's "embassy night" or a night out in Tokyo with others who will be living in the same area of Japan: national loyalty pitted against the opportunity to find a social life. Later, sitting at a long table on the roof of a Tokyo high-rise, neon billboards garnishing the sky like huge brazen planets, I am reminded at last that I am an alien here and that I'm not, as they say, in Kansas anymore. Tomorrow the buffer will be gone and I will meet new colleagues and neighbours, and begin to try and fulfill my end of the bargain.

Tokyo Orientation illustrates the extensive support network of the JET Programme. JET is ideal, I believe, for those who want to make the transition to ESL teaching abroad in the most comfortable way possible. I encountered numerous bright, capable, and independent new participants at the orientation; however, JET also accommodates many participants who are fresh out of university, may have never lived abroad, or have little or no Japanese language ability. From insurance concerns to plane tickets, JET was there. In my case there was even a weekend-long "predeparture orientation" in Toronto a month before I left for Japan that was organized by the Japanese embassy there. While I occasionally did feel lost in the herd and just a little unoriginal, I had only to remind myself what a big step coming to Japan really was and my enthusiasm returned. Nevertheless, I couldn't help feeling grateful, and a little embarrassed, for all the help and attention I was receiving.

My last two weeks have proved that JET does help new teachers to a smooth transition. After Tokyo I was whisked away to my new home in Miyagi-ken in Northeastern Honshu. The second day here my colleagues from five local schools and I met the mayor of my city in a very official-type ceremony involving local journalists and photographers. Teenagers on the street exploded with English phrases like "nice to meet you," or "Haro! Haro!" It seems everyone has been eagerly awaiting my arrival.

My apartment is more than adequate, as my JET predecessor left furniture, phone books, and other useful odds and ends in her wake. I made it my own with some minor redecorating. Shortly after my arrival, my landlord stopped by to present me with a six-pack of Sapporo beer. I was stunned but grateful. Besides this man's kindness, JET has succeeded in giving me a smooth transition into life in Japan. As I gossip with other new JETs about their first steps into teaching and living here, I find that the JET credo of "every situation is different" holds true. Nevertheless, I have yet to hear of a JET who is homeless, stranded, hungry, or pessimistic about what the coming year will bring.

I recall my initial trepidation about living overseas as I listen to the wind and rain of my first typhoon. I'm neither alarmed nor homesick. It has been easier for me to believe in myself and pursue new opportunities with the comforting support of both the Japanese government and the JET network. I find myself glad to be having the full Japanese experience, typhoon included, and I fall asleep effortlessly. The next day, I'm told that the typhoon missed my area. All I felt was the outlying storm system, but most people in the area were awakened by mild earthquakes. "I didn't feel a thing," I say. "I slept right through the night."

WORK CITED

Council of Local Authorities for International Relations (2001). *The JET programme 2001 general information handbook*. Tokyo, Japan: CLAIR.

Internet Resources on Teaching in Japan and the JET Programme

Official JET web page
http://www.mofa.go.jp/j_info/visit/jet/index.html

Unofficial JET web page
http://www.bigdaikon.com

Jetset Japan
http://www.jetsetjapan.com

Association for Japan Exchange and Teaching (AJET)
http://www.lastflightout.net/ajet/indexIE.html

A Day in the Life
http://www.geocities.com/Tokyo/Field/6511/aet/index.html

ELT News
http://www.eltnews.com/home.shtml

Appendix H

The Canadian Volunteer Service Organization: Voluntary Service Overseas Canada (A Partner of Voluntary Service Overseas International)

Elizabeth Wigful

I have always enjoyed the pleasures of letter writing. There is something exciting about going to your mailbox and finding an envelope decorated with colourful stamps and filled with tales from a faraway place. And there's something very satisfying about jotting down my thoughts in response to the new images inspired by these stories. I suppose, then, that it's only appropriate that I first had a look into the work of Voluntary Service Overseas (VSO) volunteer teachers in 1994, through the letters of my friend, Paul Seshadri. Paul and I had attended the Bachelor of Education program at the University of Ottawa together the year before. At the end of the year, he had announced that he was off to Malawi for two years with VSO. Since one of the reasons I had become a teacher was to travel overseas, I was intrigued by Paul's project. He promised to write and tell me everything.

And tell me everything he did: the excitement of his first few weeks at school, the stimulation of living in a new culture, the joys of teaching, and later on, the frustrations he faced as a Western-trained teacher working in a rural African school. Paul's stories, good and bad, both amazed and inspired me. As I put together small packages of powdered cheese and bacon bits to send so that Paul had something "interesting" to add to his daily meals of beans and rice, I dreamed of going to a new, exotic place and putting into practice the teaching skills I had learned at university. I was working as a substitute teacher in Ottawa at the time but my mind was already elsewhere. At my request, Paul provided me with the telephone number of the VSO Canada recruitment staff working in Ottawa. At the time, this staff was comprised of two people working part-time out of a basement somewhere in town. I was interviewed, along with several other prospective volunteers from a variety of professions, and selected. A few months later I was on a plane to Namibia where I spent three of the most frustrating and fantastic years of my life.

I think I had expected working in Namibia to be just like working in Malawi and in some ways, I suppose, it was: the large classes, the difficulty of the ministry's chosen syllabus, the seeming lack of organization at the school, the lack of resources, and teaching to an external examination for the first time. But there was no need to ask friends and family to send powdered cheese and bacon bits to add to my rice and beans. Food was plentiful, as long as I was prepared to travel to the "big town" to find it (and I was). Unlike Paul, I had hot water and electricity most of the time and was comfortable living with two other volunteers in our own house, surrounded by eucalyptus trees with a beautiful purple bougainvillea plant in the garden. The teaching syllabus was also very different from the one Paul was working with. Volunteer placements, it seemed, were of a wide variety, in both work and living environments.

The entire VSO experience for me was a time of great learning, both as a teacher and as a person. I took on new challenges and tackled unfamiliar situations, some successfully, others not. The result is that I have gained a lot of self-confidence. Just as important is the awareness I have gained about the lives of people in developing countries, the difficulties they face on a daily basis, as well as what we in the "developed" world can learn from them. I am convinced that those of us living in wealthier nations have an obligation to help those who are not fortunate enough to have equal access to water, food, and education. These people encompass two-thirds of the world's population. Being a VSO teacher is one way of helping to tackle the problems of poverty in developing countries.

I wouldn't change anything about the experience I had. It had its ups and downs, like all jobs, but on the whole, it was a very positive experience. I learned more than I taught and came away a richer person. I would certainly volunteer again, perhaps in an Asian country next time. Perhaps when I retire.

WHAT IS VSO?

Voluntary Service Overseas (VSO) Canada is a specialized organization sending international volunteers to communities around the world in order to share skills and change lives. And the lives they change are also their own!

The mission of VSO Canada is to enable men and women to work with people in poorer countries, sharing skills and building capabilities, and promoting international understanding and action in pursuit of a more equitable world. VSO recruits, and sends international volunteers and interns to share their professional knowledge with people in developing countries around the world. Once there, the volunteers are supported throughout their stay.

VSO Canada is a partner of VSO, an established international organization founded over forty years ago, and the world's largest independent volunteer sending agency. Since 1958, VSO has sent over 24,000 volunteers to work in Africa, Asia, the Pacific, the Caribbean, and Eastern Europe. Other partners in this growing international network include VSO UK, VSO Netherlands, VSA Kenya, and VSO Philippines.

VSO Canada was established in 1992 and federally incorporated as a charity in 1995. In 1999 there were over 124 Canadians and Americans working throughout the Pacific, Africa, Asia, the Caribbean, and Eastern Europe; in 2002, there were 140. These individuals volunteer in the fields of teaching, health care, agriculture, engineering, community development, and a range of professions where skill shortages have been identified by overseas partners.

WHAT SORTS OF TEACHING JOBS ARE AVAILABLE THROUGH VSO?

- Newly qualified English teachers—these teachers need a degree, preferably but not necessarily, in English or Modern Languages, plus a B.Ed. or Teaching English as a Foreign Language/Teaching English as a Second Language certificate. A range of placements is available in secondary schools (Africa, Asia, and the Pacific), tertiary institutions (China, other parts of Asia, and Africa) and in English for Specific Purposes placements (Asia and Africa).

- Experienced English teachers—those teachers with teaching experience, may be placed as secondary school teachers or teacher trainers in Africa, Asia, or the Pacific.

- Note, there are a few placements available to English teachers without qualifications as long as they have at least a year's experience.

- Unqualified mathematics and science teachers—a limited range of placements for those with degrees in mathematics and science, no teaching qualifications necessary, are available in secondary schools in Africa. Placements might involve teaching math or general science or focus on physics, chemistry, or biology.

- Qualified mathematics and science teachers—same as above but placements may involve in-service teacher training in addition to classroom teaching.

- Qualified and experienced mathematics and science teachers—same as above but volunteers may be placed in teacher training colleges.

- Industrial arts teachers—there are some placements in community colleges. Qualified and/or experienced teachers are preferred.

- Accounting teachers—there are some placements for qualified teachers available in African secondary schools.

- Other teachers—there are sometimes requests for teachers specializing in areas other than those mentioned above. Please call VSO for details of what is currently available.

WHAT DOES VSO PROVIDE?

VSO provides about ten days of pre-departure training to help volunteers prepare for their overseas experiences. All volunteers are required to attend a "Preparing for Change weekend that involves exploring cultural and development issues. In addition, they must attend a skills-specific course suited to their individual learning needs (e.g., "Volunteers Working in the Teaching of English," "Basic Teaching Skills," "Working with Communities," etc.). Volunteers also receive in-country training, including language training, upon arrival.

VSO covers costs for all training, travel, vaccinations and in-country health care. The volunteer's employer, or an external donor, supplies accommodation and a monthly allowance (based on a local salary—these are sometimes supplemented by VSO in very poor areas). VSO grants are available to help volunteers purchase items to equip themselves before departure and for their projects while they are overseas. Volunteers also receive a resettlement grant upon completion of their placement.

Volunteering internationally is a personal choice. It is informed by curiosity, professionalism, and a desire to help where help is needed—the experience may change a life and that life could be yours. For more information, check out the website at www.vsocanada.org or contact VSO Canada, 151 Slater Street, Suite 806, Ottawa, Ontario, Canada K1P 5H3, (613) 234–1364; FAX: (613) 234–1444.

Appendix I

Teaching Opportunities in the United States Peace Corps

Greg A. Renda

Founded by President John F. Kennedy in the 1960s, Peace Corps is an international development and community service organization funded by the U.S. federal government. Peace Corps sends U.S. citizens overseas to developing countries to do service work. Volunteers are only sent to those countries that request their presence. Assignments focus on the following areas: environment, business, civic participation, health and sanitation, community development, and education. Volunteers must be at least eighteen years of age, but the majority of assignments require postsecondary education degrees or three to five years of experience in the field of their project assignment.

Peace Corps has a three-part goal. First, Peace Corps fills the request from other countries for trained and skilled workers. The remaining two parts are designed to promote a cross-cultural exchange and understanding on the part of the communities served and the U.S. population. All three goals are equally important parts of Peace Corps's mission.

During a normal Peace Corps tour a volunteer completes a twenty-seven-month assignment. Before volunteers begin their service, Peace Corps provides three months of training that includes language instruction, technical instruction, and cultural lessons. Training also includes strategies to adapt to living in a new culture and maintaining health and safety in the developing world. After training, volunteers move to their assignment locations and proceed to not only develop their projects, but also to incorporate themselves into the community. The volunteer remains in the same community for the two years of service.

Peace Corps has programs for those that have chosen the education career path. The education programs include secondary math, secondary science, special education, secondary TEFL/English, and environmental education. There are also university English teaching, primary education teacher training, and secondary education English teacher training programs. In some of these programs a degree in the subject matter, such as math or science, can substitute for an education degree or experience.

There are many ways in which a person can make himself a more qualified candidate for Peace Corps service. Knowing a foreign language is helpful though not required. Getting involved in leadership roles and volunteering for organizations increase his qualifications. Already having cross-cultural experiences helps Peace Corps decide on the person's suitability for service. Traveling outside of the country or knowing about foreign cultures through studies can also be a benefit, but the biggest qualification is having experience in education or a degree in general education, science, engineering, math, or special education.

Volunteers that receive assignments in education are usually paired up with a school. Conditions vary in the different countries to which volunteers are assigned, as schools can be located in a large metropolitan area or a scarcely populated rural area. Working and living conditions are typical of those found in developing countries—less comfort and less amenities, but bearable. A lack of academic and educational resources should be expected. Often communities that request Peace Corps volunteers do not have financial or educational resources; thus, the need for the volunteer is clear.

Peace Corps also offers other assignment areas besides education. Teachers may qualify for other positions such as health and sanitation or agricultural-forestry extension based on their teaching skills and experience gained inside and outside the classroom. Volunteers in noneducational assignments can start their own education initiatives in their spare time.

AN EXAMPLE OF A PEACE CORPS PLACEMENT: TWO GREAT YEARS IN LATIN AMERICA

I was an agriculture and forestry volunteer in El Salvador. I worked with an agency that was in charge of managing a national park, working specifically in the buffer zone of the park. The majority of the pressure on the park's natural resources emanated from the population in the buffer zone. The main goal of my project was to teach people that lived in the area about environmental conservation and the importance of the protected area. We designed informal adult education training sessions that covered agricultural production improvement, conservation, ecology, and ecotourism. Although outside the objectives of my main assignment, I taught English at the local school in my pueblo in El Salvador. This extra work facilitated my immersion into the community. I filled the position for only two and a half months, but I was able to start up an environmental club for children in the school. I designed activities and lessons with other teachers for the club meetings. Working in the school facilitated my acceptance by the community in my transition from guest to member.

Peace Corps was not only a great adventure but also a period of personal growth for me. I learned a lot about the perception of the United States through the eyes of other nations. I redefined my world and learned about what is important to me. I gained a perspective that I could not have gained by staying in the United States.

I could not have gained the same perspective if I simply worked outside of the United States. Peace Corps volunteers grow to become members of the community, not just guests that work for a couple of years. Becoming a member of the community is part of the objective of a Peace Corps assignment and is an essential strategic component of Peace Corps's sustainable development philosophy. Peace Corps challenged me to step outside my comfort zone, which in the long run forced me to grow.

If the scope of this assignment sounds vague or daunting, be aware that while out in the field, a volunteer receives support from a host country counterpart who may be a member of any school or private or government organization working in the same field. The volunteer also receives support from the Peace Corps project director and country staff, but usually independently decides on his or her own plan of action under the general project plan's guidelines.

Monetary support comes in two forms. All volunteers receive a monthly allowance that is country specific; that is, it is adjusted so that the volunteer may live at the level and standard of the people with whom the volunteer works. Additionally, he or she receives U.S. $225 for each month of completed service at the conclusion of the assignment ($6075 total). The Peace Corps provides life insurance and full health coverage. Illnesses and injuries acquired during service are also fully covered under workman's compensation after volunteers return home. There are no out-of-pocket expenses for Peace Corps volunteers besides personal vacations. Peace Corps requires a preservice physical for which financial reimbursement is provided. Although volunteers may resign at any time and personal leave is granted, I can attest that Peace Corps is a thrilling, life-improving experience that a volunteer will never forget.

Peace Corps has eleven recruiting offices nationwide. Offices can be reached by calling 800–424–8580. Peace Corps's website http://www.peacecorps.gov, is a fountain of information. Recruiting events, including general information meetings and presentations, are held throughout the United States, usually at larger university campuses or in large cities. The application process takes about six to nine months, and the Peace Corps expects candidates to be flexible toward geographic placement.

Appendix J

What Not to Forget

Living accommodations provided?

Washer, dryer, and major appliances provided in the living accommodations?

Water filters and/or bottled water available or provided by school?

Phone line provided in living accommodations?

Cellular phone availability/provided by school?

Internet connection available?

Location of grocery or market for purchasing supplies nearby?

Transportation to and from school?

Length of contract and renewal options.

Travel allowance?

Relocation/shipping allowance provided?

Paycheck in local or U.S./Canadian dollars?

Direct deposit available?

Vaccinations needed for work/visa/safety?

Transient/tourist/work visa provided?

Temperature range throughout all seasons.

Supporting materials available per subject taught?

Teacher budget allotted for school materials?

Transportation provided for nearby weekend excursions?

Appendix K

Research

United States Department of State reports by country
http://www.state.gov/travel/

World Fact Book and other useful resources
http://www.cia.gov/cia/publications/factbook/index.html

Emergency Services to U.S. Citizens Abroad
http://travel.state.gov/acs.html

Emergency Services to Canadian Citizens Abroad
http://www.passages.gc.ca/menu-e.asp

Global Hydrology and Climate Center
http://www.ghcc.msfc.nasa.gov/GOES/

Currency conversions
http://www.xe.com/ucc/

Research on factors that affect international school settings
http://gse.gmu.edu/programs/fasttrain//schoolsetting.shtml

Research on cultural approaches to looking at international schools
http://gse.gmu.edu/programs/fasttrain//culturalapproaches.shtml

The International Baccalaureate Organization
http://www.ibo.org/

The Fulbright Program
http://www.iie.org/fulbright/

Teachers of English to Speakers of Other Languages (TESOL)
http://www.tesol.org/index.html

University of Michigan International Center (Teach Abroad without Credentials)
http://www.umich.edu/~icenter/overseas/work/teach_no_cert1.html

Index

The narrative approach of this anthology is somewhat incompatible with the convenient list of substantial references provided by a standard index. Whereas expository textbooks are structured on topics and subtopics, stories are woven with threads of theme and conflict. Consequently, instead of long, developed paragraphs or sections on a given topic, this index lists passing references to key concepts and themes.

About the Editors and Contributors

DEBORAH M. BOUCHER is currently teaching fourth grade at the American Cooperative School in La Paz, Bolivia. She and her husband, Michael, have also worked at Escuelas Asociación Lincoln in Buenos Aires, Argentina, and Colegio Nueva Granada in Bogotá, Colombia. They are based out of Mammoth Unified School District in Mammoth Lakes, California.

FORREST A. BROMAN graduated from Brown University in 1961, and received his J.D.L from Harvard Law School in 1965. He is the founder of the International Educator's Institute and publisher of TIE, its quarterly newspaper.

DAN DAVIS has a B.A. in mathematics from California State University, Fresno, and is currently teaching Algebra II through A.P. Calculus at the Lahore American School, Pakistan. Aside from living and traveling overseas, Dan enjoys anything that supplies him with his cherished adrenalin—skydiving, paragliding, bungee jumping, etc.—and passes the slower free time playing guitar and writing. His greatest personal joy at the moment, however, is watching his two young sons escape toddler-hood and become big little boys.

TREVOR DODMAN received a B.A. in English from Dartmouth College, New Hampshire. He was captain of the hockey team for two years and played in the East Coast Professional Hockey League before he spent one and one-half years teaching ESL in Hanyti, Japan. Recently he earned his

M.A. in English from Carleton University, Ottawa and he is currently enrolled in the doctoral program at Boston College.

VICTORIA EGAN graduated from the University of Waterloo, Ontario, Canada with a B.A. in English literature. She attended Althouse College, University of Western Ontario where she received her B.Ed. She also earned her E.S.L. specialist certification through the Ministry of Education, Ontario. Vici is presently teaching at Beijing al School of Singapore, Beijing, P.R.C., and is the E.S.L. Coordinator there. She loves to travel, read, and is currently working on a book of her own.

MICHELE E. GORDON has a B.A. degree in psychology from Brandeis University and a Master's degree in international education from Harvard University. In addition to her two years teaching in China, she previously taught English in France and at adult education centers in the Boston area. She is currently running training programs for international visitors at Middlesex Community College in Bedford, Massachusetts.

JOHN A. HANSEN has a B.A. in chemistry from Indiana University and has studied at the Universidad Nacional de Costa Rica. He spent his first two years teaching science and computer science in Venezuela, followed by a year teaching chemistry just outside of Washington, D.C. He is currently a doctoral student at Indiana University.

SHIRLEY HOOPER has a B.S. from Iowa State University (Ames) and a Master's degree in educational leadership from the University of Alabama. She is currently teaching in Torreon, Coahuila, Mexico.

JERI HURD has a B.A. in English from the University of Puget Sound and an M.A. in English from Gonzaga University. She is now in her fourth year of overseas teaching and currently teaches 7–12 English at Bilkent International School. From her initial plan to return home after only three months, she can't wait to move on to other countries, much to her mother's distress.

SUSAN JOHNSTAD is a doctoral candidate completing her dissertation in curriculum studies at Indiana University.

MIKE KIELKOPF has an M.A. in English and journalism from the University of Iowa, Iowa City, and is currently in his sixth year as senior English and AP English teacher and newspaper adviser at the American Community School of Abu Dhabi. He enjoys spending time with his wife, Mary, and their fifteen-year-old son Matt. Mike is a fan of the Iowa Hawkeyes, the Chicago Cubs, and good quotations—including this one: "The difference between ordinary and extraordinary is that little extra."

ROSS LAING is a graduate of the University of Manitoba (B.A.), Queen's University (B.Ed.) and the University of Ottawa (M.Ed.). In his twenty-two years of teaching he has taught a wide variety of subjects in seven different schools. For twelve years Ross was the Head of English at Sir Wilfrid Laurier Secondary School, with the exception of "detours" as an educational consultant and as an exchange teacher to Australia. He now teaches History and English in the Ottawa-Carelton Board of Education.

KEN LOCKETTE has a B.A. in theatre from the University of Missouri—Kansas City and a M.Ed. in curriculum development from DePaul University. He currently teaches writing, literature, and drama at the Almaty International School in Almaty, Kazakhstan. He enjoys traveling, writing, theatre, the blues, and spending time with his wife and son.

LAURA MANN holds both a B.A. in English and a B.S. in zoology from the University of Calgary in Alberta, Canada. She spent one year as the staff writer for a human resources company in the oil and gas business in Calgary, followed by another year as a freelance copywriter. She is currently a JET Programme participant in Miyagi Prefecture on the East Coast of Japan.

KAREN L. NEWMAN is pursuing a doctoral degree in language education at Indiana University in Bloomington, with a minor in TESOL/Applied Linguistics. She received a B.A. in German and psychology from the University of California, Irvine, and an M.A. in Germanic studies from Indiana University. Her research interests include language teaching methodology, language policy, aesthetic and social reform movements, and alternative education.

VERNON K. OLSON has a B.A. from the University of Minnesota and an M.Ed. from Goucher College. He has had both overseas and stateside positions, having taught middle school English, ESL, geography, social studies, and photography at such institutions as the Blake School in Minneapolis, the American International School in Cairo, and The Schneller School in Kirbet Kanafar, Bekaa, Lebanon. He was also Head of the Lower School at the Fay School in Southboro, Massachusetts. Currently, he teaches geography and photography at the Fessenden School in West Newton, Massachusetts.

DAVID REID has an M.A. of teaching in mathematics from the University of Chicago and an M.S. in mathematics from the University of Heidelberg (Germany), with second teaching subject physics. Although a citizen of the United States, he has not lived there for the last twenty-six years, preferring to teach, study, and wander around the world. He is presently teaching in Kuwait. He enjoys backpack-style travel (for a year or two at a time), literature of various countries, philosophy, and good friends.

GREG A. RENDA has a B.S. in biology from Indiana University and served 30 months in the Peace Corps' Agriculture and Forestry Extension Program in El Salvador. He worked for CARE International/El Salvador on the hurricane Mitch disaster relief project. He is currently working as a recruiter for the Peace Corps in Chicago.

EVAN M. SMITH has an M.A. in English from Sir Wilfrid Laurier University and a B.A. and B.Ed. from Queen's University. After teaching English for one year in Venezuela at Escuela de las Americas, and two years at a secondary school in Ottawa, he went to Peru on a professional development trip focusing on social justice and international development. In addition to writing about the experience in his career as an occasional freelance writer, he has founded an international social justice club at Waterdown District High School, near Hamilton, Ontario, where he teaches English.

LAURA L. STACHOWSKI is the director of the cultural immersion projects at Indiana University. She prepares and places student teachers in England, Wales, Scotland, Ireland, India, Australia, New Zealand, Taiwan, Kenya, and Costa Rica, and on Navajo Reservation in Arizona, New Mexico, and Utah. She earned her Ph.D. at Indiana University in 1994.

ELIZABETH WIGFUL has a B.A. in French from York University, Toronto, a certificate in Teaching of English as a Second Language from Carleton University, Ottawa, and a B.Ed. from the University of Ottawa. She currently works as a Program Officer for Voluntary Service Overseas Canada in Ottawa recruiting, training, and placing English teachers in jobs in local schools in Asia, Africa, the Pacific, and Eastern Europe. She enjoys working with teachers with an interest in international development and looks forward to working overseas again sometime in the future.